English Stress

Studies in Language: Noam Chomsky and Morris Halle, Editors

ENGLISH STRESS

Its Form, Its Growth, and Its Role in Verse

MORRIS HALLE & SAMUEL JAY KEYSER

Harper & Row, Publishers   New York•Evanston•London

ENGLISH STRESS: Its Form, Its Growth, and Its Role in Verse
Copyright © 1971 by Morris Halle and Samuel Jay Keyser

Library of Congress catalog card number: 72-125318

For Rachel, Beth, Ben, Tim, John, and Dave

I have a book here
You'd better look here
Because this book
Deserves a look
It is a book
about
Linguistics and poetry

TIM HALLE
June 11, 1969

Contents

Preface

Nisi credideritis, non intellegetis
ST. AUGUSTINE OF HIPPO
De libero arbitrio I, 11

The subtitle and the lead poem by Tim Halle announce this as a book about linguistics and poetry. In it we attempt to present a scientific account of three interrelated topics—the stress system of a dialect of contemporary English (General American), the evolution of this system from the rather different one in force in Old English, and the utilization of the stress system by English poets writing metrical verse.

In writing this book we saw our audience as one composed very largely of persons who are not professional linguists yet have a serious interest in understanding the functioning and evolution of the English stress system. We have therefore attempted to make our presentation elementary, presupposing no acquaintance or only very superficial acquaintance with the linguistic literature on the part of the reader. The presentation, however, is not simple; it requires that the reader proceed carefully and reflectively. It is our hope that this book will not only provide serious students of English with information about the nature, history, and utilization of English stress, but will also prepare them to read with some ease and understanding the important new literature on linguistic matters.

We have said that this book presents a scientific account of the stress system of English. It may be useful to dwell briefly on what we have in mind in this connection. It is easy to believe that the data available for observation about the stress system of English and about its evolution constitute merely an orderless aggregate of facts. We undertook this book on the assumption that this was not so. We assumed that, on the contrary, the facts about stress must be related in all sorts of systematic ways and that these same relations and the principles that account for them could be made explicit. We assumed that each instance of a stress distribution over an English sentence is an instance of a type which has other instances, and that the types found in any period are governed and constrained by general rules which define the stress system for that period. We also assumed that these rules change over time, but that the changes are lawful and subject to principles that could also be made explicit. We saw our task as that of constructing a theory of the stress system of English and of its evolution, such a theory being, or at least aiming at being, an explicit formulation of these various rules and principles and of their operation.

xi

A few things about such a theory need to be stressed. First, it is of necessity made up of hypotheses that go beyond the data. Such hypotheses, furthermore, cannot be derived in a mechanical or self-evident way from the evidence. They require a mixture of guesswork and good judgment. Confidence in them grows and is justified when they enable one to predict facts beyond those initially available and to construct interesting and plausible explanations of these facts.

Hypotheses of this sort, that is, hypotheses that cannot be mechanically derived from the data and that are verified by their predictive and explanatory power, are a common object of scientific efforts. A graphic illustration of the role that such hypotheses play in advancing our knowledge is provided by the decipherment of Linear B by Ventris. The facts that Ventris had at his disposal were not significantly different from those available to his predecessors. The primary difference instead lay in Ventris' choice of hypotheses through which to look at his data. Whereas prior investigators had followed Sir Arthur Evans in hypothesizing that the language of the Linear B inscriptions was *not* Greek, Ventris hypothesized that it *was* Greek. Although this latter hypothesis was not directly entailed by the data, its validity has been established with reasonable assurance by showing that its empirical implications correspond to the facts. In other words, it follows from Ventris' hypothesis that the letters in the Linear B inscriptions must represent Greek sounds or sequences of sounds, that the word endings must represent Greek inflectional endings, that the word sequences must conform to the canons of Greek syntax, and so on. As these and many other implications of Ventris' hypothesis have been shown to be true, his hypothesis has been generally accepted as being true.

While much of the value of scientific hypotheses lies precisely in their power to yield new and interesting empirically testable consequences, their ultimate virtue, to the extent that they are true, is that they explain known or knowable facts by revealing them to be consequences of underlying principles of great generality. A scientific description therefore cannot stop with a systematic account of observable phenomena but must seek a theory that purports to explain the phenomena as well as to display them. It is this explanatory goal of science that we have sought to attain in our account.

In order to achieve our aims we have had to formulate a great many of our observations in a notation which is not always readily translatable into ordinary English. This will, no doubt, make the reader's task more difficult. As we hope we have shown, however, the devices introduced perform a crucial function in enabling us to display clearly the relationships among the facts and to deduce consequences that might otherwise remain hidden. In this sense the choice of notation is an essential aspect of the theory that purports to explain and to display the phenomena under study.

One might ask whether the theory corresponds to anything real beyond the linguistic data it predicts. We would answer in the affirmative, for we wish to attribute psychological significance to our theory. It is part of the nature of language that it has elements such as words, that words are made up of sequences of sounds, that sounds are complexes of phonetic features, and that various phonetic regularities of utterances are expressible as rules that modify a few features in specific sounds in particular contexts. If our theory is correct, entities such as words, sounds, features, and rules must be crucial components of an individual's knowledge of his language. It may at first sight appear strange that such a mundane form of knowledge as that manifested in a person's ability to speak his mother tongue should pre-suppose a mastery of highly abstract principles and rules. Since, in learning their native tongue, children come in contact only with concrete words and utterances, one might suggest that there is no more to learning a language than memorizing what one hears, and that rules and abstract principles are a useless pedantry. It is, however, easy to show that children know facts about their language which they could not have acquired by memorizing what they hear. For example, children can form plurals of words that are outside their own or their parents' vocabulary, and they know how to accentuate phrases which they have demonstrably never heard. This would be impossible if their knowledge included only memorized items. On the other hand, if it is assumed that a speaker's knowledge includes also knowledge of abstract principles and rules, these perfectly ordinary abilities of children are readily explained.

The fact that at most points in our exposition we are dealing with specific technical details may make it difficult for the reader to keep the whole work in perspective. To alleviate this we give here a brief outline of the structure of the book and a summary of our main results. Novices are likely to find this summary useful only after having read the book; the more experienced reader may find it helpful to have a bird's-eye view of the whole scheme before studying its detailed exposition.

The present account of the stress system of contemporary English derives both in theoretical conception and general approach from *The Sound Pattern of English* (Chomsky and Halle (1968)). Central to this account is the discovery made in *Sound Pattern* that in the overwhelming majority of in-stances stress in contemporary English is governed by reasonably simple general rules, the most crucial of which, the Main Stress Rule, resembles rather strikingly the rule governing stress in Latin words. This observation is in sharp disagreement with the statements found in most textbooks, which, like Jones (1956a), have been teaching that "generally speaking there are no rules determining which syllable or syllables of polysyllabic English words bear the stress" (p. 248). It has, of course, always been known that particular affixes such as *-oon*, *-ion*, and *-ic* require that the main stress be located on a particular syllable in the word (see, for example, the observations in Jespersen (1909), the detailed study by Kingdon (1958), or the elaborate lists prepared by Waldo (1968)). These, however, were regarded as minor subregularities that did not controvert the fact that English stress is unpredictable, "phonemic."

The demonstration in *Sound Pattern of English* leaves little room for doubt that stress is predictable in contemporary English, and we know of no arguments from any quarter that might invalidate this claim in any way. We believe that in a number of details, however, the rules given in *Sound Pattern of English* can be improved upon, and we have incorporated the resulting alterations in our text. In particular, in line with a suggestion made to us by J. R. Ross, we have modified the Main Stress Rule so that its last alternative does not operate in accordance with the weak cluster principle but rather assigns stress to the last syllable of the word regardless of its phonetic structure. Moreover, our treatment of vowel reduction (Chapter 1, Section 9) differs to some extent from that of *Sound Pattern of English* (Chapter 3, Section 14) for reasons which we give in the appropriate place in the text. For reasons detailed in Chapter 1, we were unable to accept Ross's further suggestion that the Alternating Stress Rule be modified to allow it to handle cases of stress retraction in words such as *refectory* and *anticipatory*, which in the present study, as in *Sound Pattern of English*, are accounted for by a special option of the Main Stress Rule.

It has been known for a long time that stress in Old English was governed by very simple rules which, however, are quite unlike those governing stress in contemporary English. The gradual steps whereby the Old English stress system evolved into the stress system of the contemporary language constitute the subject matter of the second chapter. Our procedure is to establish the stress rules for certain intermediate periods and to show how these could evolve by plausible steps from the rules of the preceding period. Whenever possible we try to discover internal or external reasons for the changes.

The need to connect the stress rules of one period with those of the preceding as well as of the following period imposes constraints on the kinds of rule that can be realistically entertained as operating at a given period. These constraints have had considerable empirical consequences on our conclusions. For example, it was only by taking seriously the restrictions imposed by the historical process that we were able to appreciate the true significance of the following fact. It has been observed by some scholars that in the eighteenth century the stress contours of words such as *refectory* and *confiscate* vacillated between main stress on the second syllable and main stress on the initial syllable, whereas in the nineteenth century the stress contours were stabilized, with main stress being placed on the second syllable in *refectory* and on the first syllable in *confiscate*. As discussed in detail in the latter half of the second chapter, this change in the stress contours of individual words is a surface manifestation of a deeper change undergone by English stress rules at that time. What is especially interesting about this change is that it seems to have been caused not by external forces— not by changes in vocabulary or by the influence of foreign linguistic fashions—but rather by factors internal to the system of rules, in particular, the fact that the eighteenth-century stress rules, which allowed for vacillations in stress, were formally nonoptimal in contrast to the more optimal stress rules of nineteenth-century English that fixed the stress uniquely in each of the words under discussion. The notion of optimality is an abstract concept that is developed in some detail as our discussion proceeds. It is important to emphasize here that if this highly abstract notion is taken seriously as a force capable of determining the choice among alternative grammars, then the change in the grammar from the eighteenth century to the nineteenth, and with it the change in the accentuation of the words mentioned earlier, becomes at once understandable. The empirical evidence, therefore, appears to behave as if the postulated optimality condition plays a significant role in the development of language.

In addition to the reinterpretation of the data on stress provided by the orthoepists of the eighteenth century, we note here a further major deviation from traditional views regarding the evolution of English stress. It has been taught for a long time that in the early modern period—the sixteenth century —the Germanic stress rule became predominant. Thus, in what is apparently the most exhaustive treatment of the subject, significantly entitled "Der Übergang zur germanischen Betonung bei den Wörtern französischer Herkunft im Mittelenglischen," E. Eckhardt (1942) writes: "Der Kampf zwischen der fremden und der einheimischen Betonung dauerte bis in die erste Hälfte des 16. Jahrhunderts hinein. Um die Mitte dieses Jahrhunderts war er im wesentlichen abgeschlossen. Die heutigen Betonungsverhältnisse waren bei Wörtern französischen Ursprungs im grossen ganzen damals schon erreicht; die einheimische Betonungsweise hatte über die fremde gesiegt." We find no evidence to support the view that the non-Germanic stress patterns had been supplanted by Germanic stress patterns either in the sixteenth century or in the twentieth century. A study of the stress contours of the words given in Levins' *Manipulus vocabulorum* (1570) and other contemporary sources suggests that the non-Germanic Main Stress Rule introduced in the Middle English period must have been operative in the sixteenth century, as it still is operative today.

Since so much of the evidence for stress distribution in the earlier stages of the language must be derived from a study of metrical poetry, we have included a discussion of meter in general and of the two meters of particular interest here, namely, the alliterating verse of *Beowulf* and the iambic pentameter.

Meters in our view are simple linear arrangements of a small number of abstract entities such as the following:

XXXX

WS WS WS WS

Metric verse is produced when these patterns are encoded in linguistic utterances in accordance with specific correspondence rules. For instance a line such as

The cúrfew tólls the knéll of párting dáy

encodes the second of the two abstract patterns just given by virtue of a correspondence rule which relates W to unstressed syllables and S to stressed syllables. Since in most metrical poetry the correspondence rules that relate the abstract entities of the meter to phonetic properties of a concrete line of verse are considerably more complex than in the example just discussed, metrical evidence must be used with great caution in the reconstruction of word stress. Nonetheless, a detailed description of the relationship between meter and line of verse is a necessity if the reader is to understand the grounds on which we postulate particular stress contours for particular words.

We believe, moreover, that the theories of the alliterative verse and of the iambic pentameter presented in the present work are of interest in their own right, and we hope that they will provoke further discussion among specialists.

It is our pleasant duty to acknowledge the help we have received from various colleagues and friends. Foremost among these are the students at Brandeis, at M.I.T., and at the 1969 summer seminar of the Tokyo English Center. Their penetrating questions, their willingness to indicate to us what was unclear in our presentation, and their stimulating remarks on matters that could bear further study have helped to improve this book greatly.

We owe a great deal to our editor, Florence W. Harris, who not only improved the style of the book and corrected errors of grammar and spelling, but also put at our disposal her deep technical knowledge of linguistics and her rich experience in publishing to help us make this a book for intelligent laymen rather than an abstruse study for the edification of the small circle of our professional peers. We are aware that the book does not fully achieve this aim, but for the extent to which it does, the credit belongs in good part to her.

We have benefited from criticisms of colleagues who have read the manuscript in part or in whole in the course of the many years that it was in preparation. If we have not accepted all the advice that was offered, this is mainly due to our inability to integrate particular suggestions into the framework of the book, rather than to any shortcomings in the suggestions themselves. Needless to say, none of them is to be held responsible for any of the book's failings. We are grateful for aid received from Stephen Anderson, Michael Brame, Sylvain Bromberger, Noam Chomsky, James W. Harris, Paul Kiparsky, Charles Mazell, Wayne O'Neil, John R. Ross, James Sledd, Isabella Landon Strong, and W. K. Wimsatt. This work was supported in part by the National Institute of Mental Health, Grant MH 13300–04, and by the National Science Foundation, Grant GS2005.

MORRIS HALLE
SAMUEL JAY KEYSER

April 1, 1970

1

The Stress System of Modern English

1. The Main Stress Rule

Stress location in words differs greatly from language to language. In Finnish stress falls on the first syllable of the word; in Polish it falls on the next-to-last syllable; in French the last syllable of the word is stressed. English, however, has a far more complex system of stress contours, so that when a speaker of any of the aforementioned languages learns English, mastering the position of stress in the word is a matter of some difficulty. It is obvious that native speakers of English as well must have expended some effort on learning how to stress the words of the language, for knowing where to place stress is part and parcel of what we mean when we say that a person has command of English.

One of the most surprising discoveries of Chomsky and Halle (1968—hereafter referred to as *Sound Pattern of English*) was that in a large class of English words the stress contour was totally predictable; that is, given the sequence of consonants and vowels that compose the word, the location of the stress can be determined automatically. This discovery was so surprising because textbooks had for many years specifically denied this fact and, moreover, because the rule that was postulated to assign the stress did not resemble that of any Germanic language but rather was all but identical with the stress rule of Classical Latin.

In order to show how this rule operates, we must first consider the two columns of words in (1). The vowels in the left-hand column are phonetically different in a consistent way from those in the right-hand column. Phoneticians say that vowels of the first type are "nontense" or "lax," whereas the others are "tense":

(1)   NONTENSE   TENSE
          VOWELS   VOWELS

NONTENSE VOWELS	TENSE VOWELS
pit	*peat*
pet	*pate*
put	*pool*
putt	*pole*
	pile
	pout

Phonetic properties such as "tense" and "nontense," "stressed" and "stressless," "voiced" and "unvoiced" are referred to as "features." The feature "tense-nontense," which is found in many languages, plays a fundamental role in the principles that govern the assignment of stress to English words.

English words generally contain one vowel that is more heavily stressed than the other vowels. In accordance with a well-established tradition, we shall say that the vowel with maximum stress bears "primary stress," and we shall indicate this by writing the number "1" above the vowel. Vowels with stresses that are weaker than primary will be assigned the integers "2," "3," etc., in the obvious fashion. In general, vowels for which no integer is supplied will be assumed to be stressless.

Consider now the location of primary stress in the words in (2):

(2)

(a)	(b)	(c)	(d)
América	balaláika	agénda	Tippecanóe
génesis	arthrítis	ellípsis	capríce
alúminum	muséum	amálgam	regíme
cínnamon	albúmin	galáctin	cocaíne
médical	propósal	orchéstral	paróle

The items in (2), which have been marked for primary stress only, are arranged so that in column (a) the primary stress is on the antepenultimate vowel, in columns (b) and (c) the primary stress is on the penultimate vowel, and in column (d) the stress is on the last vowel. It can readily be seen from these examples that the location of primary stress in a word is closely correlated with the distribution of tense vowels. In particular, the regularities listed in (3) obtain:

(3) (a) If the last vowel is nontense, primary stress goes on the antepenultimate vowel when the penultimate vowel is nontense and followed by no more than one consonant (column (a)).

(b) If the last vowel is nontense, primary stress goes on the penult when the penult is itself tense (column (b)) or when it is followed by two (or more) consonants (column (c)).

(c) If the last vowel is tense, it bears primary stress (column (d)).

Let us now restate these rather unwieldy sentences in terms of a more concise and perspicuous formalism, as in (4):

(4) (a) $V \rightarrow [1\text{stress}] \ / \ [X\text{——}C_0 \begin{bmatrix} -\text{tense} \\ V \end{bmatrix} C_0^1 \begin{bmatrix} -\text{tense} \\ V \end{bmatrix} C_0]$ (3a)

(b) $V \rightarrow [1\text{stress}] \ / \ [X \begin{bmatrix} \overline{} \\ +\text{tense} \end{bmatrix} C_0 \begin{bmatrix} -\text{tense} \\ V \end{bmatrix} C_0]$ (3b)

(c) $V \rightarrow [1\text{stress}] \; / \; [X\text{——}C_2 \begin{bmatrix} -\text{tense} \\ V \end{bmatrix} C_0]$ \hfill (3b)

(d) $V \rightarrow [1\text{stress}] \; / \; [X \begin{bmatrix} \overline{} \\ +\text{tense} \end{bmatrix} C_0]$ \hfill (3c)

The formalism of (4) can be most readily understood by comparing the formulas with the corresponding verbal statements in (3). Since the notational system in (4) will be utilized throughout, we give a detailed description of the formalism at this point. The symbol V stands for "vowel"; C stands for "consonant" (used here as a synonym for "nonvowel"); and X stands for any sequence of zero or more vowels, consonants, and/or boundaries, which, however, may not include word boundary unless specifically noted. The subscripts in C_0 and C_2 denote the minimum number of consecutive consonants that must be present; thus C_0 stands for "zero or more consecutive consonants" and C_2 for "two or more consecutive consonants." Superscripts, on the other hand, indicate the maximum number of consonants that may appear: for example, C^2 stands for "no more than two consecutive consonants." This notation allows the use of subscripts and superscripts together: thus C_2^5 represents all sequences of "no more than five and no less than two consonants." The arrow is to be read as "assign to the entity on the left the feature(s) on the right"; the / stands for "provided the entity to the left of the arrow is in the position indicated by —— (dash) in the following sequence." Finally, the square brackets in light type enclose features (or cover symbols for feature complexes, e.g., V) of individual segments, and the square brackets in heavy type indicate the limits of the domain over which the regularity holds. The formula (4a), then, is to be read as "assign primary stress to a vowel provided that it is in a position where on its left is a sequence of zero or more segments not including word boundary and on its right is a sequence composed of zero or more consonants followed by a nontense vowel which is in turn followed by no more than one consonant (that is, either zero consonants or one consonant), a nontense vowel, and a sequence of zero or more consonants." When a sequence satisfies the conditions of a given statement, we shall say that the statement "applies" to the sequence in question, and the required features are then assigned to the appropriate position in the sequence.

We note for future reference that word boundaries (symbolized as ##) and certain prefix boundaries (=) must be specifically mentioned in a statement for that statement to apply to a sequence in which they appear (with the exception of = covered by a symbol like X). Morpheme boundaries (+), on the other hand, need not be specified in a statement unless their presence is obligatory.

We now illustrate how the formalism is meant to work, using the word *aluminum* as an example:

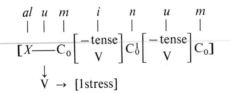

$$\text{V} \rightarrow [\text{1stress}]$$

The sentences (3) and the formulas (4) may be taken as observational statements, that is, they record in words or symbols the kinds of observations that might be made by almost anyone who has investigated stress in English words. The recording of all sorts of odd facts about language, however, cannot be said to constitute a linguistic description. The purpose of a linguistic description is to characterize explicitly the knowledge that a fluent speaker has of the language he commands. This knowledge, which all speakers of a given language have in common, must clearly be something quite different from a mere collection of odd statements about that language. It is a fact that fluent speakers of English know—though they are not necessarily able to express this knowledge in words—certain basic principles which govern the construction of English words and sentences. It is the knowledge of these principles that allows the speaker to make correct inferences with regard to English words and phrases that he demonstrably has not previously encountered. Thus, for instance, English speakers are apt to agree that the examples in (5a) are much less likely to be part of their language than those in (5b):

(a)	(b)
dnit	*glip*
tlod	*trog*
rtud	*rud*
tashk	*pask*
	thode

The point to be stressed here is that the average speaker of English will never before have come across either the items in (5a) or those in (5b); nevertheless, he will know that the former are much more "foreign" than the latter. The speaker must therefore possess knowledge that goes beyond odd facts which could be memorized. Since a satisfactory linguistic description must at the very least contain a characterization of this knowledge, it cannot be just a collection of statements about odd bits of data but rather must make explicit the general principles of which the directly observable data—the words and phrases—are special instantiations.

As a matter of fact, (3) and (4) represent more than mere recordings of factual observations, for they bring together facts in a rather special manner. The statements classify English words in terms of the location of primary stress on one of the last three vowels. There is nothing in the data that compels us to make such a classification. The facts could all be accounted for in terms of the location of primary stress on the first, second, third, etc., vowel from the *beginning* of the word. This approach would result in a larger number of classes and would require a more complicated statement than (3). However, nothing prevents us from stating the facts exhaustively and correctly in this manner. We have instead chosen the statements (3) = (4) because, as will be shown directly, these formulations bring out general principles governing the location of stress in English words which the alternative formulation fails to highlight.

Observe that the statements in (3) = (4) are mutually exclusive: a given word will satisfy one and only one of them. In ordinary discourse such situations are commonly described by means of the concept "otherwise"; that is, statements are organized in such a way that later statements apply only to cases not subject to earlier ones. As a result, statements often may be formulated more concisely. The formal apparatus developed up to this point does not allow us to take advantage of such an organization. However, it is our belief—and we shall justify this belief directly—that a formulation making use of the concept "otherwise" is of special linguistic interest. We therefore enrich our machinery by imposing upon our statements the conditions (6) and (7):

(6) Statements apply to words or other sequences of symbols in a particular order.

(7) At least some sets of statements are, moreover, "disjunctively ordered": once one of the statements in a set applies to a given sequence, then none of the later statements may apply to that same sequence.

While the machinery just introduced allows us to make use of formulations in which the notion "otherwise" figures, it does not force us to do so. Since we have stated, however, that such formulations are linguistically significant, it is natural to go one step further and stipulate that whenever the concept "otherwise" *can* be used to characterize a body of data, it *must* be used. Formally we shall achieve this result by requiring that we always choose the most concise formulation possible, where "conciseness" is to be measured as follows.

We shall distinguish between "formulaic connectives" and "symbols." The formulaic connectives include the arrow, the /, the dash, and the square brackets that delimit individual units. Among the symbols, on the other hand, we include V, C, the features, and the boundary markers. In assessing conciseness, only symbols, not formulaic connectives, are taken into account. The "conciseness condition" will then read as in (8):

(8) The "conciseness" of a statement or set of statements is inversely proportional to the number of symbols appearing in the statement(s). All other things being equal, more concise statements are to be preferred over less concise statements.

Constraints such as those in (6), (7), and (8) restrict the variety of statements that are admitted in a linguistic description. For example, because of (8) we no longer have a choice between a more or a less concise formulation of the facts but must choose the more concise formulation in every case. We shall see that additional constraints are required which have the effect of limiting even further the kinds of statements that are permitted in a linguistic description. To make explicit the fact that we are dealing with statements of a very special type, we shall adopt here the traditional terminology and refer to them as "rules" rather than statements.

Our next task is to show that the constraints we have imposed actually do work for us. Let us therefore return to the stress rules as stated in (3) and (4) and investigate the changes that result when, in conformity with the formal conditions just introduced, the notion "otherwise" is utilized. Clearly the first of the rules in the set—(3a) = (4a), which places stress on the antepenultimate vowel—cannot be affected and will therefore remain unchanged. A particular word will now be said to either satisfy all the conditions listed in (3a) = (4a) or else—"otherwise"—be subject to one of the later rules in the set.

Any word with a final nontense vowel which for some reason fails to satisfy (3a) = (4a) will receive penultimate stress. It is not necessary—and therefore, according to condition (8), no longer permissible—to state whether this word violates (3a) because its penultimate vowel is tense or because its penultimate vowel is followed by more than one consonant. We therefore replace (3b) = (4b, c) by the more concise rule (9):

(9) $\quad V \;\rightarrow\; [\text{1stress}] \;/\; [X\text{---}C_0 \begin{bmatrix} -\text{tense} \\ V \end{bmatrix} C_0]$

By a parallel argument, we no longer need to specify—and therefore, because of condition (8), cannot specify—that (3c) = (4d) will apply only to words which violate the two earlier rules by virtue of having a tense last vowel: these will be the only words to which no stress rules have yet applied. That is, words with a lax last vowel are subject to rule (4a) or rule (9); "otherwise" the final stress rule applies. Hence (4d) is replaced by the more concise rule (10):

(10) V → [1stress] / $[X\text{——}C_0]$

Observe that unless (4a), (9), and (10) are disjunctively ordered they will make incorrect predictions about the location of stress. The word *America*, for example, satisfies all three of these rules and hence, without convention (7), might be assigned stress on the three last vowels. The principle of disjunctive ordering prevents this incorrect consequence, thereby allowing the more concise formulations (9) and (10) to replace (4b, c) and (4d), respectively. Moreover, rules (9) and (10), while more concise than the statements postulated earlier, at the same time apply to a much larger class of words. Note that rules (4a–c) apply only to polysyllabic words. Thus (4d) is the only rule in this set that applies to monosyllables. However, this rule requires that the last or only vowel in the word be tense, and therefore it cannot assign stress to words such as those in the left-hand column of (1) and in (11):

(11) *list*
     sit
     husk
     bull
     bed

Given the description in (4), then, it is necessary to add still another rule to handle monosyllabic words whose vowel is lax. On the other hand, rule (10), which replaces (4d) in the disjunctively ordered set, takes care of such words automatically. Thus, the formal simplification introduced by the imposition of disjunctive order among rules simplifies not only the four statements in (4), but also avoids a further complication of the description. Observe that there is no necessity, logical or otherwise, for the words in (11) to be stressed. It is perfectly conceivable that, like prepositions and auxiliary verbs, monosyllabic words with lax vowels should be stressless. Given a formulation such as (4), this would indeed be the expected case, i.e., the situation that requires no further additions to the rules. On the other hand, given a description which, unlike that in (4), is subject to the constraints (6)–(8), words such as those in (11) would not be expected to be stressless since special rules would have to be added to account for their being without stress. The two types of description thus differ in their implications as to which of the two logically possible cases is more normal: the description with the constraints (6)–(8) implies that the words in (11) should normally be stressed; the description without these constraints implies that the words in (11) should normally be stressless. For English, as for most other languages, the former rather than the latter implication is correct, that is, the words in (11) do carry stress. This fact must therefore be taken as evidence that we are on the right track in imposing constraints (6)–(8) on our descriptive statements.

Additional evidence of the same sort is provided by the fact that rule (9), which replaces (4b) and (4c), applies not only to all the words to which the latter rules applied, but also to the bisyllabic words in (12), which (4b) and (4c) failed to handle:

(12) *venom*[1]
 edit
 weather
 valid
 cabin

This result further supports the constraints (6)–(8) for it is just as logical for the words in (12) to be stressless, or have final stress, as it is for them to have initial stress. Given the constraints (6)–(8), however, initial stress is the most expected case. The fact that the formal argument leads to empirically correct consequences in this case provides significant evidence in favor of the correctness of the theoretical apparatus that we have been employing.

There is a curious formal relationship among the main stress rules. To point this up we repeat in (13) the three rules (4a), (9), and (10), which in the framework of the present discussion constitute a disjunctive block of stress rules:

(13) (a) $V \rightarrow [1\text{stress}] \ / \ [X\text{---}C_0 \begin{bmatrix} -\text{tense} \\ V \end{bmatrix} C_0^1 \begin{bmatrix} -\text{tense} \\ V \end{bmatrix} C_0]$

 (b) $V \rightarrow [1\text{stress}] \ / \ [X\text{---}C_0 \begin{bmatrix} -\text{tense} \\ V \end{bmatrix} C_0]$

 (c) $V \rightarrow [1\text{stress}] \ / \ [X\text{---}C_0]$

Note that it is possible to obtain the later rules in (13) by deleting portions of the earlier ones. Thus, we obtain (13b) by deleting the sequence [−tense, V]C$_0^1$ from (13a), and we obtain (13c) by deleting the sequence [−tense, V]C$_0$ from (13b). It is a fact that this formal relationship is found only and always among rules that constitute disjunctive blocks. Therefore we will take account of this regularity in devising the notational conventions for disjunctively ordered sets of rules: we will give the longest rule in the set and enclose in parentheses the parts that, when deleted, yield the shorter rules. The main stress rules are now formally stated as shown in (14):

(14) MAIN STRESS RULE

$$ V \rightarrow [\text{1stress}] \ / \ [X\underline{}C_0((\begin{bmatrix} -\text{tense} \\ V \end{bmatrix}C_0^1)\begin{bmatrix} -\text{tense} \\ V \end{bmatrix}C_0)] $$

If we establish the convention that, in sets of rules abbreviated by parentheses, longer rules are ordered before shorter rules—that is, the first rule of (14) to be applied is the one including all parenthesized material, and, to obtain subsequent rules, internal parenthesized material is deleted before external parenthesized material—then (14) yields the properly ordered set (13). Rule (14) is thus nothing more than the "official" abbreviation for the three rules in (13), and in our discussion we shall refer to whichever formulation is more convenient. We shall also use the term "weak cluster" to refer to the sequence [−tense, V]C$_0^1$, that is, a lax vowel followed by no more than one consonant. Any other sequence beginning with a vowel is a "strong cluster."

Since (14) predicts the location of primary stress in English words, we shall assume that in the English lexicon, that is, in the list of words of the language that every speaker must at least in part commit to memory, there are no indications of stress. Instead, stress contours are computed as required with the help of rules such as (14). We must therefore make clear the manner in which rules function in general.

The rules in (13) are all mutually exclusive: by their very nature, that is, by virtue of the fact that they constitute a disjunctively ordered set, only a single rule in the set can apply to a given string. This, however, is not generally the case. Quite commonly, more than one rule can apply to any one word. We shall assume that this process of rule application takes place in conformity with conventions (15) and (16):

(15) When a word or other sequence of symbols satisfies the environmental conditions of a rule, the modification indicated by means of the arrow notation is executed and the string is modified accordingly.

(16) With the exception of certain well-defined cases (e.g., disjunctively ordered sets), rules are ordered linearly so that a rule appearing later in the order cannot affect a string until all earlier rules have had a chance to apply.[1]

The word *Tennessee*, for example, satisfies the environmental conditions of rule (13c) since the last vowel is tense. In conformity with (15), we modify the string *Tennessee*, which has no stress indication, as required by rule (13c) and place primary stress on the final vowel: *Tennessee*. It is our intention that a string such as *Tennessee*, with stress indicated on the last vowel, be taken as formally distinct from the same word without stress indication. In particular, if the language were also to contain a rule that required a final-stressed vowel for its application, then the rule would apply to the form *Tennessee* but not to the form *Tennessee*. Obviously, then, this rule could apply here only if it were ordered after (13c). Thus, by virtue of conventions (6), (15), and (16), the assignment of stress by rules is a stepwise procedure whereby a representation in the lexicon is changed into the phonetic representation by successive applications of ordered rules. This gradual emergence of the phonetic representation may be illustrated by the treatment of tenseness in word-final vowels in English, which we now discuss briefly.

A characteristic feature of many dialects of English is that most vowels in word-final position appear tense rather than lax: *pity, value*. To account for this fact, we shall posit that such dialects include the rule (17) (where V* stands for "certain vowels" and ## represents the word boundary):[2]

(17) $\quad$ V* $\quad \rightarrow \quad$ [+tense] $\quad / \quad$ [## X——##]

Consider, now, stress assignment in words such as those in (18):

(18) $\quad$ *Chicago* $\qquad$ *Esperanto*
$\qquad$ *Kikuyu* $\qquad$ *manifesto*
$\qquad$ *macaroni* $\qquad$ *Sephardi*

In all these items primary stress is assigned in accordance with rule (13b), the only rule which places stress on the penultimate syllable.

---

[1] As will be noted at the end of this chapter, there is a certain amount of evidence that points to the conclusion that (16) is too stringent a requirement and may have to be relaxed somewhat. Since this issue is still unsettled, we shall disregard it until we discuss exceptions to the stress rules (Section 11), where questions of rule order are clearly germane.

[2] For a fuller statement of this rule, see *Sound Pattern of English* (pp. 52, 73), as well as the end of Section 4 in this chapter.

$\qquad$ Kenyon and Knott (1944) note with regard to the suffix *-y*: "The sound varies in America from -ɪ to -i, though the -i is seldom as high (close) as in the pl of *basis* . . . The -i variant is commonest in the N and E, but rare in the S " (p. 481).

However, the forms do not appear to satisfy the conditions of this rule: (13b) requires that the last vowel in a word be nontense, but in each of the words in (18) the last vowel is tense. Note now that given (15) and (16) as conditions on rule application, we can easily explain this result. We simply assume that the words in (18) have a nontense vowel in their lexical representation and, moreover, that the stress rules precede the tensing rule (17). Thus, stress placement and final tensing will affect words in stepwise fashion, resulting in derivations such as those shown in (19). (A dash in a derivation indicates that the rule in question is not applicable; (*v*) indicates that the rule applies vacuously, i.e., that it is applicable but does not result in any modification. A macron over a vowel, as $\bar{o}$ in *macarōni*, indicates that the vowel is tense.)

(19)

LEXICAL REPRESENTATION	macarōni	manifesto	Tennessēē	
	–	–	–	RULE (13a)
	ó	é	–	RULE (13b)
	–	–	éē	RULE (13c)
	ī	ō	(*v*)	RULE (17)
PHONETIC OUTPUT	*macarōní*	*manifestō*	*Tennessēé*	

As can be seen from (19), the difference between words such as *macaroní* and words such as *Tennessee* is that the final vowel is nontense in the lexical representation of *macaroni* whereas it is tense in *Tennessee*. Note, furthermore, that the ordering of the rules in (19) is crucial: if the tensing rule (17) were ordered before the stress rules (13a–c), all the words in (18) would, incorrectly, receive final stress.

The convention (16) on rule ordering reflects a particular empirical claim about the nature of language. To demonstrate this, let us briefly examine the effects of rule ordering in a hypothetical case. Consider a group of dialects in which two rules (20) and (21) are valid:

(20) Vowels are nontense before voiceless stops (*p,t,k*).

(21) Stops are voiceless before nontense vowels.

Suppose, further, that it can be demonstrated that the dialects include the verbal stems *bā* and *bād* and that the infinitive is formed by adding *to* to stems ending in vowels and *o* to stems ending in consonants. The dialects must therefore be assumed to have the infinitive forms *bā+to* and *bād+o* (where + represents a boundary), which, in view of rules (20) and (21), cannot be taken as phonetic representations. Given the two rules and the conventions (15) and (16), which together impose a linear order on the application of rules, then the only two possible ways in which the infinitive forms in question may be pronounced are shown in the derivations (22) and (23):

(22) LEXICAL REPRESENTATION   bāto   bādo

bato	——	RULE (20)
pato	bāto	RULE (21)

      PHONETIC OUTPUT   *pato*   *bāto*

(23) LEXICAL REPRESENTATION   bāto   bādo

——	bāto	RULE (21)
bato	bato	RULE (20)

      PHONETIC OUTPUT   *bato*   *bato*

In derivation (22), the phonetic forms *pato* and *bāto* are obtained by ordering rule (20) before rule (21); in derivation (23), on the other hand, rule (21) is ordered before rule (20), and the result is *bato* in both cases. The order in which the two rules apply to the forms is, then, a critical issue. Given the claim that a rule applies to a string as modified by the preceding rule, different ordering may result in different phonetic forms.

Now consider the forms in (24):

(24)   *bato*   *bāto*

To obtain *bato* and *bāto* as phonetic forms in the dialects we have posited, it would be necessary to apply rules (20) and (21) always and only to the unmodified lexical representations, thereby violating conditions (15) and (16). Rule (20) would then not be applicable to *bādo* but would apply to *bāto*, yielding *bato*; rule (21) would not modify *bāto* but would affect *bādo*, changing it to *bāto*.

The procedure that leads to the forms in (24) is abstractly every bit as good as that resulting in the phonetic output in (22) or (23). Hence the choice between the two is purely an empirical matter. We must ask how actual languages behave. If they function in conformity with the results in (22) and (23), then we are justified in imposing the conventions (15) and (16) to establish a linear order in the application of rules. If, instead, they function in conformity with (24), then different conventions must be established. At present the evidence we have would appear to favor the hypothesis of strict ordering of rules. We shall therefore assume in this study the validity of (15) and (16) as further constraints on rule application. (See, however, note 31 for a brief discussion of work challenging this view.)

2. *Stress Contours of Compound Words and Phrases*

When words are used in phrases or in other syntactic collocations, the main stress of one word is normally subordinated or superordinated to that of other words. In the compound nouns shown in (25), the main stress of the second word is subordinated to that of the first. The location of the main stress in each word does not change, however; it remains on the syllable on which it was placed by the Main Stress Rule (14). (The integers 2, 3, etc., as mentioned earlier, will be used to indicate relative stress levels.)

(25) *rádio stàtion*   *búilding còuncil*
      commúnity cènter   *státion mànager*
      políce càptain   *lábor ùnion*

It is obvious from (25) that the language must contain a rule that weakens the stress on the second word in a compound noun. As we shall see, it is convenient to implement stress weakening indirectly. Thus, rather than formulating rules that weaken stress on certain vowels, we shall assume that stress rules are subject to the convention (26):

(26) Whenever primary stress is assigned to a vowel, the stress on every other vowel in the domain of the rule is weakened by one degree.

Given this convention, stress weakening is effected by a rule that assigns primary stress to a vowel that may already possess primary stress; this vowel will then retain its primary stress but all other stresses in the domain of the rule will be weakened by one. Unstressed vowels will remain unaffected by the rule.

Before giving a formal statement of the compound stress rule which accounts for the forms in (25), let us consider the stress contours of compound nouns such as those in (27), which themselves are composed of compound nouns:

(27) (a) *lábor union président*
      (b) *rádio stàtion mànager*
      (c) *commúnity cènter bùilding*
      (d) *políce càptain assòciation*
      (e) *lábor ùnion prèsident elèction*
      (f) *hóusing depàrtment emplòyee assòciation*

We recall that the chief effect of the compound stress rule must be to weaken the main stress of the second element of the compound. If we examine the forms in (27) from this point of view, it is not hard to see that their stress contour is also a consequence of the compound stress rule. Thus, for example, (27a) is made up of the compound noun *labor union* and the noun *president*. The stress contour of the first of these elements is a normal instance of the operation of the compound stress rule, while the stress contour of the second noun follows simply from the Main Stress Rule. If now the compound stress rule applies to the collocation of these two nouns, the effect is to weaken all but the first primary stress, turning *labor union president* into (27a). In precisely the same manner we obtain the stress contours in (27b)–(27d).

When (27a) is in turn compounded with the noun *election* to give the compound noun (27e), *labor union president election*, the correct stress contour can readily be obtained by reapplying the compound stress rule to the larger compound in exactly the same manner in which it applied to the component compound nouns. In other words, we are able to utilize the compound stress rule to account for all the examples in (27) by assuming that it is first used to calculate the stress contour of the innermost compound noun, that it then reapplies to the next largest compound noun, then to the next largest compound, and so on, until the limits of the compound word are reached. We shall call this type of repetitive rule application the principle of the "transformational cycle." An interesting feature of this cyclic application of the rules is that it is sensitive to the syntactic structure of the sequences under consideration. This will be amply illustrated as the discussion proceeds.

The reader may find the cyclical principle of rule application perfectly natural and therefore hardly worth commenting on. It should not be overlooked, however, that any number of alternative principles for rule application could readily be invented. For instance, it is certainly a logical possibility that rules apply noncyclically, or that rules apply cyclically but without regard for the syntactic structure of the compound word. To the best of our knowledge, however, the need for such conventions on rule application has never been demonstrated in any of the languages that have been studied. On the other hand, the cyclical convention is universal: there are examples of cyclical rules in all languages, if not in phonology then in syntax. This is obviously a far from trivial fact. Let us therefore examine the convention in somewhat greater detail.

As noted previously, in calculating the stress contour of larger compounds we proceed from the inside out, as it were, first applying the compound rule to the innermost compound and then, in stepwise fashion, to ever larger constituents until the limits of the word are reached. More formally, we might describe our procedure as having as its starting point a word with the constituent structure (28):[3]

(28) $[[[\overset{1}{labor}\ \overset{1}{union}]_\mathbf{N}\ \overset{1}{president}]_\mathbf{N}\ \overset{1}{election}]_\mathbf{N}$

The bracketing in (28) indicates the internal structure of the compound. On this basis, the compound rule will first apply to *labor union*, then to *labor union president*, and finally to the entire expression. In effect, this means that the application of the rules is subject to the conventions (29) and (30):

(29) Unless specifically restricted, a rule applies to a maximal sequence containing no internal brackets.

(30) After all applicable rules have applied, the brackets delimiting the sequence under consideration are erased, and the rules are reapplied to the next larger constituent.

These conventions are as formal a statement of the cyclical principle as we shall give in the present study. Their intuitive content is that the

---

[3] The labels on the brackets indicate the syntactic category to which the respective compounds belong. In (28), then, N stands for "noun." This indication is necessary since, as will be demonstrated, compounds belonging to different syntactic categories are treated differently by the stress rules.

In our discussion we have implicitly assumed that there is no upper bound on the number of levels of stress that can be distinguished in English. This is far from obvious, and a brief explanation of our procedure is therefore in order. Speakers of English can readily locate the primary stress in words in isolation, as in the examples in (2). There is also little difficulty in perceiving that in compound nouns like those in (25) the main stress in the first noun is greater than that in the second. Since these words also contain unstressed syllables, we conclude that speakers are able to distinguish at least three distinct levels of stress: primary (our [1stress]), secondary (our [2stress]), and weak (our stressless). When speakers are presented with longer and more complex compounds such as those in (27), however, they are no longer sure whether there are actual differences among the subsidiary (nonprimary) stresses. Thus, in the compound noun *labor union president*, for example, a naïve speaker may be uncertain as to whether the main stress in *union* is actually weaker than that in *president*. There is nothing unusual in this uncertainty of the average speaker with regard to phonetic properties of utterances. Naïve speakers are often unable to detect such phonetic differences. For example, many English speakers cannot determine whether the vowel in words such as *sing* is tense or lax; or Russian speakers are incapable of telling which vowel in the word bears main stress.

It has been observed that an individual's performance with regard to stress level distinctions depends only moderately on the presence of a specific acoustic cue in the utterance but is much more directly influenced by the presence of the appropriate grammatical and syntactic cues (see Lieberman (1967)). Thus, trained phoneticians may be able to distinguish only two levels of stress in nonsense syllable sequences but will distinguish reliably four or five levels of stress in meaningful utterances. This observation in no way affects the reality of the phenomenon we are studying, for the ability of a phonetician to distinguish four levels of stress is no less real than the presence of a particular physical attribute in a given stretch of sound.

phonetic form of a compound word of arbitrary length—that is, its stress contour, in the present instance—is determined by the very same rules that determine the form of its component parts, and, moreover, that these component parts are identical with the syntactic constituents of the word.

As an illustration of the operation of the rules and conventions developed here, consider the derivation (31):

(31) $[[[\overset{1}{labor}\ \overset{1}{union}]_N\ \overset{1}{president}]_N\ \overset{1}{election}]_N$

Because of convention (29), the compound stress rule applies only to the string:

$[\overset{1}{labor}\ \overset{1}{union}]_N$

and together with the stress-weakening convention (26) turns it into:

$[\overset{1}{labor}\ \overset{2}{union}]_N$.

By convention (30) the innermost brackets are erased and the compound stress rule is now applied to:

$[\overset{1}{labor}\ \overset{2}{union}\ \overset{1}{president}]_N$

which is turned into:

$[\overset{1}{labor}\ \overset{3}{union}\ \overset{2}{president}]_N$.

Innermost brackets are again erased and the compound stress rule is applied to the string:

$[\overset{1}{labor}\ \overset{3}{union}\ \overset{2}{president}\ \overset{1}{election}]_N$

which is converted into:

$[\overset{1}{labor}\ \overset{4}{union}\ \overset{3}{president}\ \overset{2}{election}]_N$.

Now consider the compound verbs and compound adjectives in (32):[4]

(32)

VERBS		ADJECTIVES	
$\overset{1}{air}\text{-}\overset{2}{condition}$	$\overset{1}{type}\overset{2}{write}$	$\overset{1}{mealy}\text{-}\overset{2}{mouthed}$	$\overset{1}{tongue}\text{-}\overset{2}{tied}$
$\overset{1}{pole}\text{-}\overset{2}{vault}$	$\overset{1}{trouble}\overset{2}{shoot}$	$\overset{1}{sea}\overset{2}{sick}$	$\overset{1}{top}\text{-}\overset{2}{heavy}$
$\overset{1}{leap}\overset{2}{frog}$	$\overset{1}{hedge}\overset{2}{hop}$	$\overset{1}{machine}\text{-}\overset{2}{made}$	$\overset{1}{heart}\overset{2}{broken}$
$\overset{1}{back}\overset{2}{bite}$	$\overset{1}{boot}\overset{2}{lick}$	$\overset{1}{ivy}\text{-}\overset{2}{covered}$	$\overset{1}{head}\overset{2}{strong}$
$\overset{1}{house}\text{-}\overset{2}{hunt}$	$\overset{1}{horse}\overset{2}{whip}$	$\overset{1}{God}\text{-}\overset{2}{fearing}$	$\overset{1}{foot}\overset{2}{sore}$

[4] In some dialects, when the second component of a compound word is a monosyllabic word, it has [3stress] rather than [2stress]. This fact can readily be taken into account by adding a rule with this effect to the description. As such a rule does not provide any new insights either into English or into language in general, we shall limit the present description to dialects where the facts are as presented in (32).

It is evident that these forms, as well as the compound nouns just discussed, are stressed in accordance with the compound stress rule. We shall therefore assume that the grammar includes three compound stress rules—one for nouns, one for verbs, and one for adjectives:

$$\begin{bmatrix} 1\text{stress} \\ V \end{bmatrix} \rightarrow [1\text{stress}] \;/\; [\#\#\,X\text{——}Y\#\#Z\#\#]_N$$

$$\begin{bmatrix} 1\text{stress} \\ V \end{bmatrix} \rightarrow [1\text{stress}] \;/\; [\#\#\,X\text{——}Y\#\#Z\#\#]_V$$

$$\begin{bmatrix} 1\text{stress} \\ V \end{bmatrix} \rightarrow [1\text{stress}] \;/\; [\#\#\,X\text{——}Y\#\#Z\#\#]_A$$

To bring out the near identity of these rules, we shall abbreviate them by factoring out all identical material and enclosing nonidentical material in braces. The Compound Rule will therefore be stated formally as (33):

(33) COMPOUND RULE

$$\begin{bmatrix} 1\text{stress} \\ V \end{bmatrix} \rightarrow [1\text{stress}] \;/\; [\#\#\,X\text{——}Y\#\#Z\#\#]_{\{N,V,A\}}$$

The symbolism used in rule (33) must be further explained. The ## symbol stands for the word boundary and corresponds roughly to the space used between words in writing and printing. The symbols X, Y, and Z represent any sequence of consonants, vowels, and boundaries, not including the ## boundary. (As mentioned previously, X, Y, and Z may also contain no segments or boundaries at all.) Thus, the compound noun *labor union*, for example, is analyzed in conformity with rule (33) as in (34):

(34) (a) $[\#\#\; l\,\overset{1}{a}\,bor\,\#\#\,\overset{1}{union}\,\#\#]_N$

(b) $[\#\#\,X\text{—}Y\;\#\#\;\;Z\;\#\#]_N$

$$\begin{bmatrix} 1\text{stress} \\ V \end{bmatrix} \rightarrow [1\text{stress}]$$

Since the $\overset{1}{a}$ of *labor union* in (34a) does occur in the position specified in (34b), rule (33) will apply to it, reassigning primary stress and, by convention (26), weakening the stress on *union* by one degree. The resulting string is therefore *l$\overset{1}{a}$bor $\overset{2}{u}$nion*, as required.

Note that the appearance of ## at the beginning and end of sequences to which (33) is applicable indicates that it applies to sequences that are made up of words. It will be recalled that in the Main Stress Rule (14) there are no word boundaries in the corresponding positions. As we shall see, rule (14) applies not only to single words but also to constituents that are components of words but are not words themselves. This difference in the domain of application of the two rules is, then, reflected in the presence versus the absence of word boundary symbols next to the outermost brackets. A rule with word boundary symbols next to its outermost brackets applies only to sequences that are constituted of one or more full words; a rule without word boundary symbols in these positions applies to other sequences as well. (We shall see in Section 8 that this notational convention has consequences of some significance.)

The question of how words are constituted from more primitive elements such as roots, stems, and affixes is one of the least understood problems in modern linguistics. We are unfortunately not in a position to shed much new light on this matter. Therefore we shall assume without discussion or justification that a grammar contains rules of word formation and that one of the effects of these rules is the correct placement of word boundaries in strings of morphemes, that is, in strings composed of primitive elements. As a first approximation we propose that word boundaries are assigned to all sequences of morphemes that constitute a member of a lexical category, i.e., a noun, verb, or adjective. As our discussion develops, however, we shall see that this straightforward principle is not fully adequate. (See (87) and (89) and the accompanying comments.)

Returning to the symbols in rule (33), recall that we have established the convention that capital letters that come late in the alphabet, such as X, Y, Z, represent any sequence of segments which may include boundaries other than word boundaries. Given this exclusion of word boundaries, however, rule (33) will not be able to handle examples such as those in (27), where the compound noun consists of three or more simple nouns. Thus it is necessary to examine more closely the conditions on X, Y, and Z in rule (33).

Consider, first, the examples in (35), which are assumed to have the indicated constituent structure:

(35) (a) $[\overset{2}{kitchen} \, [\overset{1}{towel} \, \overset{3}{rack}]_N \,]_N$
   (b) $[\overset{2}{evening} \, [\overset{1}{computer} \, \overset{3}{class}]_N \,]_N$
   (c) $[\overset{2}{theater} \, [\overset{1}{ticket} \, \overset{3}{office}]_N \,]_N$
   (d) $[[\overset{2}{community} \, \overset{3}{center}]_N \, [\overset{1}{building} \, \overset{3}{council}]_N \,]_N$

It was pointed out in *Sound Pattern of English* (p. 93) that in order to account for the stress contour of compounds such as those in (35), it is necessary to specify somewhat further the sequences covered by X, Y, and

Z in rule (33). In particular, we must impose on the rule the two conditions in (36):

(36) CONDITIONS ON COMPOUND RULE

(a) *X* and *Y* may contain ## (word boundaries)

(b) *Y* contains no vowel with [1stress]

Note that by not being mentioned in (36a), *Z* is restricted to no more than a single word. The need for this restriction can be seen from the compounds in (35). For example, in the derivation of the stress contour for (35a), we begin the last cyclical pass through the stress rules with the string [*kĭtchen tŏwel răck*]. If *Z* were allowed to contain more than one word, then *towel rack* could be analyzed as *Z*, and we would obtain the stress contour 123 in place of the desired contour 213. Moreover, *Y* must not be allowed to contain a vowel with [1stress], since otherwise *răck* could be analyzed as *Z*, and *tŏwel* as *Y*, in which case the incorrect stress contour 123 would again result. Given the conditions in (36), the only analysis of *Y* and *Z* is *-wĕl* and *răck*, respectively, with *X* being *kitchen t-*. Rule (33) will then reassign primary stress to *ŏ* in *towel*, and the other stresses will be weakened in accordance with convention (26), giving the desired contour 213.

In addition to compound nouns with falling stress contours like those in (25), English has a large number of compound nouns with rising contours, some examples of which are given in (37):

(37) *Mădison Rŏad* (versus *Mădison Strĕet*)
Ŭnion Stătion (versus *ŭnion mĕmber*)
Chrĭstmas Orătorio (versus *Chrĭstmas stŏry*)

The Compound Rule (33) places primary stress on the first word of a compound and, given the stress-weakening convention (26), will change a string such as *Madison Street* into *Mădison Strĕet*. In the case of the compounds in (37), on the other hand, the problem is to convert a string such as *Mădison Rŏad* into *Mădison Rŏad*. This can readily be achieved if we have a rule that places primary stress on the second word of the compound rather than on the first. Note that a rule with just this effect results when the string ##*Z* is removed from the Compound Rule (33), as in (38):

(38) $\begin{bmatrix} \text{1stress} \\ V \end{bmatrix}$ → [1stress] / [## *X* —— *Y* ##]$_{\{N,V,A\}}$

CONDITIONS: *X* and *Y* may contain ##

Y contains no [1stress]

The condition that *Y* may contain a word boundary is vacuous since in all compound words subject to (38) the primary stress will be on the last word. Since the condition has to be imposed on (33), however, and since the two rules should be coalesced, we have included it in (38). Observe that the two other conditions on (38) are essential to the correct application of rule (38) as well as rule (33). In particular, only the string *following* the primary-stressed vowel of the second word of the compound can be analyzed as *Y*, and stress will therefore be reassigned to that vowel, as required.

Recall now the discussion of disjunctive ordering with regard to the Main Stress Rule (14). It was observed there that disjunctively ordered sets have the property that later rules in the set may be obtained by deleting portions of earlier rules. This is precisely what was done to obtain rule (38) from rule (33). Therefore, given the ordering conventions (6) and (7) and the conciseness condition (8), we must combine the two rules into one by placing parentheses around the string *##Z*. This, in effect, orders (38) after (33). Thus we must now provide a means whereby compounds such as *Madison Road* are exempted from rule (33), since otherwise, because of the convention on disjunctive ordering, (33) will apply to them and rule (38) will be blocked. We shall avoid this difficulty by marking compound nouns such as *Madison Road* as exceptions to rule (33).[5] We can now coalesce rules (33) and (38) as (39):

(39) COMPOUND RULE

$$
\begin{bmatrix} 1\text{stress} \\ V \end{bmatrix} \rightarrow [1\text{stress}] \ / \ [\#\# X \text{------} Y(\#\# Z)\#\#]_{\{N,V,A\}}
$$

CONDITIONS: *X* and *Y* may contain *##*
Y contains no [1stress]

It is worth noting that the formulation of the second part of the Compound Rule (39), that is, the rule where the substring *##Z* is suppressed, permits application of this rule to single words as well as to compounds. In the individual words that have been considered thus far, we have been concerned only with the primary-stressed vowel. Thus, at this point in the discussion, the application of (39) to single words appears to be vacuous. We shall see in Section 3, however, that this seemingly vacuous by-product of our attempt to include the stress contours of the compound words

---

[5] We assume that there exists in language a mechanism which makes it possible to block the application of a given rule to a particular word or sequence. Since the actual device employed is not of great relevance to our discussion, and since there are also a great many open questions with regard to the nature of this device, nothing further shall be said here about the exception-marking mechanism. (For additional discussion, see *Sound Pattern of English*, pp. 172–176 and *passim*.)

in (37) in our description has real and unexpected consequences for the description of a totally different body of data. Before examining these data, we shall consider the stress contours of word collocations other than compound words.

Collocations that are not compound nouns, verbs, or adjectives generally have stress contours like the compound $\overset{2}{Madison}$ $\overset{1}{Road}$, that is, they have rising stress contours, as shown in (40):

(40) [$\overset{2}{elementary}$ $\overset{1}{proposals}$]**NOUN PHRASE**
      [$\overset{2}{Jesus}$ $\overset{1}{wept}$] **SENTENCE**
      [$\overset{2}{very}$ $\overset{1}{difficult}$]**ADJECTIVE PHRASE**
      [$\overset{2}{explain}$ $\overset{1}{theorems}$]**VERB PHRASE**
      [$\overset{2}{Jennifer's}$ $\overset{1}{relatives}$]**NOUN PHRASE**

The rule which produces these stress contours must obviously be quite similar to the second part of the Compound Rule. We shall call this rule the Nuclear Stress Rule and give a preliminary formulation as in (41):

(41) NUCLEAR STRESS RULE

$$\begin{bmatrix} 1\text{stress} \\ V \end{bmatrix} \rightarrow [1\text{stress}] \ / \ [\#\# X \text{——} Y \#\#]_{\{S,NP,VP,AP\}}$$

CONDITIONS: X and Y may contain $\#\#$
Y contains no [1stress]

The Compound Rule (39) applies to all constituents that belong to what have traditionally been called "lexical categories," that is, nouns, verbs, adjectives. The Nuclear Stress Rule (41), on the other hand, applies to constituents that belong to syntactic categories other than lexical. The two rules thus apply to mutually exclusive categories, which suggests that they may be disjunctively ordered. If we make this assumption and decide that the Nuclear Stress Rule follows the Compound Rule, then we can dispense with the indication of syntactic category in the Nuclear Stress Rule: by virtue of the disjunctive ordering, any sequence that undergoes the Compound Rule will be exempt from the Nuclear Stress Rule regardless of its syntactic category or any other considerations. We can therefore rewrite the Nuclear Stress Rule as (42):

(42) NUCLEAR STRESS RULE

$$\begin{bmatrix} 1\text{stress} \\ V \end{bmatrix} \rightarrow [1\text{stress}] \ / \ [\#\# X \text{——} Y \#\#]$$

CONDITIONS: X and Y may contain $\#\#$
Y contains no [1stress]

Recall that the Compound Rule (39) abbreviates two rules, (33) and (38), in that order. Observe further that the Nuclear Stress Rule (42) can be obtained from (38) by the deletion of the syntactic category labels. It is therefore natural to attempt to collapse the Nuclear Stress Rule and the Compound Rule into one formula by placing parentheses around the syntactic category labels of (39), as in (43):

(43) COMPOUND AND NUCLEAR STRESS RULES

$$\begin{bmatrix} 1\text{stress} \\ V \end{bmatrix} \rightarrow [1\text{stress}] \ / \ [\#\# X \text{—} Y(\#\# Z)\#\#]_{(\langle N,V,A \rangle)}$$

CONDITIONS: X and Y may contain $\#\#$
Y contains no [1stress]

Given the conventions as developed up to this point, (43) abbreviates (33), (38), (42), and also rule (44):

(44) $$\begin{bmatrix} 1\text{stress} \\ V \end{bmatrix} \rightarrow [1\text{stress}] \ / \ [\#\# X \text{—} Y \#\# Z \#\#]$$

CONDITIONS: X and Y may contain $\#\#$
Y contains no [1stress]

This rule, however, would supply a falling instead of a rising stress contour to the phrases in (40) if allowed to apply before the Nuclear Stress Rule (41), that is, before the rule abbreviated by (43) which has both parenthesized elements deleted. To prevent this, we must be in a position to impose further conditions on the deletion of parenthesized material. In particular, we must be able to require that, in reconstituting the individual rules of a formula with two sets of parentheses, the material in one set of parentheses is not deleted unless the material in the second set of parentheses is also deleted. Given the power to impose such conditions on rules, we can restate the combined Compound and Nuclear Stress Rules as in (45):

(45) COMPOUND AND NUCLEAR STRESS RULES

$$\begin{bmatrix} 1\text{stress} \\ V \end{bmatrix} \rightarrow [1\text{stress}] \ / \ [\#\# X \text{—} Y(\#\# Z)_a \#\#]_{(\langle N,V,A \rangle)_b}$$

CONDITIONS: X and Y may contain $\#\#$
Y contains no [1stress]
if a, then b

The last condition, "if a, then b," means that in reconstituting the individual rules abbreviated by (45) the material contained in the set of parentheses labeled *b* must be present if the material contained in the set of parentheses labeled *a* is present in the rule, but not vice versa. In other words, the sequence ##*Z* can be present only when the rule applies to a compound noun, verb, or adjective, which is just the desired result.

Thus, the rules abbreviated by (45) are as follows: the Compound Rule (33), which is (45) with both parenthesized strings included; the rule (38), which yields compounds like *Mádison Róad* and is obtained from (45) by the deletion of the string *a* (##*Z*) but not the string *b* ({**N,V,A**}); and the Nuclear Stress Rule (42), obtained by deleting both parenthesized strings. The fourth possibility, rule (44), which includes *a* but deletes *b*, is now eliminated by the last condition on (45), as required by the data.

There is yet another refinement that must be made in the combined rule (45). Note that the form in which the Nuclear Stress Rule was given in (42) implies that the stress contour of a noun phrase such as *elaborate questions* differs from that of a prepositional phrase such as *by elaborate questions*. The reason is that the internal structure of the prepositional phrase is more complex than that of the noun phrase, that is, there is an additional set of brackets. Therefore, according to the cyclical principle of rule application (conventions (29) and (30)), the prepositional phrase will be subject to the Nuclear Stress Rule twice rather than just once, as shown in the contrasting derivations in (46):

(46) [elaborate questions]$_{NP}$ [by [elaborate questions]$_{NP}$]$_{PP}$

1	1		1	1	
2	1		2	1	NUCLEAR STRESS (42)
			3	1	NUCLEAR STRESS (42)

To avoid the incorrect reapplication of rule (42) in the prepositional phrase, we shall impose condition (47) on the rule:

(47) *X* must contain a vowel with [1stress]

This restriction will not only prevent the weakening of 21 to 31 in prepositional phrases, but it will also account for the fact that compound nouns such as *phílosophy collóquia* do not have different stress contours when they are embedded in a prepositional phrase such as *with philosophy colloquia* or when they alone constitute a noun phrase as in *philosophy colloquia are fun*.

The combined Compound Rule (39) and the Nuclear Stress Rule

(42), with condition (47) added, will now be as in (48).[6] (The symbol ϕ stands for a string consisting of zero elements.)

(48) COMPOUND AND NUCLEAR STRESS RULES

$$\begin{bmatrix} 1\text{stress} \\ V \end{bmatrix} \rightarrow [1\text{stress}] \ / \ [\#\# X \text{——} Y(\#\# Z)_a \#\#]_{(\langle \mathbf{N,V,A}\rangle)_b}$$

CONDITIONS: X and Y may contain $\#\#$
Y contains no [1stress]
if a, then b
if $b = \phi$, then X contains [1stress]

3. The Alternating Stress Rule and the Stress Adjustment Rule

Consider the stress contours in the words in (49):

(49) (a)   (b)

       magazine   *hurricane*

       buccaneer   *anecdote*

       palisade   *pedigree*

       Tennessee   *baritone*

       chimpanzee   *matador*

       kangaroo   *cantaloupe*

       chandelier   *cavalcade*

The forms in both columns of (49) have a tense final vowel and should therefore all receive primary stress on this vowel by case (13c) of the Main Stress Rule. We see, however, that this corresponds to the phonetic facts only for the examples in column (a), not for those in column (b). It is significant here that the words in column (b) do not have a totally stressless final syllable but rather show tertiary stress in this position. Recall that, because of the stress-weakening convention (26), nonprimary stresses derive from

---

[6] Given that we already have one condition that was necessitated by the incorporation of the Nuclear Stress Rule into (39) (see (45)) and given that the Nuclear Stress Rule is further subject to condition (47) while the Compound Rule (39) is not, we must now ask whether we should, in a grammar of English, collapse (42) and (39) as in (48). This is strictly an empirical question: in the light of the necessity for imposing condition (47) on rule (42) but not on rule (39), does the striking similarity of the two rules still represent a significant generalization about language? If the answer is yes, then collapsing must be allowed. If the answer is no, then (42) and (39) must remain separate rules. Unfortunately we have no direct evidence bearing on this point. We shall simply assume, then, that the former statement is correct. For an interesting discussion of the Nuclear Stress Rule and other problems connected with it, see J. W. Bresnan (1970).

primary stresses when rules assign primary stress to other syllables in the sequence. Thus, we can account for the contrasts in (49) as follows. We assume that the examples in column (b), just like those in column (a), are subject to (13c) of the Main Stress Rule, which places primary stress on the tense vowel in the final syllable. But the forms in (b) then undergo two additional rules which assign primary stress to some syllable other than the last and thereby cause the original primary stress ultimately to be weakened to tertiary. The examples in column (a) will not be subject to these further rules.

The first of the two rules referred to will be called the Alternating Stress Rule, and its effect is to retract primary stress from the word-final syllable to the antepenultimate syllable. Formally we may state the Alternating Stress Rule as (50):

(50) ALTERNATING STRESS RULE

$$V \rightarrow [\text{1stress}] \ / \ [X\text{——}C_0VC_0 \begin{bmatrix} \text{1stress} \\ V \end{bmatrix} C_0]$$

Since this rule applies to words which must already have received stress on the last vowel by (13c) of the Main Stress Rule, it is conjunctively ordered with respect to the Main Stress Rule, that is, both rules may apply, in order, to the same sequence. Note that conjunctive ordering is essential here: only by such a successive application of stress rules, together with the connected process of stress weakening, is it possible to get a weaker stress on the final vowel than on the antepenultimate vowel in (49b). Observe also that the Alternating Stress Rule, like the Main Stress Rule, applies to sequences that are words as well as to sequences that are not words themselves but are constituents of words. This is indicated by the absence of ## next to the outermost brackets.

Once the Alternating Stress Rule has applied to words such as those in (49b), the antepenultimate vowel will have primary stress and, as a result of the stress-weakening convention (26), the final vowel will have secondary stress. In point of fact, however, the final vowel in each of these forms has tertiary rather than secondary stress. Given convention (26), there is a straightforward way to obtain the required tertiary stress. We need only postulate a Stress Adjustment Rule as in (51), which reassigns [1stress] to the vowel with [1stress] in a word:

(51) STRESS ADJUSTMENT RULE

$$\begin{bmatrix} \text{1stress} \\ V \end{bmatrix} \rightarrow [\text{1stress}] \ / \ [\#\# X\text{——}Y\#\#]_{\{N,V,A\}}$$

Before discussing this rule further, let us return briefly to the forms in column (a) of (49), that is, the forms such as *chandelĭer*, which are far less common than the words exemplified in column (b). It was noted previously that although these words undergo case (13c) of the Main Stress Rule, thereby receiving primary stress on the last syllable, they are not subject to the two additional rules, (50) and (51), which apply to the forms in column (b). We must therefore mark words such as *chandelĭer* as exceptions to the Alternating Stress Rule (50) (see note 5). There is no need, however, to mark them additionally as exceptions to the Stress Adjustment Rule (51). This rule does not actually affect primary stress at all; instead, it causes all non-primary stresses in a word to be weakened. Since at the time (51) applies to the words in (49a) they will show only primary stress, the rule will thus effect no change. (Actually, the words in question have initial [3stress] as well as final [1stress], but, as we shall see, the rule that assigns the tertiary stress applies after rule (51).)

Returning now to the Stress Adjustment Rule (51), we observe that this rule is actually available to us already: it is identical with the second Compound Rule (38), which was postulated to deal with the rising stress contours in compound nouns like *Mădison Road*. Recall that, as we noted in our discussion of this rule, the modification required to account for such compound nouns resulted in a rule that was applicable to single words as well as to compounds. At that point in our study of stress this appeared to be merely a vacuous by-product. Now, however, we find that it is precisely what we want to happen.[7] Indeed, if we wanted to prevent (38) from applying to single words, we would have to add a special condition to the rule specifically restricting it to sequences of words. Such a condition would cause further complications in combining (38) and (33) into a single rule such as (39) and in combining (39) in turn with the Nuclear Stress Rule as in (48). Thus the theoretical apparatus forces us to adopt a solution for stress contours in word collocations that happens to have the empirically correct consequences for stress subordination in single words as well. That is, our theory tells us that any language which requires a rule of the form of the Compound Rule (39) (or the combined Compound and Nuclear Stress Rules (48)) is likely also to subject its words to Stress Adjustment in accordance with (51). This is a very significant result for our notational devices because it involves

---

[7] In arguing that (51) is identical with the second Compound Rule (38), we deviate from *Sound Pattern of English*. In the earlier work the need for restriction (47) was not realized and the form of the Nuclear Stress Rule was somewhat too general. Once restriction (47) is imposed on the Nuclear Stress Rule, it is necessary to regard the Stress Adjustment Rule as a special case of the Compound Rule rather than of the Nuclear Stress Rule.

the totally unexpected prediction that the subordinate stress in noncompound words will be at most tertiary, whereas in phrases or compound words the subordinate stress may be secondary. Thus the theory tells us to expect that the subsidiary stress in *exacerbate*, for example, should be weaker than the subsidiary stress in a compound noun such as *police debate*. We illustrate the derivation of these contrasting stress contours in (52):

(52) [exacerbāte]~V~   [[polīce] [debāte]]~N~

	1	1	1	MAIN STRESS (13c)
1	2	–	–	ALTERNATING STRESS (50)
1	3	(*v*)	(*v*)	STRESS ADJUSTMENT (51) = (48)
		——	——	
			–	MAIN STRESS (13c)
		–		ALTERNATING STRESS (50)
		1	2	COMPOUND AND NUCLEAR STRESS (48)

4. *Vowel Reduction*

Unstressed vowels in English words have in many instances a special phonetic quality which is traditionally referred to as the "schwa" quality and is represented by the symbol [ə]. Phonetically, this vowel is an unrounded and somewhat backed cognate of the lax [ɛ]. Phonologically, it may be the surface reflex of many different underlying vowels, as shown in (53):

(53) *algebraic*   *algebra*
     diplomacy   *diplomat*
     torrential   *torrent*
     college   *collegiate*
     telegraphic   *telegraphy*

    To account for facts such as these, we postulate the Vowel Reduction Rule (54).

(54) VOWEL REDUCTION RULE

$$\begin{bmatrix} -\text{stress} \\ -\text{tense} \\ V \end{bmatrix} \rightarrow \quad ə \quad / \quad [\#\# X\text{——} Y \#\#]$$

Rule (54) turns unstressed lax vowels into [ə]. As shown in (55), phonetically tense vowels are not subject to reduction even when totally without stress:

(55) various¹

simultaneous¹

ambiguous¹

atheist¹

The penultimate vowels in the forms in (55) must, however, be non-tense at the point at which the Main Stress Rule applies because otherwise the words would exhibit stress on the penultimate rather than on the antepenultimate syllable. The tenseness of the penultimate vowel must therefore be the result of a tensing rule which applies after the Main Stress Rule to tense vowels occurring in prevocalic position. We state this rule as in (56):

(56) TENSING RULE—I

$$V \rightarrow [+\text{tense}] \ / \ [\#\# X \underline{\hspace{1cm}} VY \#\#]$$

Another set of examples where a tensing rule must have applied subsequent to the Main Stress Rule is given in (57a):

(57) (a) (b)

(a)	(b)
fiasco¹	magenta¹
soprano	veranda
illuminati	Bettina
ravioli	Verona
jujitsu	Matilda
Kikuyu	

Since all of these words have penultimate stress, they must undergo case (13b) of the Main Stress Rule. In order for this rule to apply, however, it is necessary that the last vowel be lax at the appropriate point in the derivation. As mentioned previously (see (17)–(19)), it follows that the phonetic tenseness observed in this position in the words in (57a) is due to a phonetic rule which applies after the Main Stress Rule and tenses word-final vowels. The examples in (57b) argue that this second tensing rule cannot apply to all vowels but must be restricted to nonlow vowels, that is, to *i, e, u, o.* This tensing rule must therefore read as in (58):

(58) TENSING RULE—II

$$V \rightarrow [+\text{tense}] \ / \ \left[\#\# X \begin{bmatrix} \underline{\hspace{1cm}} \\ -\text{low} \end{bmatrix} \#\#\right]$$

In spite of their partial identity, the two Tensing Rules (56) and (58) cannot be abbreviated with the help of our notational conventions because, as will be shown in Section 9, the rules cannot be ordered next to each other.

5. Stress Retraction and the Main Stress Rule

Consider the examples in (59):

(59) (a)

¹ ³ *inhibitory*	¹ *compulsory*
¹ ³ *admonitory*	¹ *refectory*
¹ ³ *promissory*	¹ *trajectory*
¹ ³ *interlocutory*	¹ *consistory*
¹ ³ *allegory*	¹ *advisory*
¹ ³ *category*	

(b) is in the second column above.

The tertiary stress on the suffix *-ōry* in the forms in (59a) suggests that these words were derived by means of the Main Stress Rule. If we assume that the *y* represents a lax vowel which is tensed by rule (58), then case (b) of the Main Stress Rule (13) will assign primary stress to the penultimate vowel since this vowel is tense. In terms of stress, then, we will have at this point representations such as those in (60):

(60) *inhibitory   admonitory   allegory* (each with ¹ stress)

To obtain the forms in (59a) from the intermediate representations in (60), we might consider extending the Alternating Stress Rule (50) to allow it to apply not only to words with primary stress on the last vowel but also to forms where the vowel with primary stress is followed by a syllable ending with the affix *-y*. Thus, from *inhibitory* in (60), for example, we would now have *inhibitory* (with ¹ ² stress). The Tensing Rule (58) would then tense the final vowel, and the Stress Adjustment Rule (51), which is a special case of the Compound Rule (39), would lower the stress on *-ory* from secondary to tertiary, yielding the correct output illustrated in (59a).

While this solution is in accordance with the facts of (59a), it suffers from the inadequacy that it does not permit us to derive the examples in (59b) in a parallel fashion. To obtain the latter forms we would have to assume that in these words the *o* in the suffix *-ory* is lax rather than tense so that case (13a) of the Main Stress Rule could apply to place primary stress on the antepenult as required. This lack of parallelism is furthermore only a manifestation of a deeper flaw in the analysis. The proposal just sketched fails to take explicit account of a structural difference between the two sets of forms in (59): the examples in (a) have a weak cluster in the antepenultimate syllable while those in (b) do not.[8] These facts are correlated in the familiar fashion with the position of the main stress. Stress is placed on the pre-antepenult when the antepenult is part of a weak cluster as in (59a); otherwise stress is placed on the antepenult as in (59b). In other words, the location of primary stress in all of these words is governed by the principles of the Main Stress Rule except that everything is shifted over, as it were, toward the beginning of the word.

In discussing the words in (59a), we noted that they first had to undergo case (13b) of the Main Stress Rule and then were subject to stress retraction. In the light of the preceding remarks, it is obvious that stress retraction here is governed not by the Alternating Stress Rule (50), but rather by the Main Stress Rule. Our problem, therefore, is to make the Main Stress Rule apply twice to the same string. A very mechanical solution would be to add to the grammar the rule (61c), which retracts stress in accordance with the Main Stress Rule. This rule would have to follow the Main Stress Rule but could precede the Alternating Stress Rule. As a result we would have the set of rules in (61):

(61) (a) $V \rightarrow$ [1stress] $/ [X\text{——}C_0(\begin{bmatrix} -\text{tense} \\ V \end{bmatrix} C_0^1) \begin{bmatrix} -\text{tense} \\ V \end{bmatrix} C_0]$ (13a,b)

(b) $V \rightarrow$ [1stress] $/ [X\text{——}C_0]$ (13c)

(c) $V \rightarrow$ [1stress] $/ [X\text{——}C_0(\begin{bmatrix} -\text{tense} \\ V \end{bmatrix} C_0^1) \begin{bmatrix} 1\text{stress} \\ V \end{bmatrix} C_0 y]$

We have written the Main Stress Rule in the form where its first two parts, (13a,b), are separated from the third part, (13c), giving the pair of rules (61a,b). Our purpose in doing this is simply to bring out more sharply the relevant similarities between the Main Stress Rule and the stress retraction rule (61c). It is a fact, however, that the two rules abbreviated in (61a) exhibit a certain cohesion. Thus, the overwhelming majority of words are not exceptions to one of the two rules of (61a) but rather to both. (See, for example, the forms in (143b).)

We now observe that (61b) can be obtained by partial deletions of both (61a) and (61c) and should therefore be ordered after these two rules. Indeed, forms which receive primary stress by (61b) can never be subject to (61c) since (c) applies only to words with primary stress on the penultimate rather than on the last vowel. Thus, there is no reason to order (61b) before

---

[8] In spite of forms like *locution*, the antepenultimate vowel in *interlocutory* is lax at the time the Main Stress Rule applies. See note 37 and *Sound Pattern of English*, Chapter 4, Section 4.3.4.

(61c), and, as far as the examples considered up to now are concerned, nothing would change if (c) were ordered before (b). We now have the ordered set shown in (62):

(62) (a) $V \rightarrow$ [1stress] / $[X\underline{\quad}C_0(\begin{bmatrix} -\text{tense} \\ V \end{bmatrix}C_0^1)\begin{bmatrix} -\text{tense} \\ V \end{bmatrix}C_0]$

(b) $V \rightarrow$ [1stress] / $[X\underline{\quad}C_0(\begin{bmatrix} -\text{tense} \\ V \end{bmatrix}C_0^1)\begin{bmatrix} 1\text{stress} \\ V \end{bmatrix}C_0y]$

(c) $V \rightarrow$ [1stress] / $[X\underline{\quad}C_0]$

It is evident that (62a) and (62b) are identical insofar as both embody stress assignment in accordance with the weak cluster principle. Formally this fact can be made explicit by rewriting (62) as (63):

(63)

(a) $V \rightarrow$ [1stress] / $[X\underline{\quad}C_0(\begin{bmatrix} -\text{tense} \\ V \end{bmatrix}C_0^1)\begin{Bmatrix} \begin{bmatrix} -\text{tense} \\ V \end{bmatrix}C_0 \\ \begin{bmatrix} 1\text{stress} \\ V \end{bmatrix}C_0y \end{Bmatrix}]$

(b) $V \rightarrow$ [1stress] / $[X\underline{\quad}C_0]$

In rule (63) we have made use of braces to capture formally the partial identity between (62a) and (62b). Unlike the parenthesis notation, the brace notation does not require that later rules be obtainable from earlier ones by deletion but functions rather like factoring in algebra. Moreover, later rules are conjunctively rather than disjunctively ordered with respect to earlier ones so that a given string may be subject to more than one rule in a set abbreviated by means of braces. In particular, both (62a) and (62b), abbreviated as (63a), may apply to a given string.

It is readily seen that (63b) = (13c) can be obtained by deletion from (63a) in a completely straightforward fashion. All that is required is that we add another set of parentheses. As shown in (64), when the portion of the rule enclosed in the outermost parentheses is deleted, we are left with rule (63b), as desired:

(64) MAIN STRESS RULE

$V \rightarrow$ [1stress] / $[X\underline{\quad}C_0((\begin{bmatrix} -\text{tense} \\ V \end{bmatrix}C_0^1)\begin{Bmatrix} \begin{bmatrix} -\text{tense} \\ V \end{bmatrix}C_0 \\ \begin{bmatrix} 1\text{stress} \\ V \end{bmatrix}C_0y \end{Bmatrix})]$

Given our notational conventions with regard to parentheses and braces, the ordering within the set of rules abbreviated by (64) is as follows. Rule (64) abbreviates the two disjunctively ordered rules in (62a), followed by the two disjunctively ordered rules in (62b), which are in turn followed by rule (62c). The rules of (62a) are *not* disjunctively ordered with respect to the rules of (62b). Thus, one of the rules abbreviated by (62b) may apply to the same string to which one of the rules of (62a) has just applied. Rule (62c), on the other hand, is disjunctively ordered with respect to both (62a) and (62b) and can apply only to a string that is not subject to any of the earlier rules in the set. Our notational conventions therefore produce the correct results when the ordered set of rules abbreviated by (64) is applied to the examples in both (59a) and (59b), as we will see in the sample derivations in (65) at the beginning of the next section.

We must underline at this point that the formulation (64) and the algebraic manipulations that were performed in order to arrive at it are anything but attempts to demonstrate the symbolic potentialities of the notational system. Rather, they are justified by the fact that they express a number of insights about the functioning of the language. In the case under discussion, the formulation (64) of the Main Stress Rule expresses the fact that one and the same principle—namely, the principle of the weak cluster— governs both the assignment of stress in words with a final syllable that contains a lax vowel and the retraction of stress in words that are subject to (62a). Moreover, the fact that the Alternating Stress Rule (50) is ordered after the Main Stress Rule implies that only words which are *not* subject to (62a) of the Main Stress Rule will exhibit stress retraction without regard for the weak cluster principle (i.e., by the Alternating Stress Rule).[9] These are far from trivial consequences and of themselves go a long way toward providing the needed empirical motivation for the notational manipulations of the preceding paragraphs. As the discussion proceeds, we shall point out additional empirical consequences of the formulation (64).

[9] It has been proposed on various occasions that the two stress retraction rules—(62b) of the Main Stress Rule and the Alternating Stress Rule (50)—be coalesced into a single rule, thereby making explicit the fact that both rules retract stress from a later to an earlier syllable in the word. Such a coalescence of rules would be formally less concise than the introduction of case (62b) into the Main Stress Rule. Much more important, however, is the fact that the proposed combined rule leaves totally unaccounted for the high degree of regularity with which the Alternating Stress Rule applies to words with a last vowel that is tense while case (62b) applies to words that end with *-ory* or *-ary*. We note that, as will be shown in Chapter 2, the coalescence of the two stress retraction rules was appropriate for the English of the eighteenth century, where there were many more instances than in twentieth-century English of words with a tense last vowel retracting stress by (62b) and words ending with *-ary* and *-ory* retracting stress without regard for the strong or weak clusters in intervening syllables. We will attempt to demonstrate that the change that took place in the early nineteenth century must formally be reflected by moving (62b) into the Main Stress Rule. It is therefore clear that the alternative under scrutiny here must be shown to account for a wide variety of facts about English stress if it is to be considered as a serious contender. Since no such demonstration has ever been made, we reject the proposal to coalesce the two stress retraction rules into one. For additional discussion see Sections 8 and 11 of this chapter.

6. *Further Remarks on Vowel Reduction:*
Auxiliary Reduction Rule

We examine now in detail how stress is assigned in words of the type illustrated in (59a,b). The rules as they now stand will result in derivations such as (65):[10]

(65) inhibitōry   refectōry

	1		1	MAIN STRESS (62aii)
1	2			MAIN STRESS (62bi)
		1	2	MAIN STRESS (62bii)
1	3	1	3	STRESS ADJUSTMENT (51)

While *inhíbitòry* is the desired form, *réfectòry* is not quite correct since in the actual pronunciation the penultimate vowel does not show tertiary stress. This inadequacy can readily be corrected by adding to the grammar a rule which makes vowels stressless and nontense in position after primary stress. Such vowels will then be subject to the Vowel Reduction Rule (54) and will therefore appear as schwa vowels in the phonetic output. Before formulating the needed rule, we note that it cannot apply to all vowels that follow primary stress. As shown by the examples in (66), post-stress vowels in the final syllable of the word are not subject to reduction:

(66) *prótèst*
import
vacate
kayak
tirade

The rule in question will therefore have to be restricted so as not to apply to the final syllable of the word, as in the formulation (67):[11]

(67) AUXILIARY REDUCTION RULE—I

$$V \rightarrow \begin{bmatrix} -\text{stress} \\ -\text{tense} \end{bmatrix} \Big/ \, [X \begin{bmatrix} 1\text{stress} \\ V \end{bmatrix} C_0 \text{---} C_0 VY]$$

---

[10] In the derivation (65) and elsewhere, (i) refers to the longer alternative and (ii) to the shorter alternative of rules (62a) and (62b); that is, in each case (i) represents the rule that includes the parenthesized sequence [−tense, V]C$_0^1$, and (ii) represents the rule that omits the parenthesized sequence. Recall that these alternatives are disjunctively ordered with respect to each other within (62a) and within (62b).

[11] It will be argued later (see (104) and (124b)) that (67) is a cyclic rule and applies to strings below the word level. This fact is reflected by the absence of ## inside the brackets of the rule.

The introduction of rule (67) allows us to account for an otherwise puzzling class of cases, a sample of which is cited in (68):

(68) *industry*¹
      chemistry
      liberty
      faculty
      travesty

Such words are now handled as shown in the derivation (69) and thus provide further motivation for the form of the Main Stress Rule in (64) (= (62)):¹²

(69) travesty

      1   MAIN STRESS (62aii)
      1 2   MAIN STRESS (62bii)
      1 ˇ   AUXILIARY REDUCTION—I (67)
      1 ə   VOWEL REDUCTION (54)

In stating (62b) we made use of the symbol *y*, which in the subsequent discussion was treated as equivalent to the lax vowel [i]. The reason that we did not utilize the vowel symbol [i] is that we wanted to bring out clearly that only certain words ending with [i] → [iy] are subject to stress retraction by (62b). There is another class of words with final [i] → [iy] that does not undergo this rule, as shown in (70):

(70) *Missouri*¹   *Allegheny*¹
      Israeli   *maharani*
      spumoni   *salmagundi*
      Sephardi   *Turkestani*

The symbol *y* in the Main Stress Rule is therefore to be viewed as representing the lax vowel [i] in words that are marked in the lexicon as belonging to a diacritic category. Let us label this category [B] and say that only words marked [+B] can undergo (62b). Words like those in (70) which are not subject to (62b) will be marked [−B] and hence will not undergo stress retraction.¹³

¹² We shall use ˇ to represent the feature complex [−stress, −tense], assigned here to the second vowel by the Auxiliary Reduction Rule (67).

¹³ Note that the orthography captures this distinction to a great extent, though not completely. Thus, of the words terminating in the lax vowel [i], those which are marked [+B] (and undergo (62b)) are spelled with a final -*y*, while those which are marked [−B] (and do not undergo (62b)) are spelled with a final -*i*: for example, *miscellany*¹ ³ versus *Mussolini*¹. See also note 15.

7. Complex Verbs

There is a significant number of verbs in English which are composed of prefixes such as *con-*, *per-*, *ex-*, *in-*, *re-*, *sur-* and stems such as *-sist*, *-mit*, *-vey*, and *-fer*. These verbs differ from those we have examined so far in that they receive final stress regardless of the quality of the stem vowel, as illustrated in (71):

(71) $\overset{1}{persist}$

remit

infer

extend

impel

transmit

survey

Because certain other phonological processes take place on the boundary between prefix and stem in these verbs,[14] we shall distinguish a special boundary here which will be represented by the = sign. Its status is similar to, but not identical with, the ## sign which we used earlier in this chapter to designate word boundaries. The verbs in (71) will therefore be represented as in (72):

(72) *per=sist*

re=mit

in=fer

ex=tend

im=pel

trans=mit

sur=vey

[14] Briefly, these processes include the following. In these words, stem-initial *s* is voiced when the prefix ends with a vowel but not otherwise. Thus we get *re=semble* (cf. *semblance*), *de=sign* (cf. *sign*), *pre=sume* (cf. *con=sume*), etc. The voicing of stem-initial *s* after prefixes ending with a vowel does not take place in words of all types, but only in the class under discussion; for example, there is no voicing in *para+sitic*, *chromo+somal*, *philo+sophical*, where + represents a morpheme boundary rather than the kind of affix-stem boundary we are concerned with here. (For further discussion, see *Sound Pattern of English*, pp. 95, 148, 221.) Secondly, vowel reduction in word-initial position does not take place before consonant clusters unless a = boundary intervenes: $M\overset{3}{o}nt\overset{1}{a}na$ versus $con=t\overset{1}{a}in$ (see also (109c), (110), and the discussion preceeding (125)). Finally, the Alternating Stress Rule (50) does not apply in words such as $contrad\overset{1}{i}ct$, $intro\overset{1}{s}pect$. If a = boundary is placed before the stem (e.g., *contra=dict*), this result is readily obtained with the rules given here. This last point will be discussed further later in this section.

We must now ask how forms such as those in (72) will be affected by the Main Stress Rule (62) = (64). Let us take the verb *re=mit* as an example. Beginning with case (62a), we see that the final *t* in this verb corresponds to the last C_0 mentioned in the rule, and *i* corresponds to the lax unstressed vowel. The parenthesized material in (62a) can be disregarded since we are dealing with a bisyllabic word. For the second part of (62a) to apply here and assign stress to the first vowel in *re=mit*, the sequence *=m* must correspond to C_0 in the rule. The abbreviation C_0, however, stands for a sequence of zero or more consonants, while the sequence *=m* contains, in addition to the consonant *m*, the boundary marker *=*. Subrule (62a) can therefore not apply to the verbs in (72). We can readily rule out subrule (62b) since it requires that the word contain a vowel with primary stress. This leaves only (62c). Only the final *t* in *re=mit* can correspond to the C_0 of the rule, and the sequence *re=m* properly corresponds to *X* since *X* may contain consonants, vowels, and any boundary but *##*. Hence (62c) will assign stress correctly to the last vowel of each of the verbs in (72).

By the same argument the Main Stress Rule will correctly assign final stress to the verbs in (73):

(73) *inter=cépt*
      contra=dict
      con=de=scend
      com=pre=hend
      intro=spect
      contra=vene

Note that the Alternating Stress Rule (50) will not apply to the verbs in (72) because it does not apply to bisyllabic words in general. Neither will it apply to the verbs in (73) because there is no mention of = boundaries and no cover symbol such as *X* in the appropriate position in the rule. This, however, is not entirely correct: there are words such as those in (74) where the Alternating Stress Rule must apply even though a = boundary is present:

(74) *còn=témplate*
      de=nigrate
      in=filtrate
      de=signate

The difference between the words in (73) and those in (74) is that in the former case the = boundary (plus any intervening consonants) precedes the last vowel, whereas in (74) the same boundary precedes the penultimate vowel. This suggests that the Alternating Stress Rule (50) must be modified as in (75) to allow a = boundary to appear before the penultimate vowel:

(75) ALTERNATING STRESS RULE

$$V \rightarrow [\text{1stress}] \;/\; [X\text{———}C_0(=C_0)VC_0 \begin{bmatrix} \text{1stress} \\ V \end{bmatrix} C_0]$$

Most complex verbs of the type discussed here are not subject to stress retraction by the Alternating Stress Rule either because they are bisyllabic as in (72) or because of the position of the = boundary as in (73). On the other hand, nouns that are derived from these verbs are subject to stress retraction, as shown in (76):

(76) *permit* (with superscripts 1 3 over *permit*)

survey

transfer

import

intercept

It seems natural to suppose that morphological derivation will be reflected in the syntactic structure of the words so that the nouns in (76) will have the constituent structure illustrated in (77):

(77) $[[per=mit]_V]_N$ $[[sur=vey]_V]_N$ $[[inter=cept]_V]_N$

Recall that the rules of stress assignment in phrases and compound words operate in a cyclic fashion. Let us assume, then, that the rules for stress assignment in words—namely, the Main Stress Rule and the Alternating Stress Rule—also apply cyclically. By the argument developed in connection with (72) and (73), we know that in the first pass through the rules the three examples in (77) will receive final stress. The innermost brackets will then be erased and we will have at the beginning of the second pass through the cycle the representations in (78):

(78) $[per=m\overset{1}{i}t]_N$ $[sur=v\overset{1}{e}y]_N$ $[inter=c\overset{1}{e}pt]_N$

As on the first pass through the Main Stress Rule, only the last subrule, (62c), can apply to these forms because of the = boundary. In the strings under discussion this application of (62c) would be vacuous since they already have primary stress on the last vowel. The Alternating Stress Rule (75), which comes next in the rule ordering, will not apply here for precisely the same reasons as on the first pass. Thus, given the present rules, the correct stress contours of the nouns in (78) cannot be derived. The most straightforward way to correct this is to modify the stress retraction subrule (62b) of the Main Stress Rule: we need only make the word-final *y* optional— that is, enclose it in parentheses—and admit an optional ($=C_0$) immediately before the stressed vowel. We shall see that these two modifications are actually independent of each other. There are other types of cases that require that this subrule not be limited to words ending with *y*, and these cases do not involve = boundaries (see (98)).[15]

The modified stress retraction subrule of the Main Stress Rule will now appear as in (79):

(79)   MAIN STRESS RULE: STRESS RETRACTION SUBRULE

$$V \rightarrow [\text{1stress}] \;/\; [X\text{——}C_0(\begin{bmatrix} -\text{tense} \\ V \end{bmatrix} C_0^1)(= C_0)\begin{bmatrix} \text{1stress} \\ V \end{bmatrix} C_0(y)]$$

Rule (79) will apply to the noun representations in (78) and, in conjunction with the Stress Adjustment Rule (51), will yield the correct output (80):

(80) $\overset{1}{per} = \overset{3}{mit}$ $\overset{1}{sur} = \overset{3}{vey}$ $\overset{1}{inter} = \overset{3}{cept}$

8. Further Extensions of the Main Stress Rule

An additional revision of the Main Stress Rule is required because of examples such as those in (81):

(81) $\overset{1}{undu}\overset{3}{latory}$ $\overset{1}{compen}\overset{3}{satory}$
$\overset{1}{discri}\overset{3}{minatory}$ $\overset{1}{explo}\overset{3}{ratory}$
$\overset{1}{manipu}\overset{3}{latory}$ $\overset{1}{excul}\overset{3}{patory}$
$\overset{1}{expostu}\overset{3}{latory}$ $\overset{1}{refor}\overset{3}{matory}$
$\overset{1}{antici}\overset{3}{patory}$ $\overset{1}{conser}\overset{3}{vatory}$
$\overset{1}{rever}\overset{3}{beratory}$ $\overset{1}{hor}\overset{3}{tatory}$

[15] It was pointed out in *Sound Pattern of English* that the distinction drawn by the spelling system might reflect correctly the underlying distinction between instances where stress is retracted and those where it is not (see note 13). In terms of distinctive features the glide [y] differs from the lax vowel [i] not as [+B] from [−B] but as [−syllabic] from [+syllabic]. From this point of view it is then unnecessary to have *y* in the environment of the stress retraction subrule since the symbol C_0 would include a sequence of nonvowels ending with a glide. In order for this solution to work, however, some other modifications are required. We would need a rule turning glides into vowels in word-final position, and we would have to modify somewhat case (62a) of the Main Stress Rule. Neither of these changes is unintuitive or particularly difficult to institute. This alternative, however, would involve a considerable amount of discussion of topics that are outside the main issues with which we are concerned here. Moreover, we shall see that there may be a certain advantage in regarding *y* in rule (79) as a cover symbol for [+B, +syllabic] as well as for the glide *y*; that is, there are certain cases where retraction seems to take place when primary stress is on the penultimate rather than on the final syllable. (See notes 19 and 34.) It seemed to us preferable, therefore, to depart from *Sound Pattern of English* in this matter. We note, however, that this departure is rather minor and far from adequately motivated except in terms of expository convenience.

The location of the primary stress in these words is determined by the weak cluster principle, as in the forms in (59) with the suffix *-ory*. The difference is that in (81) the weak cluster principle operates without regard for the intervening *-at-* affix. To account for this fact, we have to allow *at* to appear optionally before the stressed syllable in case (79) = (62b). But, as noted in *Sound Pattern of English* (p. 138), this situation is not limited to *at*. Thus, for instance, the words in (82a) are all stressed like *hortatory*, whereas those in (82b) are stressed like *advisory* and *refectory* (see (59b)):

(82) (a)   (b)

   sedentary   *elementary*

   voluntary   *anniversary*

   adversary   *documentary*

   momentary   *complimentary*

   legendary

The difference in the stress pattern is correlated with a difference in the phonetic structure of the words: the words in (82a) all begin with the sequence $\#\#C_0VC_0V[+\text{sonorant}]\ [+\text{consonantal}]\ldots$ (where "sonorant" refers to a liquid—i.e., *l* or *r*—or to a nasal consonant). We will therefore assume that in rule (79) $=$(62b) there may optionally appear before the stressed syllable a special vowel marked with the diacritic feature [+D]. The rules of the grammar will assign this diacritic feature to the affix *at* as well as to the second vowel in words beginning with the sequence $\#\#C_0VC_0V[+\text{sonorant}]\ [+\text{consonantal}]\ldots$. The stress retraction subrule (79) will now have the form shown in (83):

(83) MAIN STRESS RULE: STRESS RETRACTION SUBRULE

$$V \rightarrow [\text{1stress}] \quad / \ [X\text{——}C_0(\begin{bmatrix} -\text{tense} \\ V \end{bmatrix}C_0^1)(\begin{bmatrix} +D \\ V \end{bmatrix}C_0)(=C_0)\begin{bmatrix} \text{1stress} \\ V \end{bmatrix}C_0(y)]$$

There is a fair number of words which have the same structure as the forms in (82a) but which exhibit a different stress pattern. A sample is given in (84):

(84) *infirmary*

    placentary

    dispensary

These can be treated as lexically marked exceptions to the above-mentioned rule which assigns the diacritic feature [+D] to words with the specified structure.

It can be shown that the optional syllable with the diacritic mark [+D] must also be postulated in case (62a) of the Main Stress Rule. For example, although each of the words in (85) has a tense penultimate syllable—that is, the affix *at*—to which rule (62a) would assign stress if it applied, none of the forms shows such penultimate stress:[16]

(85) *generative*   *contemplative*
     speculative   *demonstrative*
     federative   *informative*
     iterative   *superlative*
     vituperative   *restorative*

Thus the syllable with the diacritic [+D] must be postulated as an optional sequence in both case (62a) and case (62b) = (83) of the Main Stress Rule. This syllable is not an optional environment for case (62c), however, since words ending with *ate* normally receive final stress by this rule: *generate, contemplate*. In the final statement of the Main Stress Rule (see (99)), the syllable with the diacritic [+D] will therefore be parenthesized and included at the end of the parenthesized expression representing the weak cluster principle. The fact that the syllable with the diacritic [+D] does not figure in the Alternating Stress Rule (75) suggests that in spite of the similarity of the effects of this rule and of (62b) = (83), the two rules are quite distinct. (For further discussion of this matter, see Section 11.)

Still a further modification in the Main Stress Rule is required to account for the examples in (86), which are pairs of verbs and nouns that are related to each other in much the same fashion as those of the *permit* type examined above:

(86)   VERB   NOUN
     delegate   *delegate*
     precipitate   *precipitate*
     advocate   *advocate*
     expatriate   *expatriate*
     predicate   *predicate*
     syndicate   *syndicate*

In view of the discussion of the complex verb-noun pairs in Section 7,

---

[16] The discussion here is limited to the stress contours indicated. Alternative stress contours such as *contemplative* must be obtained by means of different underlying representations (see *Sound Pattern of English*, p. 129). For additional discussion of these and related forms, see the end of Section 9.

it is natural to propose that the examples in (86) have the syntactic structure shown in (87):

(87) [*syndicāte*]_V   [[*syndicāte*]_V]_N

The stress contour of the verb is obtained in the normal fashion, as can be seen from the derivation (88):

(88) [syndicāte]_V

	1	MAIN STRESS (62c)
1	2	ALTERNATING STRESS (75)
1	3	STRESS ADJUSTMENT (51) = (48)

Recall now that in the statement of the combined Compound and Nuclear Stress Rules (48), of which the Stress Adjustment Rule is a constituent part, there appear word boundaries at the beginning and end of the string under consideration. They indicate that the rules subsumed under (48) apply only to constituents that are composed of one or more integral words and not to constituents smaller than a word. It has been shown, moreover, that the rules abbreviated by (48) apply in a cyclical manner to sequences with internal bracketing. The question now arises whether, in the derivation of "nested" words such as the noun *syndicate*, the Stress Adjustment Rule should apply on the first cycle when the rules consider the verb form as well as on the second cycle when the rules take into account the noun. We shall assume here that the Stress Adjustment Rule applies only once in the derivation of noncompound words, that is, at the point when the largest lexical category is under consideration. Formally we achieve this effect by constraining the convention on the placement of word boundaries in such a fashion that it assigns these boundaries to noncompound words only if they are not nested inside other noncompound words. In particular, we shall assume that the underlying representations of the verb and noun *syndicate* given in (87) are incomplete. They should read, instead, as in (89):

(89) [## *syndicāte* ##]_V   [## [*syndicāte*]_V ##]_N

Thus, the deverbal noun is delimited by only one set of word boundaries since the noun-internal verb is not supplied with boundary marks of its own. An immediate consequence of this convention is that in the derivation of the noun *syndicate* the Stress Adjustment Rule will not apply on the first pass through the cycle, as shown in (90):

(90) [## [syndicāte]_V ##]_N

	1	MAIN STRESS (62c)
1	2	ALTERNATING STRESS (75)
–	–	STRESS ADJUSTMENT (51) = (48)

The second pass through the cyclical rules will therefore start with a string of the form shown in (91):

(91) $[\#\# sy\overset{1}{n}dic\overset{2}{a}te\#\#]_N$

If this noun is to be derived in a fashion parallel to the nouns of the *permit* type discussed in Section 7, we should expect it to undergo stress retraction by subrule (83) = (62b) of the Main Stress Rule. This rule would place primary stress on the antepenultimate syllable of the word, which already carries primary stress and would thus remain unchanged. The only effect of the application of the rule, then, would be to weaken the stress on the last syllable from secondary to tertiary. The [3stress] would in turn be weakened to [4stress] by the subsequent application of the Stress Adjustment Rule (51). This would be a step in the right direction, since it is reasonable to suppose that vowels with relatively low stress will ultimately reduce, as does the last vowel of *syndicate*.

In order to achieve this result, we must do two things. We first have to modify the stress retraction subrule (83) of the Main Stress Rule so that it will apply not only if the last vowel has primary stress but also if the vowel has secondary stress. (The appropriately revised subrule is given in (100b).) Next we must add to the grammar a second Auxiliary Reduction Rule (92), which will make certain vowels with [4stress] subject to Vowel Reduction (54):[17]

(92) AUXILIARY REDUCTION RULE—II

$$\begin{bmatrix} \gamma \text{stress} \\ V \end{bmatrix} \rightarrow \begin{bmatrix} -\text{stress} \\ -\text{tense} \end{bmatrix} \ / \ [\#\# X \text{——} Y \#\#]$$

CONDITIONS: $\gamma \geq 4$
Y contains no [1stress]

The restriction of (92) to the environment $[\#\#...\#\#]$ recalls a similar restriction in the combined Compound and Nuclear Stress Rules (48). Unlike (48), however, rule (92) does not specifically admit the presence of word boundaries internal to the string. The effect of this restriction here, then, is to limit the application of the rule to a single pass through the cyclical rules, that is, at the point where we are dealing with words. This is crucial for the proper operation of the Auxiliary Reduction Rule under discussion.

---

[17] We depart here from the order of rules given in *Sound Pattern of English* and place the Auxiliary Reduction Rule (92) after rather than before the Stress Adjustment Rule. See also Section 10.

This rule subjects to reduction vowels having quarternary or weaker stress. But in the verb phrase *delegate authority*, for example, the word *delegate* has quarternary stress on the last syllable, which, unlike other syllables with [4stress], is not reduced. The reason is that the Auxiliary Reduction Rule (92) applies only at the word level (since, as already mentioned, *X* and *Y* may not include word boundaries unless specifically noted otherwise in the statement of the rule), and at that level the verb *delegate* has the stress contour 1ˇ3, which exempts the last vowel from reduction by (92). It is difficult to see how a rule of this type can be stated at all unless it is restricted to applying at one particular pass through the cyclical rules.

It is to be noted at this point that (92) must precede the Tensing Rule (58), for if (92) applied after (58) we should get a reduced vowel at the end of words such as *effigy*. That these words have no stress on the last vowel can readily be established by comparing them with such words as *refugee*. In order to obtain the correct stress assignment in *effigy*, we must assume that the last vowel is nontense in the underlying representation. The subsequent tensing of this vowel is then due to rule (58). If, however, (58) were followed by (92), its effect would be undone: rule (92) makes stressless vowels non-tense and hence subject to Vowel Reduction (54). There are a number of American dialects where word-final vowels are subject to reduction (leading to such pronunciations as *Chicag*[ə], *Missour*[ə], *potat*[ə]). It would seem that such dialects are best described as not containing the Tensing Rule (58).

The need for an additional modification of the Main Stress Rule is illustrated by verb-noun pairs such as those in (93):

(93) (a)   (b)

VERB	NOUN	VERB	NOUN
torment	torment	document	document
ferment	ferment	complement	complement
augment	augment	experiment	experiment
		instrument	instrument
		regiment	regiment

It is clear that (93a) parallels the examples of the type (72)-(76) and (93b) parallels the examples of (86). However, since all the words in (93) end with a syllable that contains a lax vowel, they are subject to (62a) of the Main Stress Rule, which will place primary stress on the penultimate vowel in (93a) and on the antepenultimate vowel in (93b). There would then be no way to obtain stress on the last vowel in the verb forms and thus no way to obtain the stress contours shown in (93). This suggests that we need some means of allowing for words with lax final vowels that are stressed. We achieve this effect by marking the forms as exceptions to case (a) of the Main Stress Rule (62). A form so marked automatically becomes subject to case (c) and thereby receives final stress. (See also Section 12.) The proper stress contours for the verbs in (93) can then be obtained in the familiar way.

The noun forms require another pass through the rules. At the start of this second cycle we will have strings such as in (94):

(94) [*tórment*]$_N$ [*dócumènt*]$_N$

These are precisely parallel to such previously discussed examples as those in (95):

(95) [*sur=véy*]$_N$ [*sýndicàte*]$_N$

It will be recalled that both representations in (95) were next subject to stress retraction by subrule (83) of the Main Stress Rule (revised, as mentioned with regard to *syndicate*, to allow secondary as well as primary stress on the final syllable). It would seem reasonable to expect, then, that the nouns in (94) would be subject to stress retraction by the same rule. Note first, however, that just as in the first cycle, case (a) of the Main Stress Rule is applicable to these forms. Were the rule allowed to apply, the results would be as in (96):

(96) *tòrmént*   *dòcumént*

Next, the revised stress retraction subrule of the Main Stress Rule would be brought to bear on (96). It would affect only the first word, yielding the representation in (97):

(97) *tórmènt*

By the operation of the Stress Adjustment and reduction rules, (97) will result in a form with a reduced vowel in the second syllable. However, as the contrast *tórmènt–tórrent* clearly indicates, the second vowel in the noun *torment* is in fact not reduced. Moreover, while the correct output *dócument*, with a reduced final vowel, ultimately is derived from the string *dòcumént* in (96), its derivation does not parallel that of *survey* or *syndicate*, which, at the very least, must be considered inelegant. It is clear, then, that case (62a) of the Main Stress Rule must not be allowed to apply in the derivation of the nouns in (93a).

Now recall that on the first pass through the rules the forms in question had to be marked as not being subject to (62a) in order to obtain the correct stress contours in the verbs. It is most natural to suppose that this marking carries over to the second cycle. Being exempt from (62a), the strings (94) are subject to the modified stress retraction subrule (62b) = (83). We obtain, therefore, the forms in (98), from which the correct stress contours are readily derived by the Stress Adjustment and reduction rules:[18]

(98) $\overset{1}{t}\overset{2}{o}rment$ $\overset{1}{d}ocu\overset{3}{m}ent$

After all of the modifications just outlined are introduced into the Main Stress Rule, the rule will appear in the form (99):[19]

(99) MAIN STRESS RULE

$$V \rightarrow [\text{1stress}] \ / \ [X\text{——}C_0((\begin{bmatrix}-\text{tense}\\V\end{bmatrix}C_0^1)(\begin{bmatrix}+D\\V\end{bmatrix}C_0)\begin{Bmatrix}\begin{pmatrix}\begin{bmatrix}-\text{stress}\\-\text{tense}\\V\end{bmatrix}C_0\end{pmatrix}\\(=C_0)\begin{bmatrix}\begin{Bmatrix}2\text{stress}\\1\text{stress}\end{Bmatrix}\\V\end{bmatrix}C_0(y)\end{Bmatrix})]$$

The Main Stress Rule (99) abbreviates the three major subrules in (100):

(100) MAIN STRESS RULE: SUBRULES

(a) $V \rightarrow [\text{1stress}] \ / \ [X\text{——}C_0(\begin{bmatrix}-\text{tense}\\V\end{bmatrix}C_0^1)(\begin{bmatrix}+D\\V\end{bmatrix}C_0)\begin{bmatrix}-\text{stress}\\-\text{tense}\\V\end{bmatrix}C_0]$

(Continued on p. 48)

[18] It has been pointed out to us by J. R. Ross that there are numerous trisyllabic verb-noun pairs in English in which no distinctions in the stress contours are to be found: *dynamite, parachute, prostitute, counterfeit, compromise, ridicule, catalog, manifest,* etc. In fact, it would appear that only words in *-ment* and *-ate* show the distinctions in stress contours just discussed. We believe that this is due to a difference in the underlying representations: the deverbal nouns in *-ment* and *-ate* have a nested constituent structure like that exemplified by (87); verb-noun pairs cited by Ross, however, are *not* deverbal nouns. We shall assume that, unlike deverbal nouns, the forms given by Ross do not have a nested constituent structure but rather are made up of unnested sequences of formatives. While a motivation for this distinction is at present unknown and would require a thorough understanding of the principles of derivational morphology, it appears to us all but certain that the devices available for word formation in a language must be rich enough to allow us to create words both with and without nested constituent structure.

[19] The ad hoc symbol *y* at the end of the lower branch of (99) represents here not only the affix *y* (as in *industry, compulsory*), but also a number of other word-final syllables marked [+B] (see end of Section 6), such as those in $\overset{1}{m}onosy\overset{3}{l}lable$, $\overset{1}{q}uanti\overset{3}{t}ati\overset{1}{v}e$, $\overset{1}{o}rchestra$, where retraction appears to take place "irregularly." See also the comments in notes 15 and 34.

   We have added to the top branch of (99) the requirement that the last vowel be not only [−tense] but also [−stress]. While this plays no role in the cases under discussion up to this point, it is crucial for some examples to be examined in Section 11.

100 (Continued)

(b) $V \rightarrow [1\text{stress}] \quad / \quad [X\text{---}C_0(\begin{bmatrix} -\text{tense} \\ V \end{bmatrix}C_0^1)(\begin{bmatrix} +D \\ V \end{bmatrix}C_0)(=C_0)\begin{bmatrix} \begin{Bmatrix} 2\text{stress} \\ 1\text{stress} \end{Bmatrix} \\ V \end{bmatrix}C_0(y)]$

(c) $V \rightarrow [1\text{stress}] \quad / \quad [X\text{---}C_0]$

The final example to be considered in this section is the noun *advocacy*. Let us assume that this noun is formed with the suffix *-y* so that its underlying representation will be as in (101):

(101) $[adv\bar{o}c\bar{a}te + y]_N$

The shift of $t \rightarrow s$ before *y* is amply attested (e.g., *diplomacy, lunacy, policy, celibacy, delicacy, candidacy, obstinacy*), and we shall therefore assume that the grammar includes a rule with this effect (see *Sound Pattern of English*, pp. 229 ff). The string (101) will be subject to subrule (100a) of the Main Stress Rule, which will place stress not on the affix *āt*, which is marked [+D] (see (85) and accompanying discussion), but rather on the preceding tense *o* (cf. *evoke, vocal*). This will give us the representation (102):

(102) $adv\bar{o}c\bar{a}te + y$

The string (102) is not subject to stress retraction by (100b) nor to any other stress rule, suggesting that the underlying representation (101) was incorrectly chosen. To obtain the correct stress contour, we must assume that the noun is in fact derived from the verb so that the underlying string is not (101) but (103):

(103) $[[adv\bar{o}c\bar{a}te]_V + y]_N$

On the first pass through the cyclical rules the verb is supplied with primary stress on the tense last vowel by (100c). This stress is then retracted to the antepenultimate vowel by the Alternating Stress Rule (75), resulting in the string in (104):

(104) $adv\overset{1}{\bar{o}}c\overset{2}{\bar{a}}te$

The sequence (104) is in turn subject to the first Auxiliary Reduction Rule (67), which, as will be recalled, is a cyclic rule (see note 11). This rule laxes the *o* in the second syllable, giving, ultimately, $adv\overset{1}{o}c\overset{2}{a}te$ for the verb form.

In the derivation of the noun form, we have at the beginning of the second pass through the cyclical rules the representation (105), where the second vowel is lax:

(105) $[adv\overset{1}{o}c\overset{2}{\bar{a}}te + y]_N$

This string is now subject to (100a). Since $\bar{a}t$ is marked $[+D]$ and the *o* in the syllable preceding $\bar{a}t$ was laxed by rule (67), the rule places primary stress on the first syllable. We therefore obtain the string shown in (106):

(106) $[\overset{1}{adv}o\overset{3}{c\bar{a}}te+y]_\mathbf{N}$

The subrule (100b) does not apply to (106) because the last stressed vowel carries tertiary rather than secondary or primary stress. Subrule (100c) is not applicable either because it is disjunctively ordered with respect to (100a), which has already applied on this pass through the cycle. The string (106) also fails to satisfy the Alternating Stress Rule (75), but the Stress Adjustment Rule (51), the Tensing Rule (58), the Auxiliary Reduction Rule (92), and Vowel Reduction (54) will all apply to yield the correct stress contour (107):

(107) $\overset{1}{æ}dvəkəs+\bar{i}y$

The example just discussed shows that by making plausible assumptions about the constituent structure of words, we can derive the correct stress contours in a fairly straightforward fashion. To the extent that this is true, our description can be regarded as being confirmed by the facts.

9. *Vowel Reduction and the Cyclical Application of Rules*

We have accounted for the reduction of vowels by postulating the Vowel Reduction Rule (54) which applies to lax unstressed vowels. As we have seen, however, certain tense vowels and vowels that have received stress at some point also reduce. To allow rule (54) to apply in these cases, we introduced the Auxiliary Reduction Rules I (67) and II (92), which make the vowels in question lax and stressless.

We also noted instances, on the other hand, where lax unstressed vowels were exempt from reduction by the Vowel Reduction Rule (54). For example, the boldface vowels in $v\overset{1}{a}rious$ and $Chic\overset{1}{a}go$, which must be lax at the point where the Main Stress Rule (100) applies, were subsequently tensed by the Tensing Rules (56) and (58) and thus prevented from undergoing reduction. Another mechanism for exempting a vowel from reduction is to assign it enough stress so that it will not be subject to any of the reduction rules. We have seen this device in operation in our discussion of the stress contour of the noun $t\overset{1}{o}rm\overset{3}{e}nt$ versus $t\overset{1}{o}rrent$ (see (97) and (98)). Consider now the words in (108), which have a tertiary stress located before the primary stress of the word:[20]

(108)

$\overset{3}{Tatamagouchi}\overset{1}{}$	$\overset{3}{Monongahela}\overset{1}{}$	$\overset{3}{Conestoga}\overset{1}{}$
$\overset{3}{Tippecanoe}\overset{1}{}$	$\overset{3}{gerontophilia}\overset{1}{}$	$\overset{3}{serendipity}\overset{1}{}$
$\overset{3}{Kalamazoo}\overset{1}{}$	$\overset{3}{Napoleonic}\overset{1}{}$	$\overset{3}{Alexandria}\overset{1}{}$
$\overset{3}{Winnipesaukee}\overset{1}{}$	$\overset{3}{aristocratic}\overset{1}{}$	$\overset{3}{opportunity}\overset{1}{}$
$\overset{3}{mulligatawny}\overset{1}{}$	$\overset{3}{arithmetician}\overset{1}{}$	

It can readily be observed that in these examples the tertiary stress appears either two or three syllables before the primary stress. The distribution is, moreover, determined by the same weak cluster principle that we have encountered in the Main Stress Rule (99). Unfortunately, there appears at present no way in which this parallelism can be formally expressed in our notations because the Main Stress Rule cannot be ordered next to the rule accounting for the forms in (108). This may be due to a shortcoming in the notational apparatus or to a lack of understanding on our part concerning the phonetic processes involved or to both. Whatever the reasons, we are unable at this point to find a solution and must for the time being be satisfied with simply flagging this inadequacy in our description. With these comments on record, we state the needed rule as (109):[21]

(109) AUXILIARY REDUCTION RULE—III

$$V \rightarrow [3\text{stress}] \ / \ [\#\#C_0 \begin{cases} X - C_0(\begin{bmatrix} -\text{tense} \\ V \end{bmatrix} C_0^1)VC_0 \begin{bmatrix} 1\text{stress} \\ V \end{bmatrix}) & \text{(a)} \\ \begin{bmatrix} \underline{\quad} \\ +\text{tense} \end{bmatrix} & Y\#\#] \quad \text{(b)} \\ \underline{\quad}C_2 & \text{(c)} \end{cases}$$

---

[20] Words formed with certain suffixes—e.g. *-ic*, *-id*, *-ion*—have stress on the presuffixal syllable even if it has a weak cluster: $\overset{1}{Napoleonic}$, $\overset{1}{aristocratic}$. There are various devices available to handle these exceptional suffixes: we can postulate bisyllabic underlying representations which then undergo certain adjustments, or we can mark the words as exceptions to subcase (100a) of the Main Stress Rule. Since at present we do not know of any systematic reason for preferring one of the possible solutions over the others, we leave the question open.

[21] It has been proposed by Kisseberth (1970) that the notational apparatus of phonology be expanded so as to allow one to value more highly rules that are partially identical, even when they are not adjacently ordered, than rules that are totally different. Although the proposal appeals to us, we have not incorporated it into our theory because we are at present far from clear about what other implications, if any, such an extension of the theory would have.

The stress-weakening convention (26) applies only in the case of rules that assign [1stress]. Hence the assignment of [3stress] by the Auxiliary Reduction Rule (109) is not accompanied by stress weakening.

Note that rule (109) as stated must be ordered after the Stress Adjustment Rule (51) since the words in (108) show [3stress] and not [4stress] in the positions affected by (109). The first branch of the rule accounts for the examples in (108). The second and third branches have been added to handle forms such as those in (110) and (111a), respectively. (It is interesting to note, incidentally, that these last two cases of the rule embody the strong cluster environment just as the first case includes the weak cluster environment.) Case (109c) has some idiosyncratic exceptions, as illustrated in (111b).

(110)
$\overset{3\ \ 1}{typhoon}$	$\overset{31}{oasis}$
$\overset{3\ 1}{iconic}$	$\overset{31}{Siam}$
$\overset{3\ \ 1}{vocation}$	$\overset{31}{hiatus}$
$\overset{3\ \ 1}{august}$	$\overset{31}{beatitude}$
$\overset{3\ 1}{event}$	$\overset{3\ 1}{geology}$

(111) (a)   (b)

(a)	(b)
$\overset{3\ \ 1}{asbestos}$	$\overset{1}{Kentucky}$
$\overset{3\ \ 1}{gestation}$	$\overset{1}{confetti}$
$\overset{3\ \ 1}{Montana}$	$\overset{1}{Atlanta}$
$\overset{3\ \ 1}{bandana}$	$\overset{1}{Saskatchewan}$

Examples such as $\overset{3\ 1}{oasis}$, $\overset{31}{Siam}$ in (110) suggest that (109b) must follow the Tensing Rule (56), for this rule insures that the first vowel in these words is tense and hence subject to (109b). This fact is important in the determination of how the rules are to be ordered (see the discussion of (118)).

We draw special attention to the fact that the syllable immediately before the one with primary stress does not receive tertiary stress by case (a) of (109). This shows up directly in the reduction to which this syllable is subject in every word in the list (108) (except in $\overset{\quad\ 1}{Napoleonic}$, in which the pre-stress vowel is tensed by rule (56)). There are, however, interesting exceptions to this regularity. As typical examples, consider the words in (112):

(112) (a)   (b)

(a)	(b)
$\overset{3\ \ 4\ \ 1}{exaltation}$	$\overset{3\quad\ 1}{devastation}$
$\overset{3\ \ 4\ \ 1}{relaxation}$	$\overset{3\quad\ 1}{illustration}$
$\overset{3\ \ 4\ \ 1}{attestation}$	$\overset{3\quad\ \ 1}{compensation}$
$\overset{3\ \ 4\ \ 1}{electricity}$	$\overset{3\quad\ \ 1}{orchestration}$
$\overset{3\ \ 4\ \ 1}{elasticity}$	$\overset{3\quad\ \ 1}{concentration}$
$\overset{3\qquad\ 4\ \ 1}{instrumentality}$	

The examples in column (a) all show nonreduced vowels in the syllable immediately preceding the one with primary stress, whereas those in column (b) show reduced vowels as before. If we examine the words somewhat more closely, we see that those in column (a) are derived from words which have primary stress on the syllable under discussion; those in column (b), on the other hand, are derived from words without stress on that syllable. We show this in (113):

(113) (a)

$$\overset{1}{exalt}$$
$$\overset{1}{relax}$$
$$\overset{1}{attest}$$
$$\overset{1}{electric}$$
$$\overset{1}{elastic}$$
$$\overset{1}{instrumental}$$

(b)

$$\overset{1}{deva}\overset{3}{state}$$
$$\overset{1}{illu}\overset{3}{strate}$$
$$\overset{1}{compen}\overset{3}{sate}$$
$$\overset{1}{orche}\overset{3}{strate}$$
$$\overset{1}{concen}\overset{3}{trate}$$

If we assume that the forms in (112) are all derived rather than primary, then the stress contours they exhibit are readily accounted for by the rules as developed, provided that these are applied in cyclical fashion, as shown in (114):[22]

(114) (a)

$$[[\text{exalt}]_V \text{ ātion}]_N$$

1		
2	1	
3	1	
3 3	1	

(b)

$$[[\text{concentrāte}]_V \text{ ion}]_N$$

	1		MAIN STRESS (100c)
1	2		ALTERNATING STRESS (75)
2	1		MAIN STRESS (100a)
3	1		STRESS ADJUSTMENT (51)
(*v*)			AUXILIARY REDUCTION—III (109)

The facts just reviewed concerning the reduction or nonreduction of pretonic vowels in words such as *concentration* and *exaltation* are everything but self-evident to the ordinary speaker of English, and the testimony of even the best phoneticians is not entirely unambiguous. In spite of this we must regard these results as the strongest possible corroboration of the theory advanced, which, as has been noted repeatedly, was developed to handle quite obvious and gross facts of English accentuation. It then turned out that the theoretical apparatus thus required had specific implications

[22] To achieve the correct stress contour for *exaltation*, a further adjustment is required which we turn to directly (see rule (115)).

The suffix *-ion* is viewed here as bisyllabic. In this way we account for the fact that it places stress in all cases on the immediately preceding vowel. By a subsequent rule the *i* of *-ion* is turned into the glide *y*, which appears in the output in such words as *rebellion* and *union* but is deleted in such words as *exaltation* and *concentration*, though not without leaving traces.

for far more subtle points of English pronunciation such as those just reviewed. The fact that these implications turn out to be empirically true constitutes, therefore, very strong confirmation of the theoretical apparatus developed. In particular, the assumption that rules apply in cyclical order is absolutely crucial to obtaining the correct results. Any theory that wishes to operate without cyclical application of rules would have to account for the same facts in an equally motivated manner. Though not impossible in principle, it is quite unlikely that this challenge will be easily met. And unless and until it is met, the assumption that cyclical rules apply below the word level must be accepted.

Returning now to the derivations in (114), we note that although *concentration* $\overset{3}{}\overset{1}{}$ is correctly derived, our rules give the contour 331ᵛ for *exaltation* rather than the necessary 341ᵛ. A very simple way to correct this is to add a special rule that applies before the Auxiliary Reduction Rule (109) and weakens the pretonic vowel from [3stress] to [4stress]. We formulate the rule as in (115):

(115) [3stress] $\rightarrow$ [4stress] / **[## X——C₀ [1stress] Y ##]**

This not only remedies the defect just noted but also provides some additional machinery that appears to be needed quite independently. The word *electricity* has, according to Kenyon and Knott (1944), two possible stress contours: it can be pronounced [ə͵lɛkˈtrɪsətɪ] or [͵ilɛkˈtrɪsətɪ], that is, with the stress contour ᵛ31ᵛᵛ or 341ᵛᵛ. We cannot account for the former stress contour with the rules we now have, for (115) will assign [4stress] to the pretonic syllable and the Auxiliary Reduction Rule (109a) in its present form will assign [3stress] to the first syllable. To remedy this, we will complicate rule (109) somewhat and require that the pretonic vowel have quaternary or weaker stress. We can then account for the stress contour ᵛ31ᵛᵛ in *electricity* by saying that this word is exempt from (115) and consequently also from the Auxiliary Reduction Rule (109a) as just modified. The stress contour 341ᵛᵛ, on the other hand, is obtained by allowing (115) to apply, which then means that the revised (109a) will also apply. The modified Auxiliary Reduction Rule—III is given as (116):

(116) AUXILIARY REDUCTION RULE—III

$$V \rightarrow [3\text{stress}] \ / \ [\#\# C_0 \left\{ \begin{array}{l} X\!\!-\!\!-\!\!C_0(\begin{bmatrix} -\text{tense} \\ V \end{bmatrix} C_0^1)\begin{bmatrix} \gamma\text{stress} \\ V \end{bmatrix} C_0 \begin{bmatrix} 1\text{stress} \\ V \end{bmatrix}) \quad \text{(a)} \\ \begin{bmatrix} \rule{1.5em}{0.4pt} \\ +\text{tense} \end{bmatrix} \quad \text{(b)} \\ \rule{1.5em}{0.4pt}C_2 \quad \text{(c)} \end{array} \right\} Y \ \#\#]$$

CONDITION: $\gamma \geq 4$

Rule (116), in conjunction with rule (115), accounts properly for all the words in (112), in particular, for the differences between the words in column (a) and column (b). Note, by the way, that the unreduced pretonic vowels in (112a) are invariably lax and followed by two or more consonants. There are no cases where the unreduced pretonic syllable is tense. Thus, there is a lack of parallelism between noninitial syllables and the initial syllable, where, as shown in (111a), both types of strong cluster appear unreduced pretonically. Now compare the examples in (112a) with those in (117):

(117) $\overset{3}{e}xpl\overset{1}{a}nation$ $\overset{3}{a}tom\overset{1}{i}city$

       intonation   *canonicity*

       divination   *periodicity*

       consolation   *historicity*

       $\overset{3}{o}rgan\overset{1}{i}zation$ *chromaticity*

       interposition

All these words are parallel in structure to (112a) in that the phonetically pretonic vowel has received primary stress in the immediately preceding cycle: e.g., *expláin–expláination*, *atómic–atómicity*. The analogy with the words in (112a) would then lead us to expect an unreduced pretonic vowel with [4stress]. As a matter of fact, however, the pretonic vowel in (117) is consistently reduced. Now note that, as opposed to (112a), the pretonic vowel in (117) is followed by one consonant rather than two. We may, then, account for (117) with an additional auxiliary reduction rule which is similar to (92) (and which will therefore be combined with it—(see (125-IX)) in that it turns a stressed vowel into one that is both nontense and unstressed and, moreover, applies at the word level only. The environment in which this takes place may be given provisionally as in (118):

(118) $\begin{bmatrix} \gamma\text{stress} \\ V \end{bmatrix} \rightarrow \begin{bmatrix} -\text{stress} \\ -\text{tense} \end{bmatrix} \; / \; [\#\# X\text{——}C_0^1 \begin{bmatrix} 1\text{stress} \\ V \end{bmatrix} Y \#\#]$

CONDITION: $\gamma \geq 4$

Rule (118) must be ordered after (116b): if (118) were to apply to the words in (110) (e.g., $typh\overset{3}{o}\overset{1}{o}n$, $o\overset{3}{a}\overset{1}{s}is$), the vowel in the first syllable would be laxed and there would be no way for (116b) to assign it [3stress].[23] We must also note that if the Auxiliary Reduction Rules (67), (92), and (118), which all have very similar effects, are to be ordered together, the two Tensing

---

[23] This is technically an improvement over the treatment in *Sound Pattern of English*, where additional conditions had to be imposed on the counterpart of rule (118) (cf. (113) of Chapter Three in *Sound Pattern*).

Rules (56) and (58) cannot be collapsed. It was pointed out in the discussion accompanying the Auxiliary Reduction Rule (92) that (58) must follow (92), whereas, as shown in the discussion of (109)=(116), the Tensing Rule (56) must precede (116b), which, as just shown, must in turn precede (118). Since we wish to order (92), (118), and (67) together, the Tensing Rule (56) will precede not only (118) but also (92). The order of the rules must therefore be (56), (116), (67)-(118)-(92), (58).

Recall, now, that the nonreduction of the pretonic vowels in (112a) has been attributed to the fact that they received primary stress on a previous pass through the cycle. As illustrated in the derivations (114a,b), this account is contingent upon attributing to the words in question a nested constituent structure. Such an approach is not implausible in view of the fact that these words are clearly cognate to the verbs from which they are said to be derived. There are, however, a great many words which are quite similar to those in (112a) but which show a reduced pretonic vowel instead of the expected unreduced vowel. Some examples are given in (119):

(119) *consultation*

      transformation

      information

      conversation

      lamentation

Note that these words, like (112a) but unlike (117), have two consonants before the primary stress and thus cannot be explained by rule (118). Given the rules developed here, then, the reduction of the pretonic vowel can be achieved only by assuming that the words in (119) do not have a nested constituent structure like the words in (112a) but are instead formed by a simple linear collocation of morphemes, as illustrated in (120):[24]

(120) $[con = sult + \bar{a}t + ion]_N$

	1	MAIN STRESS (100a)
3	1	AUXILIARY REDUCTION—III (116a)

It must be stressed here that the proposed account, while not implausible, lacks full justification. It yields the required results but it leaves unexplained why *exaltation* should have a nested constituent structure while *consultation* does not. As noted previously, the answer to such questions is not likely to be found until deeper understanding is gained of the intricate topic of word formation, which, at present, is one of the least understood chapters in linguistics. These gaps in our knowledge, however, do not affect

---

[24] The application of rule (116a) to a sequence with the boundary = in the position indicated in (120) presumes a slight modification that will be made in Section 10.

the primary point at issue here: the stress contours of certain classes of words can readily be accounted for if they are assumed to have a nested constituent structure and if rules are applied in cyclical order to this structure. No serious alternatives to this procedure have as yet been advanced.

A new class of examples supporting the proposed cyclical analysis has been brought to our attention in an unpublished paper by M. K. Brame (1969). Brame notes that in spite of great superficial similarities, the two sets of words in (121) show striking differences in their stress contours:

(121) (a)

$\overset{1}{div}\overset{3}{inatory}$
$\overset{1}{obl}\overset{3}{igatory}$
$\overset{1}{inflamm}\overset{3}{atory}$
$\overset{1}{expl}\overset{3}{anatory}$

$\overset{1}{prov}ocative$
$\overset{1}{comm}utative$
$\overset{1}{disp}utative$
$\overset{1}{decl}arative$
$\overset{1}{comp}arative$

(b)

$\overset{1}{assim}\overset{3}{ilatory}$
$\overset{1}{obl}\overset{3}{igatory}$
$\overset{1}{sal}\overset{3}{ivatory}$
$\overset{1}{reverb}\overset{3}{eratory}$

$\overset{1}{iter}ative$
$\overset{1}{gen}erative$
$\overset{1}{cop}ulative$
$\overset{1}{cum}ulative$
$\overset{1}{ejac}ulative$

All these words end with the prefinal affix *at* followed by a final suffix *-ory* or *-ive*. In the forms in column (a) the primary stress is on the syllable preceding *at*; in those in column (b) the primary stress is two syllables before *at*. Since in all the examples a weak cluster precedes the affix *at*, column (b) is readily seen to be regular while column (a) appears at first glance to be irregular. Brame observes, however, that the forms in column (a) all have related verbs without *at* which, moreover, end with a tense vowel (e.g., *divinatory–divine*); the forms in (b), on the other hand, have related verbs with *-ate* (e.g., *assimilatory–assimilate*). We can express this difference by positing that the words in (a) have a different syntactic structure from those in (b), as illustrated in (122):

(122) (a) $[[\text{pro}=\text{vōk}]_V +\text{āt}+\text{iv}]_A$

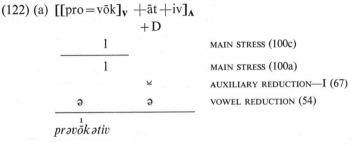

(b) $[[\text{iterāt}]_V +\text{iv}]_A$
$+D$

	1		MAIN STRESS (100c)
1	2		ALTERNATING STRESS (75)
1	3		MAIN STRESS (100a)
1	4		STRESS ADJUSTMENT (51)
1	ᴗ		AUXILIARY REDUCTION—II (92)
ə	ə		VOWEL REDUCTION (54)

$\overset{1}{\textit{itərətiv}}$

These underlying representations, which parallel those in (114a) and
(114b), lead to the correct output with one exception: they fail to explain
why the stem vowel in $\overset{1}{provocative}$ is lax although in the underlying representation it has to be tense. The answer is to be found in the well-known
Trisyllabic Laxing Rule (123), which has to be included in a phonology of
English in any case (see *Sound Pattern of English*, p. 52 and *passim*):

(123) TRISYLLABIC LAXING RULE

$$V \rightarrow [-\text{tense}] \ / \ [\#\# X \text{——} C_0 V C_0 V Y \#\#]$$

Since the $\bar{o}$ in *provocative* is in the third syllable from the end of the
word, it will be subject to this rule, and we will have a lax vowel in the phonetic
output.

A word must be said about the dual forms $\overset{13}{obligatory}$ versus $\overset{13}{obligatory}$.
The natural move is to interpret the former as being derived from the verb
oblige and the latter from the verb *obligate*, as shown in (124):

(124) (a) $[[\text{oblīg}]_V +\text{āt}+\bar{\text{o}}\text{ry}]_A$
$+D$

1			MAIN STRESS (100c)
2		1	MAIN STRESS (100a)
1		2	MAIN STRESS (100b)
1		3	STRESS ADJUSTMENT (51)
ĭ			TRISYLLABIC LAXING (123)
		ᴗ	AUXILIARY REDUCTION—I (67)
ə		ə	VOWEL REDUCTION (54)

$\overset{13}{\textit{əblĭgətŏry}}$

(*Continued on p. 58*)

124 (*Continued*)

(b) [[oblīgāt]$_V$ +ōry]$_A$

	+D		
	1		MAIN STRESS (100c)
1	2		ALTERNATING STRESS (51)
	⌣		AUXILIARY REDUCTION—I (67)
2	3	1	MAIN STRESS (100a)
1	4	2	MAIN STRESS (100b)
1	5	3	STRESS ADJUSTMENT (51)
1	⌣	3	AUXILIARY REDUCTION—II (92)
	ə ə		VOWEL REDUCTION (54)

$\overset{1}{o}bl\overset{}{ə}g\overset{}{ə}t\overset{3}{o}ry$

Nothing needs to be said about $\overset{1}{o}blig\overset{3}{a}tory$ in (124a) since its derivation is similar to that of *provocative* in (122a). The derivation of $\overset{1}{o}blig\overset{3}{a}tory$, on the other hand, merits some comment. In view of the obviously related *oblige*, the underlying form of *obligate* must have a tense [ī]. It might appear that this would cause difficulty on the second pass through the cyclical rules since the stress retraction subrule (100b) would place primary stress on this *i*, if tense, rather than on the initial syllable as required. We now recall that the Auxiliary Reduction Rule (67), which laxes and unstresses vowels in immediately post-tonic position, applies cyclically (see note 11). Since rule (67) is therefore applicable to the string $obl\overset{1}{i}g\overset{2}{a}te$, it will lax the *i* on the first pass through the cyclical rules. The rest of the derivation then proceeds without difficulty as shown in (124b). Words like $\overset{1}{o}blig\overset{3}{a}tory$ therefore represent another class of examples (see also (104) and the derivation of *advocacy*) where the Auxiliary Reduction Rule (67) must apply cyclically. This is of some interest since valid examples of cyclical rules affecting segmental as opposed to prosodic features of utterances are far from plentiful.

10. Summary of Rules

In this section we list in the appropriate order in (125) all the rules which we have had occasion to formulate up to this point. The set of rules presented here differs somewhat from that in Section 14 of Chapter Three in *Sound Pattern of English*. In part the present account attempts to correct certain inconsistencies that crept into the earlier work as a result of various changes in the ordering of the rules. In particular, the account in *Sound Pattern of*

English assumes that the Auxiliary Reduction Rule that assigns less than primary stress early in the word (the analog of our (125-VII)) follows the Auxiliary Reduction Rule that laxes and unstresses quaternary- and weaker-stressed vowels (the analog of our (125-IX)). The reason was the desire to include the latter rule among the various laxing rules, which must precede the tensing rules and hence also the stress-assigning Auxiliary Reduction Rule. This order, however, was not carried through in the illustrative derivations in *Sound Pattern of English* (see, for example, (112) and (116) there). Moreover, it had the somewhat unfortunate consequence of requiring a special complication in the Auxiliary Reduction Rule that laxes and unstresses vowels (see *Sound Pattern of English* (118a) and the discussion of (118) here) which did nothing but repeat case (c) of the second Auxiliary Reduction Rule.

The present account, furthermore, corrects the inconsistency in the rule order as given in Chapter Three, page 124, of *Sound Pattern of English* as against that given in Chapter Five. In the former, the Auxiliary Reduction Rules precede the Stress Adjustment Rule whereas in the latter the order is reversed. We have adopted the latter order here.

The formulation of the Main Stress Rule (99) differs in certain ways from its counterpart in *Sound Pattern of English* (p. 110). The implications of this revision are taken up in the discussion accompanying (141) and at the beginning of Section 12.

Finally, we note that in order to account for the nonreduction of the first syllable in *consultation* (see (120)) we have optionally admitted the boundary = to the environment of the Auxiliary Reduction Rule—III (125-VIIa), while to handle the reduction of the first syllable in *contemplative* the same optional boundary has been admitted to the Auxiliary Reduction Rule—II (125-IX). The latter modification will also explain why the first syllable reduces in words like *continue, persist, admit*, which have = between the two consonants, while there is no reduction in the initial syllable of *asbestos* and the other forms of (111) where there is no such boundary.

(125)

(I)   MAIN STRESS RULE (99)

$$V \rightarrow [\text{1stress}] \; / \; [X\text{---}C_0((\begin{bmatrix} -\text{tense} \\ V \end{bmatrix}C_0^1)(\begin{bmatrix} +D \\ V \end{bmatrix}C_0)\begin{Bmatrix} \begin{bmatrix} -\text{stress} \\ -\text{tense} \\ V \end{bmatrix}C_0 \\ (=C_0)\begin{bmatrix} \begin{Bmatrix} 2\text{stress} \\ 1\text{stress} \end{Bmatrix} \\ V \end{bmatrix}C_0(y) \end{Bmatrix})]$$

(*Continued on p. 60*)

125 (*Continued*)

(II) ALTERNATING STRESS RULE (75)

$$V \rightarrow [\text{1stress}] \ / \ [X\text{———}C_0(=C_0)VC_0\begin{bmatrix}\text{1stress}\\V\end{bmatrix}C_0]$$

(III) COMPOUND, NUCLEAR STRESS, AND STRESS ADJUSTMENT RULES (48), (51)

$$\begin{bmatrix}\text{1stress}\\V\end{bmatrix} \rightarrow [\text{1stress}] \ / \ [\#\#\,X\text{———}Y(\#\#Z)_a\#\#]_{(\{N,V,A\})_b}$$

CONDITIONS: X and Y may contain $\#\#$
Y contains no [1stress]
if a, then b
if $b = \phi$, then X contains [1stress]

(IV) TRISYLLABIC LAXING RULE (123)

$$V \rightarrow [-\text{tense}] \ / \ [\#\#\,X\text{———}C_0VC_0VY\#\#]$$

(V) RULE (115)

$$[\text{3stress}] \rightarrow [\text{4stress}] \ / \ [\#\#\,X\text{———}C_0[\text{1stress}]Y\#\#]$$

(VI) TENSING RULE—I (56)

$$V \rightarrow [+\text{tense}] \ / \ [\#\#\,X\text{———}VY\#\#]$$

(VII) AUXILIARY REDUCTION RULE—III (116)

$$V \rightarrow [\text{3stress}] \ / \ [\#\#\,C_0\left\{\begin{array}{l}X\text{———}(C_0=)C_0(\begin{bmatrix}-\text{tense}\\V\end{bmatrix}C_0^1)\begin{bmatrix}\gamma\text{stress}\\V\end{bmatrix}C_0\begin{bmatrix}\text{1stress}\\V\end{bmatrix})\quad\text{(a)}\\[2ex]\begin{bmatrix}\text{———}\\+\text{tense}\end{bmatrix}\qquad\qquad\qquad\qquad\qquad\qquad\text{(b)}\\[2ex]\text{———}C_2\qquad\qquad\qquad\qquad\qquad\qquad\text{(c)}\end{array}\right\}Y\#\#]$$

CONDITION: $\gamma \geq 4$

(VIII) AUXILIARY REDUCTION RULE—I (67)

$$V \rightarrow \begin{bmatrix}-\text{stress}\\-\text{tense}\end{bmatrix} \ / \ [X\begin{bmatrix}\text{1stress}\\V\end{bmatrix}C_0\text{———}C_0VY]$$

(IX) AUXILIARY REDUCTION RULE—II (118)(=(a)), (92)(=(b))

$$V \rightarrow \begin{bmatrix}-\text{stress}\\-\text{tense}\end{bmatrix} \ / \ [\#\#\,X\begin{bmatrix}\text{———}\\\gamma\text{stress}\end{bmatrix}\left\{\begin{array}{l}C_0^1(=C_0)\begin{bmatrix}\text{1stress}\\V\end{bmatrix}Y\quad\text{(a)}\\[2ex]Z\qquad\qquad\qquad\qquad\text{(b)}\end{array}\right\}\#\#]$$

CONDITIONS: $\gamma \geq 4$
Z contains no [1stress]

(X)   TENSING RULE—II (58)

$$V \rightarrow [+\text{tense}] \quad / \quad [\#\# X \begin{bmatrix} \rule{1.2em}{0.4pt} \\ -\text{low} \end{bmatrix} \#\#]$$

(XI)   VOWEL REDUCTION RULE (54)

$$\begin{bmatrix} -\text{stress} \\ -\text{tense} \\ V \end{bmatrix} \rightarrow \text{ə} \ / \ [\#\# X \rule{1.5em}{0.4pt} Y \#\#]$$

11. Exceptions

Among the consequences of the Main Stress Rule (99) and the Alternating Stress Rule (75) and of the conventions that determine their operation, those listed in (126) are of special interest to the present discussion. (To simplify the exposition we shall restrict ourselves here to words that have unnested constituent structure and exclude from consideration words like those in (90), (103), (114), (122), and (124), where nesting is motivated.)

(126) (a) Bisyllabic words with a tense last vowel in their underlying representation[25] must always have final stress.
   (b) (i) Trisyllabic and longer words with a tense last vowel in their underlying representation[25] must always have a stress contour that terminates with the sequence 1ˇ3 (where ˇ represents a stressless vowel).
       (ii) No word without nesting may have a stress contour that terminates with the sequence 13.
   (c) Polysyllabic words with a lax last vowel may not have stress—neither primary nor weaker—on the last syllable unless they are complex verbs of the type *permit*.

   The claims in (126) follow from two facts: (a) words with a tense last vowel are subject to (100c) and not to (100a), and (b) the Alternating Stress Rule applies only to trisyllabic or longer words. Unfortunately, however, these claims are controverted by certain data. In (127) we give examples that violate the corresponding statements in (126):

---

[25] The restriction "in their underlying representation" is necessary to exclude words which in their underlying form end with a lax vowel which later becomes tense by the Tensing Rule (125-X).

(127)   (a)   (b)
                                          (i)   (ii)

Móscow¹³   vácate¹³   adúmbrate¹²   Láertes¹³
alcove   locate   elongate   Archimedes
encore   steroid   enfranchise   molluscoid
Azores   senile   projectile
Magyar   feline

                        (c)

Brázil¹   tórment¹   Mónadnock¹³   phálanx¹³   dócument¹³ (vb)
Japan   lament   Adirondacks   Adolph   complement¹³ (vb)
Ceylon   cement   kapok
Berlin   erect   Kellogg
Peking   sumac
                                        Slovak
                                        Ahab

Some of these "irregularities" would become regular if the Alternating Stress Rule were to retract stress not only to the antepenultimate syllable but also to the penult. This extension is technically a rather minor change, requiring only that we introduce one more set of parentheses into the structural description of the rule, as shown in (128):

$$(128)\quad V \;\to\; [\text{1stress}] \;\; / \;\; [X\text{———}C_0(=C_0)(VC_0)\begin{bmatrix}\text{1stress}\\ V\end{bmatrix}C_0]$$

Such a modification, however, results in a considerable weakening of the grammar since the fact that the overwhelming majority of bisyllabic words without internal nesting is not subject to stress retraction now becomes a fortuitous coincidence. Moreover, by revising the Alternating Stress Rule so that it retracts stress both to the antepenultimate and the penultimate syllables, we make the rule extremely similar to the stress retraction subrule (100b) of the Main Stress Rule. The question then arises as to whether there is still any justification for having both retraction rules in the grammar. Mechanically, all of the correct stress contours could be obtained by the weakened Alternating Stress Rule alone. We should, however, be forced to express certain generalizations in an ad hoc manner. We would no longer be able to account for the fact that stress retraction in words ending with -ory obeys the weak cluster principle of the Main Stress Rule whereas in words that end with a tense syllable stress is retracted to the antepenultimate syllable without regard for the nature of the penultimate syllable (e.g., refectory and *confiscate* rather than *refectory* and *confiscate*). We could not explain why nouns with a nested constituent structure undergo stress retraction whereas nouns without nesting do not (e.g., *combine* (n) but *ravine*). We would have no explanation for the fact that bisyllabic words are only exceptionally subject to stress retraction whereas trisyllabic words are only exceptionally exempt from stress retraction. Given a single stress retraction rule, namely, (128), all these facts would be totally ad hoc; they would be as plausible as the situation where the converse relations among the cited nouns obtained or where there was no regularity whatever in the behavior of forms with regard to stress retraction. This seems to us to be clearly wrong. An observed regularity does not cease to exist as soon as the discovery is made that it is not completely general, that there are forms where the regularity is not to be found. It is for this reason that we prefer not to modify the Alternating Stress Rule as in (128) but instead to account for the "irregular" stress contours by other means. As the discussion of exceptions proceeds, we shall point out particular cases that seem to support the alternative chosen here.

Consider first the examples in (127a). These consist exclusively of unnested bisyllabic words with a tense vowel in the final syllable. If the Alternating Stress Rule were changed as proposed in (128), these words could readily be handled. Such a solution, however, would also require that we mark in the lexicon all words of this type where stress retraction does not take place. That is, by revising the Alternating Stress Rule as in (128) we are asserting that bisyllabic words are normally subject to stress retraction and that the cases where stress retraction does not take place in such words are to be marked as exceptions. This seems wrong to us since the majority of bisyllabic words do not undergo stress retraction. In (129) we give a list of all the unsuffixed words of this type with stress retraction that we have been able to find:

(129)

argyle	*archive*	*mohair*	*Ambrose*	*Moscow*
microbe	*enzyme*	*alcove*	*console*	*Osage*
Magyar	*Azores*	*topaz*	*satire*	*protein*
alloy	*envoy*	*ozone*	*gangrene*	*tirade*
ampere	*cashmere*	*gargoyle*	*encore*	

These are to be compared with the much more numerous list (130), which contains only a sampling of the bisyllabic words that do not undergo stress retraction:

(130)

antique	*amount*	*bamboo*	*canoe*	*caprice*
catarrh	*chicane*	*critique*	*debate*	*debauch*
delight	*domain*	*esteem*	*embrace*	*extreme*
fatigue	*guitar*	*attire*	*patrol*	*parole*
perfume	*police*	*ragout*	*taboo*	*veneer*
parade	*crusade*	*tableau*	*cahoots*	*esprit*
pecan	*bazaar*	*jabot*	*adieu*	*July*
mirage	*cortege*	*physique*	*cliché*	*touché*
regime	*latrine*	*marine*	*mundane*	*routine*
ravine	*escape*	*brochure*	*manure*	*valise*
demise	*chemise*	*marquis*	*cheroot*	*trapeze*
malaise	*papoose*	*caboose*	*boutique*	*ménage*
tattoo	*Louise*	*spittoon*	*roué*	*technique*

(The words in the first row — *antique*, *amount*, *bamboo*, *canoe*, *caprice* — are each marked with primary stress `1` over the final vowel.)

In view of this numerical disparity it is natural to regard the words in (130) as regular and those in (129) as irregular.

The proper place to reflect the fact that a given form is irregular is the lexicon, for, as Bloomfield (1933) has remarked, "the lexicon is really an appendix of the grammar, a list of basic irregularities" (p. 274). But the decision to reflect the irregularities in the lexicon does not determine fully the device to be used. We choose not to mark the forms in (129) with an ad hoc diacritic feature; rather, we shall supply the lexical representations with primary stress on the last vowel. In this way we state explicitly that these forms differ from others in that their stress contour is not wholly determined by the rules but is instead partially idiosyncratic and hence marked in the lexicon. The lexicon will therefore contain words with inherent stress, such as *alcove* and the other words in (129), in contrast to the majority of words, such as *antique* and *patrol*, which will be entered without stressed vowels. It should be noted here that stress needs to be marked in the lexicon on only one syllable, namely, the last.

At this point, then, we have two types of lexical representations exemplified by *alcove* and *antique*. Neither of these words is subject to (100a) of the Main Stress Rule since the last vowel is tense. *Alcove*, because it has inherent stress on the last vowel, is subject to retraction by (100b). By virtue of the disjunctive ordering that obtains between (100b) and (100c), the resulting string *alcove* is not subject to the latter subrule, and, being bisyllabic as well as without primary stress on the last vowel, it is also not subject to the Alternating Stress Rule (75). The Stress Adjustment Rule (51) then yields the correct contour 13. The word *antique*, on the other hand, fails to satisfy subrule (100b) and is therefore subject to (100c), which assigns stress on the last vowel. It is subsequently subject to the Auxiliary Reduction Rule—III (125-VIIc), which supplies [3stress] to the initial vowel.

Let us now consider nouns formed with the suffix *-oid*, which are illustrated in (131):

(131) *mollúscóid*   *hóminóid*
       cylindroid   *anthropoid*
       ellipsoid   *celluloid*
       epicycloid   *alkaloid*
       steroid

It is clear that these words undergo stress retraction by the weak cluster principle and must therefore be subject to subrule (100b) of the Main Stress Rule. This, however, is impossible by our rules. Since the words under discussion end with a syllable containing a tense vowel, namely, *-oid*, they will first be subject to subrule (100c) of the Main Stress Rule, and words that are subject to (100c) cannot subsequently be subject to (100b): by the principle of disjunctive ordering, (100b) must always precede (100c) and cannot apply to the same string as (100c). The problem raised by these examples is not difficult to resolve, however. We need only assume that the suffix *-oid*, like most suffixes with a tense vowel (e.g., *-ine*, *-ize*), is supplied with primary stress by a special rule which applies before the Main Stress Rule (see rule (158), p. 152, *Sound Pattern of English*). As a result, the words in (131) will undergo derivations such as those shown in (132):

(132) mollusc + ȯid			homin + ȯid			
—	—	—	—	—	—	SPECIAL
—	—		1	2		MAIN STRESS (100a)
	1	2	—	—		MAIN STRESS (100bi)
—			—			MAIN STRESS (100bii)
	1	3	1	3		ALTERNATING STRESS (75)
						STRESS ADJUSTMENT (51)

It has been observed that in many cases words with particular terminations undergo identical treatment regardless of whether the termination constitutes a particular morpheme or not. Thus, for instance, words terminating in [īyr] (spelled *-eer*, *-ier*, or *-ere*) are never subject to stress retraction, as illustrated in (133) on the next page.

In the grammar that is being proposed here, this fact would be reflected by a rule which would mark all words having this termination as

(133) (a)

frontíer

veneer

vizier

cashier

sincere

revere

austere

career

(b)

engíneer

mutineer

mountaineer

auctioneer

grenadier

musketeer

volunteer

cavalier

exceptions to the Alternating Stress Rule. In the case of bisyllabic words this marking would be vacuous, but the generalization need not be weakened on this count. Note that cases of this type would have to be handled in exactly the same manner given the revised Alternating Stress Rule considered earlier.

A few words terminating in [īyr] do undergo stress retraction, as shown in (134):

(134) cáshmère

ámpère

Cásimìr

chánticlèer

These forms will be entered in the lexicon with inherent primary stress, and the generalization that words ending in [īyr] are exceptions to the Alternating Stress Rule will then be restricted to words without inherent stress.

The differences between our treatment of exceptions and the alterna-tive proposal with the revised Alternating Stress Rule (128) become somewhat more substantive when we study another termination. Words ending in [āyn] undergo retraction quite generally, as we see from the examples in (135):

(135)

(a)	(b)		(c)
c$\overset{1}{a}$rb$\overset{3}{i}$ne	*c$\overset{1}{o}$lumb$\overset{3}{i}$ne*	*$\overset{1}{i}$$\overset{3}{o}$dine*	*eleph$\overset{1}{a}$nt$\overset{3}{i}$ne*
Sabine	*saturnine*	*aquiline*	*adamantine*
turbine	*Byzantine*	*asinine*	
quinine	*levantine*	*leonine*	
feline	*valentine*	*porcupine*	
bovine			
porcine			
canine			
alpine			
cosine			

The only exceptions we were able to find are listed in (136a). The words in (136b) show retraction but, as we shall see, retraction according to a different principle.

(136)

(a)	(b)
div$\overset{1}{i}$ne	*P$\overset{1}{a}$lest$\overset{3}{i}$ne*
opine	*Wittgenstein*
supine	
benign	

The first point to be observed is that the majority of the examples in (135) are formed with the suffix *-ine* (*alp+ine*, *saturn+ine*, *elephant+ine*), whereas none of the examples in (136) can be said to have this suffix. Since the words in (136) will therefore not be subject to the rule assigning stress to tense suffixes, they will receive final stress by (100c) of the Main Stress Rule. They will then undergo retraction if they satisfy the environment of the Alternating Stress Rule, which in its unmodified form (75) will apply only to words of at least three syllables, without regard for the structure of the pretonic syllable. The retraction that we observe in the bisyllabic words in (135a) must therefore be the result of the stress retraction subrule (100b). This presupposes that the words in question have received stress by the special tense affix rule or, alternatively, have been supplied with lexical stress on the last syllable. In either case, rule (100b) will apply and yield the correct output. The same is true of the examples in (135c). Turning now to (135b), it might appear at first sight that it is the Alternating Stress Rule rather than rule (100b) that is responsible for the stress retraction. This would be embarrassing, for it would force us to treat *elephantine*, for example, differently than *saturnine*. We observe now, however, that the examples in (135b) are all trisyllabic words in which the medial cluster is either weak or ends with a sonorant consonant followed by a consonant. The former cases will be treated identically by both retraction rules. The latter cases, on the other hand, are subject to the rule, mentioned previously with regard to examples (82a), which assigns the special diacritic feature [+D] to the second syllable in trisyllabic words if that syllable ends with a sonorant consonant followed by another consonant. Syllables marked [+D] are disregarded in the application of case (100b) of the Main Stress Rule, which will then retract primary stress to the initial syllable of words such as *columbine*. In (135c), on the other hand, the syllable ending with a sonorant and a consonant is not the second syllable of the word; therefore, it is not assigned the diacritic feature [+D] and receives the retracted stress by subrule (100b). Thus, all the words in (135) can be shown to be subject to stress retraction by the same retraction rule, namely, (100b) of the Main Stress Rule. Were we to adopt the alternative proposal with the Alternating Stress Rule (128), the fact that all the forms in (135) retract stress in what is basically the same way could not be expressed.[26]

A somewhat different situation is exemplified by the treatment of the termination *-ate*. As shown in (137), stress retraction occurs in a large number of verbs in which *-ate* functions as a real suffix:

(137)

aerate	*migrate*
gyrate	*pulsate*
phonate	*donate*
vibrate	*mutate*
castrate	*rotate*
locate	*frustrate*
placate	*orate*
dictate	*stagnate*

[26] Words with the termination *-ile* are treated in the same manner as those terminating with [āyn]. We can distinguish here three types of cases:

(a) *agile, docile, gentile, labile, profile, reptile, senile*
    crocodile, domicile, juvenile
(b) *infantile, mercantile*
(c) *projectile, percentile*

In the solution with the unmodified Alternating Stress Rule (75), all these words will have to be subject to the rule assigning [1stress] to tense affixes, and, as a result, they will retract this stress by subrule (100b). This is totally obvious in the examples in (a). In the forms in (b), the second syllable terminates with a sonorant consonant + consonant sequence which is marked [+D] and disregarded in the application of (100b). The examples in (c) differ from those in (b) in that they have a prefix boundary: *pro=ject+ile, per=cent+ile*. Given the formulation of (100b) and the convention that rules cannot apply to sequences containing = unless the boundary is specified in the rule in the appropriate position, stress can be retracted no further than the second syllable of the word, regardless of the way this syllable terminates.

These contrast with the nonsuffixed forms in (138), which do not retract stress:

(138) abáte   reláte
      eláte   debáte
      beráte   transláte
      infláte   defláte
      creáte   diláte

In the approach that keeps the Alternating Stress Rule (75) intact, it would be necessary to assume that in the forms in (137) the suffix *-ate* has inherent stress. This, however, is not particularly elegant since *-ate* is commonly without inherent stress when it forms trisyllabic and longer words, as in (139):

(139) íntegràte
      confíscate
      élevate
      contémplate
      antícipate

On closer examination the situation appears to be even more complicated. On the one hand, as shown in (140a), there are bisyllabic words formed with the suffix *-ate* which do not undergo stress retraction and in which *-ate* therefore does not have inherent lexical stress; on the other hand, as shown in (140b), there are trisyllabic and longer words where *-ate* behaves exactly like *-oid* and thus must have inherent stress:[27]

(140) (a)   (b)
       negáte   remónstràte   defálcàte
       equáte   erúctate   elóngate
                  adúmbrate   incúlcate

We find, thus, that the suffix *-ate* sometimes figures in words that have stress retraction in accordance with the weak cluster principle and at other times in words that have stress retraction in accordance with the Alternating Stress Rule. This fact must be taken into account with either of the Alternating Stress Rules being considered here; that is, both proposals will have

---

[27] The forms in (140b) can all be analyzed as being composed of a prefix plus stem: *de=falc+ate*. This fact, however, does not account for the retraction of the stress to the penultimate syllable since words having this structure normally retract the stress to the antepenult by the Alternating Stress Rule (75): *con=fisc+ate*. Note, incidentally, that because of the special treatment of syllables ending with a sonorant + consonant sequence, the three words in the second column of (140b) must be entered in the lexicon with a = boundary if they are to have the stress contour ˇ13. (See also note 26.)

to recognize that not all -*ate* terminations function uniformly and will have to incorporate special, more or less ad hoc devices to handle some of the cases. The difference between the alternatives concerns only the cases that will be marked as exceptional. Given the unmodified Alternating Stress Rule (75), the suffix -*ate* will be supplied with inherent stress in cases such as those in (137) and (140b); of these, the forms in (137) represent a subregularity that can be captured by a redundancy rule. In the alternative proposal with the Alternating Stress Rule modified as in (128), the words in (138) and (140a) will have to be marked as exceptions; moreover, it will be necessary to distinguish by an additional mark the cases in (140b) from the more regular *confiscate*, *contemplate* type in (139). It is obvious that the latter solution is somewhat more cumbersome than the former. What inclines us strongly in favor of the former solution, however, is not so much this fact but rather that it embodies the important insight that, as already noted here, bisyllabic words with a tense vowel in the last syllable are generally not subject to stress retraction (see (129) and (130)).

Before examining words with a lax vowel in the final syllable, we summarize our results thus far. We began by noting that certain claims implicit in the Main Stress and Alternating Stress Rules (see (126)) seemed to be violated by examples such as those in (127). After a closer consideration of forms with a tense vowel in the last syllable, we found that bisyllabic words of this type normally have primary stress on the last syllable and only exceptionally exhibit the stress contour 13. Thus, it was assumed that in the former case the words appear in the lexicon without stress indication, but in the latter case primary stress is assigned to the last vowel of the word in the lexical representation. All words with lexical stress undergo stress retraction by subrule (100b) of the Main Stress Rule. Bisyllabic words can undergo stress retraction only by this route. A curious fact is that trisyllabic and longer words with a tense final vowel receive lexical stress on the last syllable only if the vowel is part of a separate suffix. Thus, to the best of our knowledge, there are no unsuffixed counterparts to *molluscoid* and *adumbrate*; that is, words like [timbʌktōwk] or [bærōwlēym] do not appear to exist in English. This is in contrast to the situation with regard to bisyllabic words, where we have both suffixed and unsuffixed forms with final stress: *vacate* and *Azores*, *senile* and *enzyme*. This means that trisyllabic and longer words do not have stress marked in the lexicon. They receive stress either by the special tense affix rule or by case (100c) of the Main Stress Rule.

Words with a lax vowel in the final syllable generally are subject to (100a), which never places stress on the last vowel. Thus, such words do not generally show final stress and, moreover, do not undergo stress retraction, which is contingent upon the word having received stress on the last syllable by a prior rule. It is for this reason that (126c) is a formal claim implicit in our rules. The only apparent exceptions to this claim have been deverbal nouns of the *per = mit* type (see Section 7) and words ending with *-y* (see Section 5), and we have seen how these are naturally incorporated into our system. There are, however, the examples in (141), which on the surface seem to violate (126c):[28]

(141) (a) (b)

$\overset{1}{\quad}\overset{3}{\quad}$	$\overset{1}{\quad}\overset{3}{\quad}$	$\overset{1}{\quad}$
kapok	*capon*	*Berlin*
moron	*iamb*	*Brazil*
Boaz	*phalanx*	*Japan*
nomad	*Adolph*	*Madrid*
gonad	*Kalmuck*	*Peking*
coupon	*syntax*	*Saigon*
boycott	*incest*	*Siam*
apex	*insect*	*Smolensk*
Yokut	*Bagdad*	*Verdun*

The examples in (141a) are completely parallel to (129) and will be handled in the same way. We therefore postulate that these words have inherent stress on the last syllable, meaning their lexical representations will be as in (142):

(142) $\overset{1}{ins}ect$ $\overset{1}{syn}tax$ $\overset{1}{Bag}dad$ $\overset{1}{iamb}$

These forms will not be subject to (100a) of the Main Stress Rule since the lax last vowel is stressed (see note 19), but they will undergo stress retraction by (100b), which will produce the correct stress contour.

The words in (141b) cannot be treated in the same way because they are not subject to stress retraction. Hence, if they were represented lexically with [1stress] on the last vowel, they would also have to be marked as exceptions to the stress retraction subrule (100b). Instead, we may handle these cases by marking them as exceptions to (100a) of the Main Stress Rule. They will thus be unmarked for stress when (100b) becomes applicable and the rule will not apply. Rule (100c) will then assign stress on the last syllable, and, since the words in question are bisyllabic, this final stress will not be

---

[28] Elaborate lists of words of this type have been prepared by Fidelholtz (1967), who points out that reduction does not take place in words of this kind when the *first* syllable has a strong cluster. In terms of the system proposed here, this would mean that primary stress can be assigned in the lexicon to bisyllabic words only if their first syllable ends with a strong cluster.

retracted by the Alternating Stress Rule (75). It should be noted here that the words in (141b) represent our main reason for deviating from *Sound Pattern of English* in the matter of rule (100c). The analog there to (100c) is case (e) of the Main Stress Rule (see, for example, page 110 of *Sound Pattern of English*). This case differs from our (100c) in two respects: first, it applies to nouns ending with a lax vowel only exceptionally, and, second, it assigns stress to the last or to the penultimate syllable in accordance with the weak cluster principle. Nouns such as those in (141b) would therefore have to be marked as doubly exceptional: they would have to be excluded from case (a,b) of the *Sound Pattern* Main Stress Rule, and, in addition, they would have to be marked as receiving final stress in spite of the fact that they end with a weak cluster. The formulation given in the present work accepts the suggestion made by J. R. Ross that words which are not stressed in accordance with (100a) receive final stress in all cases.[29]

The question to be treated next is whether the two classes of nouns in (141) are also to be found among trisyllabic and longer words. In (143) a number of examples of this type are listed:

(143) (a)
$\overset{1}{\text{A}}\text{dir}\overset{3}{\text{o}}\text{ndacks}$
Agamemnon
Monadnock
Aroostook

(b)
$\overset{1}{\text{F}}\text{lor}\overset{3}{\text{e}}\text{stan}$
Algernon
Serendip
Baluchistan

Like the bisyllabic forms in (141a), the words in (143a) will be lexically represented with [1stress] on the last vowel and will undergo stress retraction by (100b). Note that because of the requirement in (100a) that the last vowel be unstressed, the rule cannot apply to these words, just as it did not apply to the bisyllabic forms in (141a). This is important, because if (100a) did apply as well as (100b), the stress on the final vowel would, after the Stress Adjustment Rule, be low enough to be subject to reduction.

The examples in (143b), like those in (141b), will be marked as exceptions to (100a), will thus not be subject to (100b) either, and will receive

---

[29] In Chapter 2 we give some historical justification for this decision. The words that are not stressed in accordance with the weak cluster principle were originally largely of French origin and therefore came into the language with final stress.

The solution proposed here encounters certain problems when extended to adjectives and verbs. These are discussed in Section 12. J. R. Ross has proposed that case (100a) of the Main Stress Rule regularly applies to words ending with a vowel or with a dental consonant; words ending with consonants other than dental are never subject to subrule (100a) of the Main Stress Rule, but are instead subject to case (100c). We are not in a position to confirm or reject Ross's proposals. If they should prove correct, they would require only very minor changes in the system of rules proposed here.

final stress by (100c).[30] These words, however, being trisyllabic rather than bisyllabic, will then undergo retraction by the Alternating Stress Rule (75).

We must now inquire whether such different classes are also to be found among words that are composed of a stem and suffix. Suffixes with lax vowels that must be provided with [1stress] by a special rule are exemplified in (144):

(144)
$$\begin{array}{ll}
\overset{1}{encep}\overset{3}{halon} & \overset{1}{Dunc}\overset{3}{iad} \\
\overset{1}{elec}\overset{3}{tron} & \overset{13}{Jeremiad} \\
\overset{1}{pro}\overset{3}{ton} & \overset{1}{mon}\overset{3}{ad}
\end{array}$$

We postpone consideration of verbs such as *document* and *torment* to the next section.[31]

---

[30] The two words *Algernon* and *Serendip* may also be represented with an inherent stress on the last vowel. Their stress contour would then result from the fact that the words are of the form $\#\#C_0VC_0V[+\text{sonorant}][+\text{consonantal}] \ldots$, in which case the second vowel is disregarded in the application of the stress retraction subrule (100b) of the Main Stress Rule. The contrast $\overset{1}{Agamem}\overset{3}{non}$ versus $\overset{1}{Alger}\overset{3}{non}$ is thus a precise parallel of $\overset{1}{elementary}$ versus $\overset{1}{seden}\overset{3}{tary}$. (See (82) here and *Sound Pattern of English*, p. 138.)

[31] In our discussion it has been taken for granted that the rules of a grammar are uniquely ordered so that rules must apply in the same order in the derivation of every form. This assumption has been challenged by Anderson (1969). Anderson proposes that certain facts in phonology require that specified pairs of rules apply in one order in the derivation of some forms and in another order in the derivation of others. For example, Anderson has shown that in Sanskrit, cluster deaspiration (CD) must precede Grassmann's Law (GL) in the derivation of most forms; in the derivation of forms that are also subject to Bartholomae's Law (BL), however, Grassmann's Law must apply before cluster deaspiration. Thus, for most forms the order of the rules is CD, GL, but for a restricted class the order is GL, BL, CD.

In view of Anderson's work, it seemed of interest to investigate the possibility that the "irregular" examples of (127) are a result of the rules operating not in their usual order but rather in a special "aberrant" sequence. As shown below, the examples of (127) fall into two classes. In the first of these, the subrules in the Main Stress Rule have to apply in an order that is the reverse of that found in the standard cases, that is, the order (100c), (100b), (100a). In the second set of cases, the subrules have to apply in the order (100b), (100c), (100a). We are at present unable to comment on the significance of this alternative account, but we think it sufficiently intriguing to warrant mention here.

(a) Azores	Laertes	Monadnock	
1	1	1	MAIN STRESS (100c)
1 2	1 2	1 2	MAIN STRESS (100b)
– –	– –	– –	MAIN STRESS (100a)
–	–	–	ALTERNATING STRESS (75)
1 3	1 3	1 3	STRESS ADJUSTMENT (51)

(b) torment	document	Brazil	
– –	– – –	– –	MAIN STRESS (100b)
1	1	1	MAIN STRESS (100c)
– –	– – –	– –	MAIN STRESS (100a)
–	1 2	–	ALTERNATING STRESS (75)
– –	1 3	– –	STRESS ADJUSTMENT (51)

An interesting class of words which resembles the forms under discussion is exemplified in (145):[32]

(145)

¹anti³christ	³anti¹labor	¹micro³volt	³micro¹am³peres
¹anti³pope	³anti¹slavery	¹micro³watt	³micro¹farad
¹anti³cline	³anti¹toxin	¹micro³cosm	³micro¹or³ganism
¹anti³type	³anti¹cy³clone	¹micro³scope	³micro¹biology
¹anti³dote	³anti¹macassar	¹micro³film	³micro¹analysis

These complex words evidently are composed of a prefix and a word, as in *antichrist* and *microampere*, or a prefix and a stem morpheme which does not function as an independent word, as in *antimacassar* and *microcosm*. This is an important observation since it makes it unlikely that the stress contours in (145) are derived with the help of the Compound Rule (39): in order for (39) to assign stress in these cases, the rule would have to be extended so that it could apply to nonwords, which is so radical a modification as to be quite implausible. Note, furthermore, that stress retraction takes place in (145) when the second component is monosyllabic but not when it is polysyllabic. Since consideration of the number of syllables in a word is foreign to the Compound Rule, this is a second reason for assuming that rule (39) is not likely to be involved here.

The fact that retraction takes place only when the second element is monosyllabic suggests that the examples in (145) should be handled by one of the rules that account for stress retraction in words, namely, the Alternating Stress Rule (75) or case (100b) of the Main Stress Rule. To decide which rule is involved, we must investigate words with longer prefixes, such as those in (146):

(146)

¹hetero³nym	¹kaleido³scope
sideroscope	laryngoscope
cardiogram	electrograph
mimeograph	aristocrat

It is clear that retraction proceeds here in accordance with the weak cluster principle of the Main Stress Rule. Note, however, that just as in adjectives such as ¹antici³patory, ¹compen³satory (see Section 8), the stress is retracted without regard to the pre-tonic syllable. Thus, we must treat the

[32] The tertiary stress on the initial syllable in the examples in the second and fourth columns is provided by the Auxiliary Reduction Rule (116).

We assume that the last vowel of the prefixes under discussion is lax in the underlying representation.

connecting vowel -*o*- in the same way as -*at*-, that is, we mark *o* [+D].[33]
The stress retraction in the first and third columns of (145) and in (146) can
then readily be accounted for by the stress retraction subrule (100b) of the
Main Stress Rule. Since stress retraction generally occurs only when the
primary-stressed vowel is on the last syllable, stress is not retracted in the
second and fourth columns of (145). The one problem remaining, then, is
how to assign stress to the last syllable in the words under discussion. We
have two alternatives available. On the one hand, we can utilize a special
rule analogous to the rule that assigns primary stress to tense affixes such as
-*oid* (see (131) and (132) and the accompanying discussion) to assign stress
to the second element in complex words of this type provided that they are
monosyllabic. On the other hand, we can follow the suggestion of *Sound
Pattern of English* (p. 100) and postulate that the words under discussion all
have a constituent structure similar to that shown in (147):

(147) $[anti \; [cyclone]_N \;]_N$ $[micro \; [scope]_{STEM} \;]_N$

If we adopted the former alternative, we would account for the facts
and no more. A rule such as the one just described is no more motivated
than a rule that would assign final stress to trisyllabic words or to words that
end with nasal consonants or to words whose last two syllables have rounded
vowels. We may have to utilize a rule of this kind, but it is certainly not as
fully motivated as one would wish.

The second proposal, which assumes that the words in question have a
constituent structure as in (147), is much more directly tied in with the internal
makeup of the word. Unfortunately we can provide no unassailable justification for the postulated constituent structure since at the present time we
have only the most superficial idea about the nature of the rules of word
formation. It seems to us, however, that it is not implausible that the words
under discussion should have the constituent structure proposed here, that is,
that when the word-formation component of a grammar is ultimately developed, it will assign constituent structure in the fashion indicated. If our
assumption is correct, the second alternative is to be preferred over the first;
if our assumption is wrong, the two alternatives are equally arbitrary and
there is little reason to choose between them.[34]

---

[33] The assignment of the feature [+D] to the connecting vowel *o* is apparently not completely
automatic since in words such as *Germanophile*, *cinematograph*, *galvanoscope*, the *o* cannot
be so marked. (See *Sound Pattern of English*, p. 104n.)

[34] An important difference between the Main Stress subrule (100b) and the Alternating Stress
Rule is that only in the former does stress retraction occur when an extra syllable follows
the vowel that has received primary stress by a prior stress rule. As mentioned briefly in

12. *Remarks on Stress in Adjectives and Verbs*

In *Sound Pattern of English* a distinction was drawn between nouns and other lexical categories, that is, verbs and adjectives. Whereas nouns were said normally to be subject to the *Sound Pattern of English* counterpart of (100a) of the Main Stress Rule, verbs and adjectives were not subject to this rule unless they were formed with a suffix containing a lax vowel. If they did not contain such a suffix, verbs and adjectives were subject to the *Sound Pattern* counterpart of (100c), which differed from the rule here in that it placed stress on the penultimate syllable when the word ended with a weak cluster (see *Sound Pattern of English*, rule (102), p. 110). Since we feel that such a rule can no longer be justified (for reasons given in the discussion of (141)), it is necessary to reconsider here the treatment of verbs and adjectives in *Sound Pattern of English*. There is nothing to be added with regard to suffixed verbs and adjectives since these are treated here in the same manner as in *Sound Pattern*. Questions arise only with regard to unsuffixed forms in these categories, and among these only with regard to those whose last vowel is lax.

We begin with adjectives since they are somewhat less varied than the verbs. As shown in (148), adjectives ending with a lax vowel as in (148a) (recall that final vowels are tensed by rule (58) and are thus lax in their underlying form) or with a lax vowel followed by a single consonant as in (148b) exhibit only one type of accentual behavior, whereas adjectives ending with a lax vowel followed by two or more consonants split up into two groups as in (148c):[35]

---

note 19, there is reason to generalize from the affix *-y* to a small class of syllables marked with the diacritic feature [+B] which permits retraction by (100b). Thus the admissibility of an extra syllable (symbolized by the letter *y*) after the syllable with primary stress allows us to account for such puzzling stress contours as *orchestr+al* but *orchestr+a*: the latter form is now treated exactly like *industry*, and we mark the final syllable [+B]. Words such as *quantitātive*, *qualitātive* might perhaps also be handled in this fashion. In addition (see *Sound Pattern of English*, Chapter Three, Section 13), when the second component of a complex word under discussion contains a real word, stress retraction frequently takes place even when the primary stress is on the penult: *monosyllable*, *antibody*, *metalanguage*. The retraction, however, is highly idiosyncratic, and there are many words where it does not occur: *monoacid*, *biophysics*, and the already cited *anticyclone*, *microfarad*. The fact that retraction may take place in cases where an extra syllable follows the one with primary stress provides a certain amount of support for treating the complex words under discussion as being subject to stress retraction by rule (100b).

[35] We assume that in the underlying representation the words *sinister* (148ci) and *minister* (149ci) end with the consonant cluster *str*. Support for this analysis is provided by such related forms as *sinistral*, *ministry*, where no vowel is present. See also the discussion at the end of this section.

(148) (a) *shallow*[1] (b) *certain*[1]
  mellow *common*
  yellow *novel*
  narrow *wanton*
  callow *dapper*
  sallow *neuter*
  thorough *clever*
  meager

(c) (i) (ii)
  earnest[1] *august*[1] *manifest*[1][3]
  honest *robust* *difficult*
  modest *inert* *moribund*
  haggard *overt* *derelict*
  ribald *alert*
  covert *absurd*
  fecund *rotund*
  awkward *occult*
  jocund *abstract*
  sinister *direct*
  succinct

The words in (148cii) evidently receive stress by (100c) of the Main Stress Rule and are then subject to stress retraction by the Alternating Stress Rule. We cannot assume that these words were entered in the lexicon with a stressed final vowel because then we would expect stress retraction in the bisyllabic forms as well as in the trisyllabic forms.

The examples in (148cii) contrast with those in (148ci), all of which would receive the correct stress by rule (100a) of the Main Stress Rule. In *Sound Pattern of English* this distinction was ascribed to the fact that the adjectives in (cii) were suffixed and hence automatically subject to (100a). While this is not implausible in the case of a few of the words listed, it is quite farfetched in such cases as *fecund* and *jocund* (cf. *rotund*) or *covert* (cf. *alert, overt, inert*).

The examples in (148a,b) do not show the same split in accentual behavior. All of them are properly handled as words regularly subject to (100a) of the Main Stress Rule. We conclude, therefore, that unsuffixed adjectives ending with a strong cluster are lexically subcategorized as to whether they do or do not undergo (100a); all other adjectives are subject to (100a).

The situation with regard to verbs is illustrated in (149):

(149) (a) fóllow
swallow
borrow
carry
hurry
bury
argue
value

(b)
	(i)		(ii)
gállop	delíver	jéttison	equíp
harass	develop		attack
rollick	envelop		caress
frolic	determine		rebel
cover	consider		
conquer	discover		
	embarrass		
	continue		

(c)
(i)	(ii)	
góvern	molést	flábbergást
bollix	cavort	galivant
flummox	bombard	document
minister	accost	complement
scavenge	arrest	regiment
	adorn	
	lament	
	cement	
	augment	
	ferment	

Verbs ending with vowels, as in (149a), are normally subject to (100a); therefore, they parallel the behavior of adjectives in this respect. Verbs ending with a lax vowel followed by a single consonant, as in (149b), differ from adjectives in that there are some that have final stress (149bii) and thus seem not to be subject to (100a). Observe that the penultimate stress in most of the trisyllabic verbs in (149bi) is due to the fact that these forms are composed of prefix + stem, completely parallel to such verbs as *permit, resist*.[36] This analysis is confirmed by the verb *jettison*, where there is no prefix and the stress is therefore placed on the antepenultimate syllable. The third class of verbs, those ending with a strong cluster as in (149c), split into the same two groups as the adjectives of the same type; that is, some are subject to (100a) and others are not. The situation with regard to verbs is therefore similar to that encountered with nouns (see (141)) in that verbs ending with a consonant may not be subject to (100a). The difference between verbs and nouns, however, is that at least in the case of verbs ending with more than one consonant a majority appears not to undergo (100a), whereas in the case of nouns the proportions are reversed.

The accentuation of verbs provides an instructive example of cases where the underlying representation must contain elements that never appear on the surface. In Section 4 we noted that unstressed nonlow vowels in word-final position were subject to tensing by rule (58). When we examine the actual words to which this rule applies, we become aware of a curious gap in the distribution. As shown in (150) we have examples of the vowels [i,u,o] but none of the vowel [e] :[37]

(150)

Garibaldi	*continue*	*chiaroscuro*
carry	*avenue*	*soprano*
hurry	*virtue*	*momento*
bury	*value*	*bellow*
marry	*argue*	*swallow*
		follow
		winnow
		borrow

[36] To account for the stress contour of the cognate noun *envelope*, we assume that there is a special noun-forming process that tenses the final vowel of the stem. The noun then receives final stress by (100c) and subsequently undergoes the Alternating Stress Rule, which yields the correct output. The same noun-forming process may account for the stress contours of the nouns *retinue* and *attribute* (cf. the verbs *continue* and *attribute*). We would thus assume the representations [re=tini] and [æt=tribite] for the verbs (See *Sound Pattern of English*, Section 4.3.4 of Chapter 4, for an explanation of the relationship between i and u.) Incidentally, we owe to J. R. Ross the observation that tense [i] must be assumed in underlying representations in order to account for the different stress contours in such pairs as *Bermuda* (with a tense [i]) and *uvula* (with a lax [i] in the penultimate syllable).

[37] The forms in the middle column of (150) all end in phonetic [yūw]. In *Sound Pattern of English* (p. 194) it was argued that the source of this phonetic triphthong is [i]. We shall suppose, in keeping with that discussion, that the forms in the middle column contain a word-final underlying lax *u* which is subject to a rule of the form u → i/——#. Words such as *voodoo*, *hindu*, *jujitsu*, which end in a phonetic [ūw], will also be assumed to terminate in a word-final lax *u*. Unlike *argue*, *continue*, etc., these words will be considered as exceptions to the unrounding rule just postulated.

To account for the absence of word-final [e], we shall postulate, following *Sound Pattern of English* (p. 147), a rule which deletes this vowel in word-final position:

(151) e → φ / ——##

The existence of rule (151) allows us to explain not only the gap illustrated in (150), but also some additional phonetic peculiarities. As argued in *Sound Pattern of English* (pp. 219–223), before the vowels [i,e] velars undergo "softening": *medicine* but *medical*, *regicide* but *regal*. We can readily account for the parallel alternations in the stems of the verbs in (152) if we assume that these verbs end with a final [e] which is subsequently deleted by (151):

(152) *práctice* (cf. *practical*)   *allége* (cf. *allegation*)
      redúce (cf. *reduction*)   *oblíge* (cf. *obligation*)
      convínce (cf. *conviction*) *púrge* (cf. *purgatory*)

The verbs ending with a vowel in (150) receive stress by (100a) of the Main Stress Rule. It is therefore quite natural to propose that the verbs in (152) receive their stress by (100a) as well. This can readily be done, provided that we represent *allege* and *reduce* as [æl=lege] and [re=duke], respectively, which is perfectly plausible in view of the fact that these verbs are of the same type as [æl=lude] and [re=mit].

The postulation in verbs of a final vowel that is subsequently deleted, as J. R. Ross has noted, also makes it possible to account for the fact that in verbs ending with *-it* or *-ish* the stress is on the penultimate vowel and this vowel is, moreover, lax, as illustrated in (153):

(153) (a)   (b)
      crédit   *vánish*
      cóvet   *estáblish*
      édit   *abólish*
      inhérit   *demólish*
      inhábit   *dimínish*
      límit   *fínish*
      pósit   *flóurish*

A final *-e* in (153a,b) provides for penultimate stress placement in accordance with (100a) of the Main Stress Rule. This is crucial, of course, only with trisyllabic verbs such as *establish, abolish, demolish, diminish*, since the bisyllabic verbs would receive penultimate stress by (100a) in any case.

However, note further that all of these verbs contain a lax vowel in the penultimate syllable. This fact is an automatic consequence of the supposition of a final *-e*, since the postulation of such a vowel would make these verbs subject to the Trisyllabic Laxing Rule (123). It also explains the absence in English of such hypothetical verbs as [crīydət] or [vēynəš].

This proposal, however, runs into some minor difficulties. Because of alternations such as *elliptic* versus *ellipse*, it is necessary to posit the rule (154):

(154) t → s / ——e

Hence, if the verbs in (153a) were to be represented with a final *-e*, we should expect a final [s] rather than [t] in the output. This difficulty can be overcome by preventing the verbs in question from undergoing rule (154). Several devices are available for accomplishing this. One, suggested by J. R. Ross, would be to represent the word-final vowel not as [e] but rather as its back cognate [ɤ]. This would prevent (154) from applying. The postulated [ɤ] would then be deleted by (151), which would have to be generalized to unrounded mid vowels.

Yet another argument in support of a final *-e* which is subsequently deleted is the stress contour in a verb like *acquiesce*, which has stress on its final (phonetic) syllable. If we posit the underlying form [ak=kwieske], we will get the correct penultimate stress assigned by (100a) of the Main Stress Rule. This representation is supported by the penultimate stress of the obviously related adjective *qu$\overset{3}{i}\overset{1}{e}$scent* from [kwieskent] (cf. *$\overset{1}{i}$nnocent*). Notice, moreover, that the postulation of the final *-e* (which is not marked [+B]) will block (100b) from retracting stress and will also prevent the Alternating Stress Rule (75) from shifting stress as it does in a verb like [kon=pensǣt].

It is not the case that all verbs have a final *-e*. Consider, for example, verbs ending in *-ent*. One might assume that the final stress in bisyllabic verbs such as *torm$\overset{1}{e}$nt*, *lam$\overset{1}{e}$nt* in (127) could be accounted for by positing a final *-e* which is subsequently deleted. This *-e* would block both (100b) and the Alternating Stress Rule as in *acquiesce*. We see that this alternative is wrong, however, when we look at trisyllabic verbs in *-ent*: *d$\overset{1}{o}$cum$\overset{3}{e}$nt*, *r$\overset{1}{e}$gim$\overset{3}{e}$nt*, *exp$\overset{1}{e}$rim$\overset{3}{e}$nt* (see (93)). Here the 1⌣3 stress contour can only be achieved if we assume that final stress is assigned to these verbs and subsequently shifted by the Alternating Stress Rule, which would be blocked if there were a final *-e*.

There are certain other verbs which cannot have a final *-e* in their underlying form—*j$\overset{1}{e}$ttison*, *m$\overset{1}{i}$nister*—since they would not have initial stress if the last consonant were followed by a vowel. Because *st* is a strong cluster, the verb *minister*, moreover, must be represented without a vowel in the last syllable: *ministr*. The adjectival form *ministerial*, then, requires the assumption that the vowel [e] is inserted in the final cluster before the adjectival suffix *-ial*. In view of the absence of the vowel in *ministry*, this is quite plausible. We recall, moreover, that vowel insertion under very similar circumstances is well attested: [ɨ] is inserted before a cluster consisting of a labial followed by [l] before *-ar*: *table* versus *tabular*, *constable* versus *constabulary*; whereas [i] is inserted in these clusters before *-ity*: *noble* versus *nobility*, *humble* versus *humility*. The insertion of [e] in dental clusters is considerably less common, but in view of the insertion of vowels in other consonant clusters, it is hardly implausible. Incidentally, the pair *Áristotle* versus *Aristotélian* could also be accounted for in the same fashion. In the adjective the vowel is inserted and then (100a) correctly assigns the stress. The noun would have to be marked as not being subject to (100a). It would then receive final stress by (100c) and be subject to stress retraction by the Alternating Stress Rule (75).

13. *Conclusion*

In the discussion of English stress just concluded, we have attempted to bring out a specific relationship between the formal constraints one imposes on a theory and the empirical consequences which these formal constraints entail. In particular, we have tried to show that a correct formal notation designed to account for one set of phenomena will often have implications in quite independent areas of the grammar. Indeed, it is in this sense that one may speak of a correct formalism leading to new discoveries about the language under consideration.

Very early in this chapter, for example, we listed four statements (see (4)) which accounted for stress in nouns such as *América, balaláika, agénda,* and *Tippecanóe* (see (2)). We then pointed out that by the introduction of a formalism which allowed us to express the notion "otherwise," it was possible to replace the rules in (4) by a technically "simpler" set of rules. This simplification had certain further empirical consequences which the formulation in (4) did not have: among others, it predicted initial stress in bisyllabic words with a lax final vowel, such as *vénom, spírit*. This is of special interest since, on purely logical grounds, one could just as well have expected to find final stress in such words.

In the discussion of the Compound Rule (39), we showed that the need to modify the rule to account for the stress contour in compounds like

$\overset{2}{Madison}$ $\overset{1}{Road}$, $\overset{2}{Columbia}$ $\overset{1}{Point}$, $\overset{2}{Fifth}$ $\overset{1}{Avenue}$ entailed a further empirical consequence of a totally unexpected and rather subtle nature, namely, that the subordinate stress in a noncompound word will be at most tertiary.

In our discussion of the retraction rules in English, we pointed out that it was necessary to postulate a rule to deal with such cases as $\overset{1}{compulsory}$, $\overset{1}{inhibitory}$, $\overset{1}{refectory}$. Since the proposed rule assigned stress according to the weak cluster principle, our formal notations allowed it to be incorporated into the rules that constituted the Main Stress Rule. This incorporation gave rise to a technically simpler rule. Moreover, it provided formal expression of a generalization about English stress which would otherwise have remained unstated, namely, that in words which show stress retraction, those which receive stress by (100a) of the Main Stress Rule will retract according to the weak cluster principle, while those which receive stress by (100c) will retract according to another principle altogether, one embodied in the Alternating Stress Rule (75), which ignores the character of the intervening syllable.

In our discussion of compounds as well as of other collocations of words, we found it necessary, in order to account for some fairly obvious facts of English accentuation, to allow our rules to apply in cyclical fashion, beginning with the smallest immediate constituent of the collocation and continuing until the limits of the phonological phrase are reached. We then showed that when our rules were applied in this fashion to immediate constituents below that of the word, certain extremely obscure stress contours were accounted for, in particular the differences in stress and vowel reduction in pairs like *exaltation–devastation*.

Thus, in the four cases just mentioned, obscure and subtle empirical data are accounted for automatically by means of a set of rules required to deal with an entirely different and much more obvious set of facts. This constitutes the strongest possible corroboration for the theoretical foundations that underlie our description.

2

The Evolution of the English Stress System

1. Introduction

It is assumed here that a speaker's knowledge of a language can be adequately characterized with the help of a system of rules such as that given in the preceding chapter. Different systems of rules will therefore be necessary for different languages. On this view, a history of a language must consist of showing how one system of rules (e.g., that of Old English) evolved by plausible steps into another system (e.g., that of modern English). It is obvious that the process must be a gradual one since we know that people belonging to contiguous or near generations are rather similar in their speech. Specifically this means that changes in rule systems of successive generations must be of a very limited kind. To account for the pronunciation of certain new words or for new modes of pronunciation of old words, a rule may be added to the grammar, an existing rule may be altered or even dropped, or other relatively minor adjustments may be made in the rules. If modern English differs radically from Old English, this is due not to any radical changes, but rather to the cumulative effects of relatively minor changes introduced at various points in the course of a thousand or more years.

2. Old English Stress

Our prime source of data for the stress contours of Old English is the alliterative poetry of the period. As discussed in greater detail in Chapter 3, Section 2, poets of the time adhered to the following metrical convention: each line of poetry had to contain at least two alliterating "staves," that is, at least two words in which the syllable bearing primary stress begins with the same consonant or with zero consonants. Thus, this type of verse affords evidence for the location of primary stress in a word when the word in question is attested in stave position. Examples of such verse lines are given in (1) and (2), where the alliterating staves are indicated by boldface type. Observe that in (1) there are only two alliterating staves while in (2) there are three:

(1) *þæt **h**ealreced **h**ātan wolde*   *(Beowulf 68)*
     that he would command a hall-building

(2) *wēox under **w**olcnum **w**eorðmyndum þāh*   *(Beowulf 8)*
     he prospered under the heavens; he thrived in honor

        It is essential to note that second elements of compound words do not satisfy the requirements of the meter. A hypothetical line such as (3) is therefore unmetrical:[1]

(3) *þone bétstan sǽbằt wolde*
the best vessel (sea-boat) he wanted

The explanation is that in Old English, much as in modern English, second elements of compound words had nonprimary stress, and the meter requires that the two alliterating syllables have primary stress. Alternatively one might assume that lines such as (3) are unmetrical because alliterating syllables had to be word initial. This explanation can be ruled out, however, since lines such as (4) are perfectly metrical:

(4) *þone þīn fǽder tō geféohte bær*   (*Beowulf 2048*)
the one thy father into battle bore

Like other Germanic languages, Old English placed stress on the first syllable of the stem rather than the word. Since *geféohte* in (4) has the prefix *ge-* before the stem, the primary stress is on the second rather than on the first syllable.

The assignment of stress to the initial syllable of the stem was a productive process in Old English, as shown by the fact that words borrowed from the classical languages received initial stress regardless of their original accentuation. Some examples of this are given in (5)–(7), where the loan words appear in nonitalic type:

(5) *égesful éorla dryhten. Ða wearð* **Hó**lofernus   (*Judith 21*)
the dread lord of warriors. Then Holofernus became

(6) *tō ðǣre béorhtan býrig* **Bé**thuliam   (*Judith 327*)
to the fair city of Bethulia

(7) *ond* **Á**lexandreas *éalra ricost*   (*Widsith 15*)
and Alexander mightiest of all

As in modern Germanic languages, deverbal nouns in Old English were subject to a rule which retracted the primary stress from the stem in the verb to the prefix in the noun (cf. German *missbráuchen* "to misuse" versus *Míssbràuch* "misuse"). We exemplify this process in (8):

(8) (a) *Forþan bið ándgit ǽghwǣr sēlest*   (*Beowulf 1059*)
therefore understanding shall be best in every way

[1] In this chapter we use the mark ′ to represent primary stress and the mark ‵ to represent subsidiary (nonprimary) stress, as in (3). Since nothing is known about the level of subsidiary stresses in Old and Middle English, there is little point in making finer distinctions in the transcription.

(b) *þæt hie Gḗata clifu ongítan meahton* (*Beowulf 1911*)
until they could make out the Geatish cliffs

In the verb *ongítan* in (8b), it is the stem rather than the prefix that carries primary stress. In the related noun *ándgit* in (8a), however, primary stress is on the prefix.

Metrical poetry is the most direct but not the only source for Old English stress. There were phonological processes in the language that occurred only in the presence of stress as well as processes that took place only in the absence of stress. Among the former we mention the diphthongization of stressed *e* to *ie* after palatal consonants, which is exemplified in the verb *ongíetan* "to understand" and in the noun derived from it, *ándgìet* "intelligence," both of which are cited in (8).[2] (See Campbell (1959, §185).) Since diphthongization takes place not only in the verb but also in the noun, which no longer has primary stress on the relevant syllable, this process clearly does not depend on primary stress alone but rather on stress of any degree. Unstressed vowels, on the other hand, do not diphthongize, as shown by the absence of a diphthong after *g* in *geféoht* "fight," *strénge* "strong," *wérgend* "defender," and similar forms.

Among the processes that take place only in the absence of stress are various types of reduction, one of which has already been exemplified by the pair *ándgìet–ongíetan* in (8): when the prefix here is stressed, its shape is *and-*; when it is unstressed, it undergoes reduction and is realized as *on-*.[3] A different type of reduction in stressless syllables is that undergone by the prefix of the verb *wiþsácan* "refuse" as compared with the related nominal *wíþersàca* "adversary" in which the unreduced prefix *wiþer-* appears. Still another kind of reduction is illustrated by the noun *bígàng* "practice" and its related verb *begángen* "practice." Here the change of tense *ī* to lax *ĕ* is conditioned by the absence of stress.

The most salient features of Old English accentuation are listed in (9):

(9) (a) Prefixed nouns have primary stress on the prefix and some lower stress on the stem vowel.

(b) Other words have primary stress on the first syllable of the word stem (not the prefix).

(c) In compound nouns the first element has primary stress.

---

[2] The examples in (8) show *i* rather than *ie* because of the subsequent monophthongization that *ie* underwent in late Old English. (See Campbell (1959, §300).)

[3] This process is described in Sievers/Brunner (1951): "Auslautendes *d* ist geschwunden in proklitischem *on*-aus *ond*-wie in *onfón* empfangen, ws. *ongietan* verstehen, *onsácan* widerstehen, vgl. *óndfenga* Empfänger, *óndgiet* Verstand, *óndsaca* Widersacher, usw." (§198, note 2).

In order to account for the facts of Old English stress in (a) and (b), we postulate the two stress assignment rules (10) and (11), which apply in the order given.[4] (We shall account for (c) later—see (26).)

(10) INITIAL STRESS RULE

$$V \rightarrow [\text{1stress}] \ / \ [(X\#)C_0\text{——}Y]$$

(11) STRESS RETRACTION RULE (Old English)

$$V \rightarrow [\text{1stress}] \ / \ [C_0\text{——}X\#C_0 \begin{bmatrix} \text{1stress} \\ V \end{bmatrix} C_0]_N$$

Rule 10 places stress on the stem-initial syllable, and rule (11), which is restricted to nouns, retracts the stress from the last, or only, syllable of the stem to the first syllable of the word. Consider, for example, the noun *andgiet*, which is assumed to have the nested constituent structure shown in (12):

(12) $[[and\#giet]_V]_N$

Rules (10) and (11) will apply to the representation (12) as shown in the derivation (13):

(13) $[[and\#giet]_V]_N$

	1	INITIAL STRESS (10)
−		STRESS RETRACTION (11)
	1	INITIAL STRESS (10)
1	2	STRESS RETRACTION (11)

On the first pass through the cyclical rules,[5] rule (10) assigns stress to the stem of the underlying verb, but (11) cannot retract the stress since it is restricted so as to apply only to nouns. On the second cycle, however, the internal brackets are erased and the noun form becomes subject to the rules. Thus, after (10) vacuously reassigns primary stress to the stem, (11) can now apply to retract the stress to the prefix, yielding the correctly stressed noun *ándgìet*.

A peculiar feature of the Stress Retraction Rule as stated is that it applies only when the form has final stress, just as in modern English. This fact is implicit in the traditional descriptions of Old English, but as far as we know its true significance has never been fully appreciated. Campbell (1959, §73) notes that complex nouns and verbs differ with respect to stress

---

[4] The symbol # represents the internal word boundary which separates prefixes from stems. It is to be distinguished from ##, which represents the true word boundary (as throughout Chapter 1), and also from the boundary = (see, for example, (61) in the present chapter).

[5] See Chapter 1, (29) and (30), for the relevant conventions on rule application.

on their prefix, the stressed prefix appearing in the nouns and the unstressed prefix in the verbs (see (8)). Contradicting the principle just cited, Campbell states elsewhere that "... nouns derived from compound verbs have un-accented prefixes: *forgífness* forgiveness, *alýsing* redemption " (§77). The apparent contradiction is readily resolved when it is observed that with the exception of the noun *ǽtspỳrning* "offense" (about which we shall say more shortly), the nouns derived from prefixed verbs cited by Campbell in §73 all have monosyllabic stems: *ǽwielm* "fountain," *ǽfþunca* "source of offense," *ándsaca* "apostate," *bígenga* "inhabitant," *órþanc* "mind," *wíþersaca* "adversary." (We shall discuss the declensional ending -*a* in these forms directly.) They are therefore all subject to the Stress Retraction Rule (11). This is not the case with forms such as *forgífness*, which instead, if we assume a nested constituent structure, will be derived as in (14):

(14) [[for # gif]$_V$ ness]$_N$

1	INITIAL STRESS (10)
—	STRESS RETRACTION (11)
1	INITIAL STRESS (10)
—	STRESS RETRACTION (11)

On the first cycle, rule (10) places primary stress on the stem of [*for # gif*]$_V$, and rule (11), which is restricted to nouns, does not retract the stress. On the second pass through the rules, (10) vacuously reassigns primary stress to the string [*for # gif+ness*]$_N$, and again rule (11) does not apply, this time because it retracts stress only in nouns with monosyllabic stems. If we instead assume the unnested constituent structure [*for # gif+ness*]$_N$, we achieve the same result with just one pass through the rules.

Observe that initial stress in forms like *ándsaca, bígenga, wíþersaca* indicates that declensional endings do not block stress retraction. We must distinguish, therefore, between declensional endings like -*a* and -*u* and conjugational endings such as the infinitival -*an*, on the one hand, and true suffixes such as -*ness*, on the other: the former set of endings has no effect on the operation of the Stress Retraction Rule; the latter group of suffixes, as shown with -*ness* in (14), does affect the retraction of stress. Thus we must extend the Stress Retraction Rule to allow for this, and we reformulate (11) as (15):

(15) STRESS RETRACTION RULE (Old English)

$$V \rightarrow [\text{1stress}] \ / \ [C_0\text{———}X \# C_0 \begin{bmatrix} \text{1stress} \\ V \end{bmatrix} C_0 (C_0 \begin{bmatrix} V \\ +B \end{bmatrix} C_0)]_N$$

We assume that the feature [+B] is automatically assigned by a lexical rule to declensional and conjugational endings. In addition, we find that in certain cases true suffixes are also idiosyncratically marked with this feature. Consider, for example, the near minimal pair *ǽtspỳrning–alýsing*. If we assume that *-ing* is marked [+B] in the first form but not in the second, then we can account for the stress contrast here by the rules as developed thus far. (It appears that subsequently the suffix *-ing* was marked [+B] in all words, for accentual doublets such as the one just cited are not attested in later stages of the language.) Recall from Chapter 1 that the retraction rule (100b) of modern English also allows an extra syllable position to the right of the [1stress] syllable and that this position can be occupied by one of a restricted set of syllables (see Chapter 1, notes 15, 19, and 34). The situation in Old English is not unlike this.

The fact that rule (15) must be limited as to lexical category is shown by the representative sample of adverbs in (16):

(16)

todǽg	*beínnan*	*wiþnéoþan*
onwég	*benéoþan*	*wiþŭtan*
onbǽc	*onúfan*	*undernéoþan*
beǽftan	*onúppan*	*tofóran*
befóran	*wiþǽftan*	*togǽdere*
begéondan	*wiþfóran*	*ætfóran*
behíndan	*wiþínnan*	*ætgǽdere*

Each of the forms in (16) is composed of a prefix followed by another element, and the stress is always on the root element rather than on the prefix. Given a constituent structure such as $[to \# dæg]_{ADV}$, rule (10) will assign primary stress to the root syllable, but rule (15) will not retract stress since it does not apply to adverbs. Thus the restriction of (15) to nouns produces the correct results for the forms in (16).

With rule (15), then, we are able to account not only for initial stress in prefixed nouns like *ándswàru* and in deverbal nouns like *ándgìet*, but also for noninitial stress in prefixed verbs like *ongíetan* and *ofergán* "traverse" and in adverbs like *todǽg*. Moreover, (15) also explains the fact that participles in Old English normally do not show stress retraction when preceded by prefixes. Thus, forms such as *underþéoded* "subjected" or *wiþerwínnende* "fighting against" cited by Campbell (1959, §81) would receive root stress by rule (10) but would be subject to no other rules. These examples are problematic for Campbell since participles are inflected like adjectives in

Old English and, in Campbell's view, all adjectives exhibit stress retraction like nouns.[6]

Up to now we have limited rule (15) to nouns; however, it appears that at least some adjectives as well exhibited retraction in Old English. Wright (1925) notes: "Derivative adjectives often have the same inseparable prefixes as nouns, as *andfenge* 'acceptable', *ansund* 'entire', 'sound', *edgeong* 'growing young', *gecynde* 'innate, natural', *sammǣle* 'agreed', *unsynnig* 'innocent'" (§621). The poetry shows that these adjectives, with the exception of *gecynde*, exhibit initial stress. They are, moreover, composed of a prefix and a stem. As our rules are now formulated, the adjectives will receive root stress by (10), but, because (15) is limited to nouns, retraction will not take place. The natural modification of (15), then, is to extend it to adjectives, and we therefore replace (15) by (17):

(17) STRESS RETRACTION RULE (Old English)

$$V \rightarrow [1\text{stress}] \ / \ [C_0 \underline{\quad\quad} X \# C_0 \begin{bmatrix} 1\text{stress} \\ V \end{bmatrix} C_0 (C_0 \begin{bmatrix} V \\ +B \end{bmatrix} C_0)]_{\{N,A\}}$$

The extension of the Stress Retraction Rule to adjectives does not cause difficulty with prefixed participles, which, as we have seen, normally do not exhibit stress retraction. The reason is that participles are formed by the addition of a syllabic suffix to the root of the verb— *-ende* in the case of present participles, and *-en* or *-ed* in the case of past participles, depending upon whether the verb is strong or weak. As we have already seen in (14), the addition of a syllabic suffix to a monosyllabic root will normally have the effect of blocking stress retraction, and this is precisely what one finds in forms such as *underþḗoded*, *wiþerwínnende*.

There are other environments in which rule (17) must be blocked. Certain Old English prefixes are always stressless, for example the prefix *ge-*. (Notice that the prefix vowel does not exhibit the diphthongization that would be expected after a palatal consonant if the vowel were stressed.) Such nouns as *geféoht* "fight" and *getrúm* "troop" contain root stress only, as can be seen from the lines in (18) and (19):

[6] Campbell (1959, §81) cites a small number of prefixed participles, both adjectives and nouns, with initial stress: *wiþerfeohtend* "enemy," *wiþerhycgende* "hostile," and *únderþēoded* "subjected" (a variant of *underþéoded*). We shall assume that *wiþer* and *under* here are prepositional adverbs. The forms just cited, therefore, are not single words and hence not subject to retraction by (15). Rather, the rules for stress in compound words will apply to them. The apparent absence of reduction in the prefix in unretracted participles such as *underþéoded* may be due to the failure of the orthography to indicate such processes consistently or perhaps to a special stress rule that assigns nonprimary stress to some clitics.

(18) *þone þīn fǽder to geféohte bær*   (*Beowulf 2048*)
      the one thy father into battle bore

(19) *trýddode tírfæst getrúme micle*   (*Beowulf 922*)
      the illustrious one went forth with a great company

      Several alternatives are available to account for these facts. We might suppose that words with the prefix *ge-* are all marked as exceptions to the Stress Retraction Rule (17). This would handle the forms just cited in a satisfactory fashion. However, a problem arises with regard to certain roots that take two prefixes, one of which is *ge-* while the other is a prefix quite capable of taking stress: *úngeþýldig* "impatient." To account for such forms as well, one might suppose that *ge-* is marked as an exception to rule (17) just in case it occupies word-initial position. This would permit retraction in *úngeþýldig* while blocking it in *geféohte*, etc. Another alternative is to extend our theory to allow certain morphemes to be marked [−stressable], with morphemes so marked then being exempt from any rule that has the effect of assigning stress. A category such as the one just proposed implies that a morpheme may be an exception to a particular phonological process rather than just a particular rule. The need for being able to refer to processes rather than merely rules has been noted previously in phonological studies, but at this point we are unable to specify precisely what this means in terms of the theory. Thus, we leave open the question of specifically how to deal with prefixes like *ge-* and assume only that they are somehow marked as exceptions to the stress assignment rules.

      There is evidence in Old English which suggests that certain other prefixes, in particular *be-* and *for-*, behaved like *ge-* at some stage in the history of English, although they did not always do so. Consider the examples in (20) and (21), drawn from Wright (1925, §12):

(20) *bebéodan*   to command
      belífan   to keep
      begángan   to provide
      forbéodan   to forbid

(21) *bebód*   command
      beláf   remainder
      begáng   practice
      forbód   prohibition

      In (20) root stress is assigned normally by rule (10) and retraction fails since (17) does not apply to verbs. The list in (21) contains nouns which are clearly the deverbal counterparts of the verbs in (20) and which should therefore show retraction by (17); however, noninitial stress is recorded instead. Thus we must assume that *be-* and *for-* are somehow prevented from acquiring stress. Indeed, the doublets *fórwyrd* "ruin" and *forwýrd* suggest that there was considerable shifting of categories with respect to the stress-ability of prefixes. (Cf. also *bígang* versus *begáng*.)

We recall now that stress in compound words (see (9c)) still remains unaccounted for. It has usually been assumed that Old English compound nouns, verbs, adjectives, and adverbs—in effect, any compound word whose elements are themselves words—had primary stress on the first element and lesser stresses on the remaining elements. Limiting ourselves to compound words with two elements, we illustrate with the forms in (22)–(25):

(22) COMPOUND NOUNS

wǽldrèor	blood of slaughter
fýrgenstrèam	mountain stream
þéodcỳning	king of a people

(23) COMPOUND ADJECTIVES

gámolfèax	gray haired
góldwlànc	proud with gold
fýrhèard	hardened by fire

(24) COMPOUND VERBS

ǽfter-spỳrian	inquire
fóre-gescrìfan	preordain
óf-adrìfan	drive away

(25) COMPOUND ADVERBS

gĕardàgum	formerly
hlúdswège	loudly
éalswằ	quite so

To account for such examples, we shall suppose a structure of the form $[\# \; [\# gamol \#]_A \; [\# feax \#]_N \; \#]_A$ and the rule (26):

(26) COMPOUND RULE

$$\begin{bmatrix} 1\text{stress} \\ V \end{bmatrix} \rightarrow [1\text{stress}] \; / \; [\#\# X \text{—} Y \#\# Z \#\#]_{\{N,V,A\}}$$

        CONDITIONS: X and Y may contain $\#\#$

                           Y contains no [1stress]

This rule is identical with that postulated for modern English (see (33) and (36) in Chapter 1), since as far as we know there is no reason to suppose that the Compound Rule has changed fundamentally since Old

English times. The compound forms in (22)–(25) are now derived as illustrated with *gámolfèax* in (27) (where only the relevant steps are shown):

(27) $[\# \; [\# \text{gamol} \#]_A \; [\# \text{feax} \#]_N \; \#]_A$

1	1	INITIAL STRESS (10)
1	2	COMPOUND (26)

Like modern English (see Section 7 of Chapter 1), Old English contains a great many prefixed verbs like *ofergán* which have primary stress on the stem. In contrast with these are the verbs exemplified in (24), in which both elements are full-fledged words. Thus *æfter-spỳrian* differs from *ofergán*, for example, in that *æfter* is not a prefix like *ofer-* but rather an adverb, that is, a full word, which in construction with the verb *spyrian* forms a compound verb that takes initial stress by (26). Indeed, the examples *fóre-gescrìfan* and *óf-adrìfan* in (24) indicate that the second elements of such compound verbs may themselves be composed of a prefix and a root: $[\# \; [\# of \#] \; [\# a \# dr\bar{\imath} fan \#] \; \#]$.

In a similar fashion we can compare compound adverbs like *géardàgum* "in days of yore" with prefixed adverbs like *todǽg*. The correlation of initial stress in compound words and noninitial stress in prefixed words breaks down, however, when we come to nouns and adjectives. Thus both *gámolfèax* and *wǽldrèor*, which have no prefix, and *ánsùnd* and *ándgìet*, which do have one, exhibit initial stress. The similarity in stress contour of compound nouns and adjectives and deverbal nouns and prefixed adjectives, respectively, might lead one to suppose that both are derived by the same rule and that the Stress Retraction Rule (17) has no separate existence in Old English. What argues against this, however, is precisely the fact that initial stress in noncompound prefixed words is found only in nouns and adjectives. While compound verbs and adverbs show initial stress, prefixed verbs and adverbs do not. If the Compound Rule (26) were responsible for initial stress in nouns and adjectives with prefixes, one would expect to find initial stress in all other lexical categories when forms are composed of a prefix and a root. Since this is not the case, it is clear that two separate rules are involved, one which places initial stress on all categories of words composed of elements which are words, and one which places initial stress on prefixed nouns and adjectives only.

Finally, we must consider a modification of the Initial Stress Rule (10) which is motivated by verb-noun pairs such as *ándswàrian* "to answer," *ándswàru* "answer" and *ándwỳrdan* "to answer," *ándwỳrde* "answer." Evidence from alliterative poetry and the lack of orthographical indication of reduction in the prefix *and-* point toward prefixal stress on the verb as well as the noun, as opposed to pairs such as *ongíetan–ándgìet*. We shall therefore make the natural assumption that in the pairs under discussion here the verb is derived from the noun, resulting in the following nested constituent structure and partial derivation:

$$[[\text{and} \# \text{swar}]_N + \text{ian}]_V$$

	1	INITIAL STRESS (10)
1	2	STRESS RETRACTION (17)

As this derivation shows, at the beginning of the second pass through the cycle we have the string $[\overset{1}{and} \# \overset{2}{swar} + ian]_V$, which is identical to the desired output. The difficulty is that rule (10) will now apply to this sequence to alter the stress contour incorrectly to 21. (Rule (11) is blocked since it does not apply to strings categorized as verbs.) To achieve the desired result, then, we must block the application of (10) on the second pass. This can be done either by adding to the rule the restriction that X contains no [1stress] or else by restricting the application of the rule to vowels with [−stress]. We shall choose the latter method, though without strong motivation, and reformulate rule (10) as in (28):

(28) INITIAL STRESS RULE

$$\begin{bmatrix} -\text{stress} \\ V \end{bmatrix} \rightarrow [\text{1stress}] \quad / \quad [(X\#)C_0 \text{——} Y]$$

To summarize, Old English was subject to the following three stress rules: the Initial Stress Rule (28), which placed stress on the first syllable of the stem; the Stress Retraction Rule (17), which retracted stress from the stem to the prefix mainly in derived nouns and adjectives; and the Compound Rule (26), which greatly resembled the analogous rule in the modern language. Our task now is to sketch the steps whereby these three rules evolved in a plausible manner into the stress rules of modern English as described in the first chapter.

3. *Late Middle English Stress*

In the three hundred years that intervened between the Norman Conquest and Chaucer, the language was inundated by Romance words. In spite of the assertions to be found in the handbooks,[7] these words generally were not

---

[7] See, for example, Sweet (1891): "In Old French the stress generally fell on the same syllable as in Latin, as in *na·ture = nā·tūram*. Through the dropping of final Latin syllables many French words thus came to have the stress on the last syllable, as in *o·nour ho·norem*, *pi·te = pie·tātem*. When first introduced into ME, French words kept their original stress: *nā·tūre, o·nūr, pi·te*; but such words afterwards threw the stress back on to the first syllable by the analogy of the native E. words, such as *·fader, ·bodi*, becoming *·nātūre*, etc." (§786).

subject to the prevalent Germanic stress pattern expressed in the Initial Stress Rule (28). While a portion of the newly introduced words were Anglicized and did receive stress by rule (28), a large number maintained the Romance stress. In (29) we cite a number of lines from Chaucer containing nonprefixed words with noninitial stress, that is, words that could not have been subject to rule (28):[8]

(29) *Of which* vertú *engéndred is the flóur*   *(A.Prol.4)*
   Wel kóudĕ hé fortúnen *the⌢*ascendént   *(A.Prol.417)*
   But Í, that ám exíled *and* baréyne   *(A.Kn.1244)*
   In ál Egípte *that she kóude* espýc   *(LGW.674)*
   That fórsight of divínĕ purveyáunce   *(TC.4.961)*

We recall that we view a grammar of a language as the formal analog of the (largely tacit) knowledge that a speaker has of his language, that is, the knowledge by virtue of which it is possible to assert that a certain individual knows English whereas another does not or that Chaucer's contemporaries spoke a language different from ours. From this perspective, the question that arises from (29) is how the grammar of English would have to have changed from that presented in the preceding section in order to accommodate these new facts. We note that as long as the number of words that violate one of the rules of the language is small, they can be handled as lexical exceptions. Thus, if such were the case with the nonitalic words in (29), they could be marked in the lexicon as exceptions to rule (28) and be provided there with noninitial stress. It is in a similar fashion that we account for the appearance

---

[8] The metrical verse of Chaucer is our primary source of information about Middle English accentuation. Since there is no generally accepted theory of Chaucerian metrical practice, we have included a detailed account of our views on this matter in Chapter 3. For the convenience of the reader we summarize briefly here the main consequences of our theory with regard to the utilization of Chaucer's verse as a source of Middle English stress.

  Iambic verses, in which the overwhelming majority of Chaucer's poems was composed, are constituted by alternating sequences of weak and strong positions. The even-numbered, strong positions may be freely occupied by both stressed and unstressed syllables. The odd-numbered, weak positions may be occupied freely only by unstressed syllables; they may be occupied by stressed syllables only if the two adjacent syllables are *not* both unstressed. Since a great variety of sequences of stressed and unstressed syllables therefore constitute lawful embodiments of the iambic meter, in many cases the verses will not help us to establish the correct accentuation of a word. On the other hand, not every arrangement of syllables is allowed, so that at least a certain amount of evidence for determining stress is provided. For instance, the word *service* in

   Fúl wéel she sóong the sérvĭcĕ *dyvýne*   *(A.Prol.122)*

must be trisyllabic and bear initial stress. Any other stress assignment in this word would render the line unmetrical since an odd position may be occupied by a stressed syllable only when it is not adjacent to unstressed syllables on both sides. For further discussion the reader is referred to Chapter 3.

in our idiolect of modern English of a velar fricative in words such as *Bach*. Such a procedure, however, is clearly inappropriate for the words under discussion since it would imply not only that there was a huge number of exceptions to the normal stress rules of the language but also that these exceptions exhibited no regularities of their own, that is, that stress in these forms could be placed on any vowel whatever. In actuality, stress placement in the words that do not follow rule (28) is as regular as in those that do; it is just governed by different principles.

This is by no means an unusual situation in language. For instance the words constituting the chemical terminology in contemporary English are constructed in accordance with certain general principles which are productively utilized by workers in the field when new chemicals have to be named. There is thus a special subdivision in the grammar of these speakers which deals with the morphology and phonology of this portion of their vocabulary. In much the same fashion the grammar of Chaucer and his contemporaries contained a special subdivision dealing with stress placement in words that were being introduced from medieval French and other, primarily Romance, languages. We shall try to demonstrate that this part of the grammar was deliberately utilized by Chaucer and his contemporaries to produce Romance stress patterns in words that were clearly of Germanic origin and vice versa, showing that both the Initial Stress Rule (28) and the Romance Stress Rule to be given (see (35)) were productive in the language. But first we must describe the stress pattern of the newly introduced words.

The nonnative vocabulary of Chaucer consisted of two types of words, namely, learned words largely of Latin origin and everyday words borrowed from Old French or Anglo-Norman. These two classes had different stress patterns. The words of Latin origin were stressed on the antepenultimate vowel if the penultimate syllable ended with a weak cluster; otherwise, they were stressed on the penultimate vowel. Examples of such accentuations are given in (30):

(30) (a) *"For if my fader* Týdĕŭs," *he seyde* (TC.5.932)
    (b) *And also how* Čappánĕŭs *the proude* (TC.5.1504)
    (c) *The snowes molte, and* Zéphĕrŭs *as ofte* (TC.5.10)
    (d) Sătúrnĕs *doughter, Juno, thorugh hire might* (TC.4.1538)
    (e) *My ship and me* Căríbdĭs *wol devoure* (TC.5.644)
    (f) *For certein, Phebus and* Nĕptúnŭs *bothe* (TC.4.120)

While in classical Latin the last vowel in a word could be either tense or lax, in medieval Latin all unstressed vowels had become lax.[9] We shall

[9] Thus Meyer-Lübke (1890) notes: "In tonloser Silbe ist jeder Quantitätsunterschied verwischt" (p. 53).

assume, then, that in Chaucer's pronunciation words borrowed from Latin, such as those in nonitalic type in (30), contained a last vowel that was lax.

The stress in Latin words can therefore be accounted for with the help of the two disjunctively ordered rules in (31):

(31) (a) V → [1stress] / $[X\text{——}C_0 \begin{bmatrix} -\text{tense} \\ V \end{bmatrix} C_0^1 \begin{bmatrix} -\text{tense} \\ V \end{bmatrix} C_0]$

    (b) V → [1stress] / $[X\text{——}C_0 \begin{bmatrix} -\text{tense} \\ V \end{bmatrix} C_0]$

Words borrowed from Old French do not quite follow the pattern in (31), as shown in (32), in particular (32e–l):

(32) (a) *And honestly* govérne *wel oure hous*   *(B.Sh.1434)*
    (b) Egíste *to his chambre fast hym spedde*   *(LGW.2623)*
    (c) *A lymytour, a ful* solémpne *man*   *(A.Prol.209)*
    (d) *In al* Egípte *that she koude espye*   *(LGW.674)*
    (e) *To doon* honóur *to May, and for to ryse*   *(A.Kn.1047)*
    (f) *In no* degrée *the value of a flye*   *(B.Sh.1361)*
    (g) *Quod the* chanoún, *"and farewel, grant* mercý!"   *(G.C Y.1380)*
    (h) *And after this* Jhesús, *of his mercy*   *(B.ML.690)*
    (i) *And after that the⌢*abbót *with his covent*   *(B.Pri.1827)*
    (j) *Who yaf* Judíth *corage or hardynesse*   *(B.ML.939)*
    (k) *In mount* Oréb, *er he hadde any speche*   *(D.Sum.1891)*
    (l) *But ever crie agayn* tempést *and rayn*   *(H.Mcp.301)*

In the words of Pope (1934): "The wholesale reduction and elimination of atonic syllables made of Old French a language in which all words were either oxytone or paroxytone, and, if paroxytone, then always in a syllable containing e" (§223). More formally this stress assignment principle can be expressed by the rules in (33), which are disjunctively ordered:

(33) (a) V → [1stress] / $[X\text{——}C_0 e]$
    (b) V → [1stress] / $[X\text{——}C_0]$

Consider first the words with final e (32a–d). Old French was subject to a rule that tensed vowels in open syllable, that is, before another vowel or before a single consonant followed by a vowel.[10] Thus the penultimate vowel

---

[10] Meyer-Lübke (1920): "Dieser ersten Umgestaltung . . . folgt nun eine zweite, die eine völlige Umgestaltung der alten Längeverhältnisse mit sich bringt. Vokale in geschlossener Silbe werden nämlich durchweg gekürzt, in offener durchweg gedehnt . . . und da teils sprachliche, teils sachliche Erwägungen die Aufnahme dieser und anderer entsprechend behandelter Wörter nach dem 6. Jahrh. und vor das 9. setzen lassen, so hätte man zwar noch einen weiten Spielraum, aber immerhin namentlich eine Grenze rückwärts, hinter die nicht gegangen werden darf" (§116).

in words ending with e was either tensed by this rule or was followed by more than one consonant, meaning that there were no weak clusters in the penultimate syllable of such words. Since e is, moreover, a lax vowel, all words ending with e will be handled properly by case (b) of rule (31), and case (a) of (33) is redundant.

The remaining cases in (32), that is, the nonitalic words in (e)–(l), all have final stress. Two subcategories must be distinguished. First, there are words like *honóur* and *degrée* which have a tense vowel in the last syllable. These contrast, then, with forms that have antepenult or penult stress since, as we have seen, the latter all have a lax vowel in the last syllable. Second, there appears in Chaucer a number of words, mainly bisyllabic, which have final stress but in which the last vowel apparently is lax: *Jhesús, abbót, Judíth, Oréb, tempést.* (Many of these are also found in Chaucer with initial stress.) Since words of the second type would receive nonfinal stress by rule (31b), we suggest that they are marked as exceptions to this rule (and possibly also to (31a), but clear cases are missing). Forms so marked will then receive stress on the last vowel by rule (33b), as will the previously cited words with a tense vowel in the final syllable.

We have thus established that in Chaucer's grammar there was need for the three rules of stress assignment in (34):

(34) (a) $V \rightarrow [\text{1stress}] \ / \ [X\text{———}C_0 \begin{bmatrix} -\text{tense} \\ V \end{bmatrix} C_0^1 \begin{bmatrix} -\text{tense} \\ V \end{bmatrix} C_0]$ (31a)

(b) $V \rightarrow [\text{1stress}] \ / \ [X\text{———}C_0 \begin{bmatrix} -\text{tense} \\ V \end{bmatrix} C_0]$ (31b), (33a)

(c) $V \rightarrow [\text{1stress}] \ / \ [X\text{———}C_0]$ (33b)

It has been assumed that these rules constitute a disjunctively ordered set. Like all such sets, the rules of (34) have the property that the later rules can be derived by deleting portions of the earlier ones. As noted in Chapter 1, we reflect this property by means of the parenthesis notation, and we therefore abbreviate the stress rules for the borrowed portion of Chaucer's vocabulary as in (35):

(35) ROMANCE STRESS RULE

$V \rightarrow [\text{1stress}] \ / \ [X\text{———}C_0((\begin{bmatrix} -\text{tense} \\ V \end{bmatrix} C_0^1) \begin{bmatrix} -\text{tense} \\ V \end{bmatrix} C_0)]$

In sum, in order to account for the stress contours of words found in the language of Chaucer and his contemporaries, it is necessary to assume that the words are subdivided into two lexical classes with regard to the rules that assign stress. Unmarked words are assumed to be subject to the Initial Stress Rule (28) and the Stress Retraction Rule (17); others are marked as being subject to the Romance Stress Rule (35). Among the latter, certain words are further marked as exceptions to rule (34b) (and perhaps also (34a)) of the Romance Stress Rule. There is hardly any need to draw attention to the fact that (35) is formally identical with cases (100a) and (100c) of the Main Stress Rule of modern English as formulated in Chapter 1.

The class of words subject to rules (28) and (17) consisted largely of words of native Germanic origin, whereas those subject to rule (35) were of Romance origin. This observation, of course, is one that can be made only by a linguist. As far as the speaker of the language was concerned, we claim only that he was aware of the existence of two classes of words with distinctly different stress patterns. To the speaker of Middle English, the historical origins of these two classes were at most of marginal interest.

It has often been observed that in Chaucer and other poets of the same period there is a large number of stress doublets where Germanic forms are stressed in accordance with the Romance Stress Rule (35) and where words clearly of Romance origin are stressed in accordance with the Initial Stress Rule (28). Such doublets are naturally explained as shifts of a given word from one lexical category to another. The idea that these doublets might be accounted for in this way is not altogether new. A shift in lexical category is clearly implicit in the following passage by Luick (1896), who, in commenting on stress alternants, noted:

> Ich möchte glauben, dass diese erscheinung [the stress shift] eine gewisse sprachliche grundlage hat, aber eine vorübergehende und ganz anders geartete: dass sich nämlich in ihr die betonungsweise widerspiegelt, welche diese wörter im munde der Normannen erheilten, als sie anfingen, englisch zu lernen und es unvollkommen nachbildeten—in der weise ungefähr, wie heute Franzosen vielfach deutsch sprechen. Ihre sprache kannte nach der tonsilbe nur schwaches *e* (in den ausgängen -*e* und -*es*), nicht andere vokale. Englische wörter wie *tale* oder *tales* und auch wohl solche wie *rīden, rideþ, better* konnten sie daher nachbilden. Anders dagegen bei nachtonigen silben mit vollvokal: ein englisches *hŏli*, wurde in ihrem munde nach muster wie *hardí* zu *holí* oder doch *hòlí*, ein englisches *rídinge* zu *ridínge* oder *rìdínge*: indem sie die englischen wörter in ihre artikulationsweise hineinzogen oder doch ihr stark annäherten, verschoben sie in allen zweisilbigen wörtern dieser art den akzent auf die schlusssilbe, in allen dreisilbigen auf die mittelsilbe.

In addition to this shift from the Germanic to the Romance category, we can also find in Chaucer instances of a shift in the opposite direction, that is, from the expected Romance accentuation to the Germanic initial stress.

Examples of such stress doublets are given in (36):

(36) (a) *Ŏf whĭch Ĭ spéke, thér hĕ Cŭstáncĕ fónd*   (B.ML.576)

 (b) *"Ĭ ām youre dóghtĕr Cústăncĕ," quŏd shé*   (B.ML.1107)

 (c) *Lóo, hówthĭs théef kŏude hĭs sĕrvícĕ béedĕ*   (G.CY.1065)

 (d) *Fúl wéel shĕ sóong thĕ sérvicĕ dўvýnĕ*   (A.Prol.122)

The final lax *ĕ* in the nonitalicized words in these lines must be assumed
to have been pronounced, for otherwise the lines would lack the required
number of syllables. Since in both *Custance* and *service* the penultimate
syllable ends with a strong cluster, these words would receive penultimate
stress if they were subject to the Romance Stress Rule (35). Hence the only
way in which they could receive the initial stress they exhibit in (36b) and (36d)
is by being shifted into the unmarked category of words which receive stress
by the Initial Stress Rule (28).

The stress doublets in (37) are apparently to be explained in a somewhat different fashion:

(37) comfórt   *Thus hath my freend with gret comfort*   (RR.3467)
      cómfort   *That myght me ease or comfort gete*   (RR.2965)

      discórd   *And for ther hath ben gret discord*   (RR.6705)
      díscord   *But aftir discord they accorded*   (RR.5815)

      rewárd   *To myn estat have more reward, I preye*   (TC.2.1133)
      réward   *That han no reward but at tyrannye*   (LGW.375)

      covént   *And after that the abbot with his covent*   (B.Pri.1827)
      cóvent   *And up I roos, and al oure covent eke*   (D.Sum.1863)

      geáunt   *Til that ther cam a greet geaunt*   (B.Th.1997)
      géant   *He slow the geant Antheus the stronge*   (B.Mk.3298)

      presént   *Caliope, thy vois be now present*   (TC.3.45)
      présent   *What tyme that nowe present is*   (RR.377)

      serváunt   *So fareth it by a riotous servaunt*   (A.Co.4408)
      sérvant   *Emforth my myght, thy trewe servant be*   (A.Kn.2235)

      tormént   *To thee clepe I, thou Goddesse of torment*   (TC.1.8)
      tórment   *That evere derk in torment night by night*   (TC.5.640)

      tiráunt   *Right so bitwixe a titleless tiraunt*   (H.Mcp.223)
      týrant   *Som tyrant is, as ther be many con*   (E.Mch.1989)

When the words in (37) appear with final stress, they must be stressed
in accordance with case (34c) of the Romance Stress Rule. When they appear

with initial stress, however, there are two possible explanations. On the one hand, their stress pattern may be explained in the same manner as that of the forms in (36b) and (36d), that is, by assuming that the words were shifted into the unmarked lexical category of native words and received stress by rule (28). Alternatively, the words may have had two possible pronunciations, one with a lax vowel in the last syllable, the other with a tense vowel. Such vowel quality doublets are quite common in different languages, for example the [īy]–[e] alternation in the modern American pronunciation of *economics* or [ēy]–[ə] in the last syllable of nouns such as *candidate*, *delegate*.

The latter explanation, however, will not handle the examples in (38):

(38) (a) *Wĭth prḗchy̆ng ĭn thĕ púlpĭt thĕr hĕ stóod*   (*D.Sum.2282*)

     (b) *Ĭ stónde ly̆k ă clérk ĭn my̆ púlpét*   (*C.Pard.391*)

It is unlikely that *pulpét* (38b) had a nonetymological tense vowel in the last syllable since it rimes with *yset* in the next line of the verse. Instead, we propose that *pulpét* in (38b) was treated like the Romance words that were marked as exceptions to rule (34b) and therefore received final stress by rule (34c) (see (32h–l)). In (38a), on the other hand, *púlpit* is treated as if it were a regular word of the Romance portion of the vocabulary.

The fact that words in the Romance portion of the vocabulary could be subcategorized with respect to whether or not they were subject to (34b) of the Romance Stress Rule, this in turn determining whether they received final stress by (34c), seems also to have been utilized by Chaucer to create stress doublets. This was noted by Ten Brink (1901) with regard to the stress doublets found in classical names such as *Appóllo–Appolló*, *Pláto–Plató*, *Cléo–Cleó*. Ten Brink remarked that in "proper names under the influence of French accentuation, the final syllable of a Latin paroxytone acquires the primary, or at least the secondary stress . . ." (§94). It seems to us that this is the appropriate explanation for the numerous instances, a few of which are cited in (39), where the Latin ending *-us* receives final stress:

(39) (a) *That specially oure sweete Lord* Jhesús   (*D.Sum.1921*)

     (b) *She, this in blak, liking to* Troilús   (*TC.1.309*)

     (c) *Bitwix this and the mount of* Kaukasóus   (*D.WB.1140*)

     (d) *Faireste of faire, o lady myn,* Venús   (*A.Kn.2221*)

     (e) *Ther was a duc that highte* Theseús   (*A.Kn.860*)

     (f) *Dispitously, of daun* Pirrús   (*HF.1.161*)

Ten Brink thought that these instances could all be explained by assuming that the vowel was "lengthened for the sake of the rhyme: Kaukasous (:hous)" (§94). The difficulty with this view is that it overlooks the fact that rimes of tense and lax vowels are attested elsewhere in Chaucer (cf. *hade–blade*, *A.Prol.617–18*) and especially that *Troilus* in (39b) rimes with *thus* which clearly has a lax vowel. This ad hoc tensing need not be postulated if it is assumed that the lexical categorization of such words was changed so that they were made exceptions to (34a,b) of the Romance Stress Rule.

In (40) we give examples which show one word undergoing all of the possible lexical shifts:

(40) (a) *Fŏr thílkĕ nýght Ĭ lást* Crĭséydĕ *saý*   *(TC.5.1187)*

      (b) *Ămóng thĭse óthĕre fólk wăs* Crĭséydá   *(TC.1.169)*

      (c) *"*Crĭséydă, *mў frénd?" Hĕ séydĕ, "Yís,"*   *(TC.2.1424)*

In (40a) *Criseyde* is stressed with its normal penultimate stress pattern: since it belongs to the Romance vocabulary and ends with a lax vowel, it receives stress on the tense penultimate vowel by rule (34b). In (40b) the word is still treated as part of the Romance vocabulary but is marked as an exception to (34b) and receives final stress by (34c). In (40c) we have an example of a headless line, in which stress on the first syllable is found almost exclusively. We can explain the initial stress in *Criseyda* in this line by assuming that here the word was stressed not in accordance with the Romance Stress Rule, as would normally be the case, but rather that it was shifted from the Romance to the unmarked Germanic category.[11]

---

[11] The explanation proposed here for stress alternants found in Chaucer and his contemporaries makes no use of the fact that in Middle English lax [e] was optionally deleted in word-final position or that certain vowels underwent changes in tenseness, primarily in word-final position. In an earlier study (Halle and Keyser (1966)) we expressed the opinion that these two facts, rather than shift in lexical category, were directly responsible for the stress doublets observed. As a result, however, trisyllabic words such as *knowynge*, *sownynge*, *service*, *Custance* could never have initial stress if the final *e* was not elided. But there are a number of lines which require precisely this configuration in order to be deemed metrical. Our former theory, then, forced us to classify as metrically deviant perfectly ordinary lines such as the following:

(1) *The cóper téyne, noght* knówўngĕ *this préest*   *(G.CY.1324)*

(2) *As férforth as my* kónnўngĕ *may strécche*   *(G.CY.1087)*

(3) *So swéte a* sównўngĕ *facóunde*   *(BD.926)*

(4) *Fúl wéel she sóong the* sérvĭcĕ *dyvýne*   *(A.Prol.122)*

(5) *"I am youre dóghter* Cústăncĕ," *quod shé*   *(B.ML.1107)*

The present explanation does not deny that *e*-elision or the changes in tenseness that certain vowels underwent were correlated with the shift in main stress; it simply no longer takes the view that the stress shifts resulted from these phenomena. The account here is thus closer to the traditional view expressed by Ten Brink (1901) that *e*-elision and laxing of the penultimate vowel in words such as *manner*, *nature*, *bataille* "battle" were consequences rather than causes of the shift in stress: "After a syllable which, though unaccented, is capable of stress, weak *e* must become mute: apocope, for instance, in *báner*, *máner*, instead of *bánere*, *mánere*, also, though not indicated graphically, in *míllere*, *lóvere*, *náture*, *bátaille* . . ." (§257).

There are other instances where the existence of rules that provided a number of alternatives for stressing a given word was put to poetic use by Chaucer and his contemporaries. Thus we frequently find the same word with different stress contours in neighboring lines or in the same line, as in (41):

(41) *A bettre* félăwe *sholde men noght fynde*   (*A.Prol.648*)
      A good felăwe *to have his concubyn*   (*A.Prol.650*)
      In dívĕrs *art and in* divérse *figures*   (*D.Fri.1486*)

A particularly striking example of this type is the famous passage in the Pardoner's Tale dealing with the evils of swearing, which is given in (42):

(42) *Gret* swéryng *is a thyng abhominable,*
      And fals swerýng *is yet moore reprevable.*
      The heighe God forbad swerýng *at al,*
      Witnesse on Mathew; but in special
      Of swéryng *seith the hooly Jeremye,*
      "Thou shalt swere sooth thyne othes, and nat lye,
      And swere in doom, and eek in rightwisnesse";
      But ydel swéryng *is a cursednesse.*
      Bihoold and se that in the firste table
      Of heighe Goddes heestes honurable,
      Hou that the seconde heeste of hym is this:
      "Take nat my name in ydel or amys."
      Lo, rather he forbedeth swich swerýng
      Than homycide or many a cursed thyng;   (*C.Pard.631–44*)

The examples in (41) and (42) serve mainly to add variety to the language but do not appear to have a particular structural function in the poem. We shall now consider two cases where, on the other hand, stress doublets have a clear function in conveying the message of the poem.

Given in (43) are lines from a ballad in Chaucer's *Complaint of Venus* dealing with the reversal of feeling experienced by a person in love:[12]

---

[12] We assume a structure of the form $[com=plain+ing+e]_V$ for the last word in line four. When this underlying representation is treated as belonging to the Romance portion of the vocabulary, it receives stress on *-ing* by rule (34b). (See note 11 on the subsequent deletion of final *e*.) Notice that this same underlying form will be stressed on *-plain* by rule (28) if it is instead treated as part of the native portion of the vocabulary (assuming the generalization of the rule to include the boundary $=$ as well as $\#$). In a similar fashion, observe that *wepinge* in the same line receives initial stress when treated as a native word but would receive stress on the suffix *-ing* (with or without subsequent loss of the final *-e*) if treated as a foreign word.

(43) *Now certis, Love, hit is right covenable*
  That men ful dere abye thy nobil thing,
  As wake abedde, and fasten at the table,
  Wépinge to laughe, and singe in compleynýng,
  And doun to caste visage and lokyng,
  Often to chaunge hewe and contenaunce
  Pleye in slepýng, and drémyng at the daunce,
  Al the revers of any glad felýng.

Note that in the fourth line the *-ing* forms are at the two ends of the line, while two different deverbal forms appear in the middle of the line. In line seven the order is reversed: the *-ing* forms are verse medial; the non-*ing* forms are at the two ends. This reverse symmetry, graphically illustrating the reversal of feelings that is the poem's theme, is further underlined by the stress patterns of the *-ing* forms. In the fourth line the first *-ing* form is stressed on the stem in accordance with the Germanic stress rule, but the second *-ing* form has suffixal stress, which it can receive only from the Romance Stress Rule (35). This difference in the stress of the *-ing* forms is also observed in the seventh line, but the order is reversed. The poetic motivation is so clear here that it is exceedingly unlikely that these are accidental stress shifts to conform to the exigencies of the meter.[13]

Another interesting example is found in *Gawain and the Green Knight*. This fourteenth-century poem is composed in stanzas that incorporate two distinct metrical schemes. The major portion of the stanza is composed in Germanic alliterative verse, while the concluding four lines are written in rimed iambic trimeter, a verse form that was imported into English poetry from the continent. Mirroring the different national origins of the metrical patterns, the poet uses the same word with Germanic stem stress in the alliterating portion of the stanza (44a) but with Romance suffixal stress in the riming couplet (44b):

(44) (a) *þus wiþ* lázande *lótez þe lórde hit tayt make*   *(988)*
  (b) *wyþ chynne and cheke ful swete*
    boþe quit and red and blánde
    ful lufly con he lete
    wyþ lyppez small lazánde   *(1204–7)*

It is not our purpose to argue that participial forms were stressed on the suffix in any actually spoken dialect of English. Such forms are always

---

[13] For additional discussion of this poem, including a defense of the reading of line seven, see Halle and Keyser (1966, pp. 216–217).

artificial creations of the poet. In order to create them, however, he must have been able to make active use of the principle in accordance with which Romance words were stressed. But this is just another way of saying that the poet's dialect contained two stress rules, one inherited from Old English (rule (28)), and the other introduced into the language together with the newly acquired Romance words (rule (35)).

We recall that, in addition to a rule governing the stress in simple words, Old English also had rules that assigned stress to certain prefixed words and to compounds. The evidence at our disposal would make it appear that these two rules of Old English—rules (17) and (26)—remained unchanged in Chaucer's language.

Evidence for retraction in prefixed nouns through the operation of the Old English Stress Retraction Rule (17) appears in lines such as those in (45):

(45) (a) *Men clepen hym an* óutlawe *or a theef*   (*H.Mcp.234*)
      (b) *An* óutridere, *that lovede venerie*   (*A.Prol.166*)
      (c) *That* fórsight *of divine purveyaunce*   (*TC.4.961*)

The initial stress in the nonitalicized forms is accounted for if we assume the following constituent structure: $[out \# lawe]_N$, $[out \# r\bar{i}d + ere]_N$, $[for \# sight]_N$. The derivations would then proceed as in (46):

(46) $[out \# lawe]_N$ $[out \# r\bar{i}d + ere]_N$

	1			1	INITIAL STRESS (28)
1	2		1	2	STRESS RETRACTION (17)

with $+B$ under $[out \# r\bar{i}d + ere]_N$.

Notice that the same result is achieved whether or not we derive these nouns from the associated verbs *ouláw*, *outríde*, and *forsée*. Although none of these verbs is attested in Chaucer, *outláw* and *forsée* occur in Peter Levins some 150 years later (see the next section), and the gap in Chaucer is, therefore, accidental.

Turning now to the Compound Rule, its presence in Old English and modern English (rule (26) here and rule (33) in Chapter 1) is sufficient to motivate its existence in Chaucer's time. Still, there is rather interesting metrical evidence in lines such as (47) which is worth noting:

(47) (a) *Ther nas* qúyk-sìlver, *lytarge, ne* brýmstòon   (*A.Prol.629*)
      (b) *For* qúyk-sìlver, *that we hadde it anon*   (*G.CY.1103*)
      (c) *He understood, and* brýmstòon *by his brother*   (*G.CY.1439*)

The two nouns *quyk-silver* and *brymstoon* occur with their first elements occupying sometimes an even position and sometimes an odd position in the line. In (47a), *quyk-* and *brym-* occupy the third and ninth positions, respectively, that is, odd-numbered weak positions, while these same elements occupy the second and sixth positions, respectively, that is, even-numbered strong positions, in lines (47b) and (47c). In terms of the metrical theory sketched in note 8 and to be detailed in Chapter 3, these occurrences are consistent with the stress contour 12 since a weak position may be occupied by a stressed syllable provided that a stressed syllable is adjacent to it. The metrical theory predicts that one would find such lines in iambic poetry, but only infrequently, since they are, from a metrical point of view, highly complicated. The poetry of Chaucer bears out this prediction.

Since these words exhibit metrical behavior consistent with a 12 stress contour and since they receive this contour in modern English through the Compound Rule, it seems reasonable to suppose that this same rule was operative in Chaucer's English as well.

To summarize, the change that the Old English stress rules underwent as a result of the influx of Romance words was quite moderate. A second word stress rule—the Romance Stress Rule (35)—was added and a special subcategorization in the lexicon was provided which determined which of the two stress rules applied to a given word. All other rules remained as before.

4. *Early Modern English Stress*

The Sixteenth and Seventeenth Centuries (Levins, Shakespeare, Cooper)

A major landmark for the study of the evolution of the English stress pattern is Peter Levins' *Manipulus vocabulorum*, printed in 1570. This book is essentially a riming dictionary and indicates the location of the main stress (and the main stress only) for many, though not all, of its entries. A striking feature of the Levins list is that, with the exception of a handful of words (which may, moreover, be due to printing errors), it includes no stress doublets. We see no reason to doubt that this accurately reflects the state of the language, which therefore differed from that of Chaucer's language in that uniformity was imposed where two centuries before there had been much diversity.[14] We propose that this uniformity in the assignment of stress was formally

---

[14] A number of stress doublets are attested in Shakespeare and other poets contemporary with Levins. The character of these doublets, however, is quite different from that of the doublets in Chaucer, and they do not require the postulation of two distinct stress rules. For some additional discussion of this question, see the comments preceding (63).

achieved by the replacement of the two distinct stress rules found in Chaucer with a single rule. As a result, lexical categorization no longer played the same role in Levins' dialect that it had played in Chaucer's, at least insofar as stress assignment was concerned. Whereas in Chaucer's dialect a word received stress either by the Initial Stress Rule (28) or by the Romance Stress Rule (35), depending on how it was marked in the lexicon, in Levins' dialect such a lexical subcategorization no longer existed and all words received stress by one and the same rule.

That stress assignment was much more uniform in the sixteenth century than it had been two centuries earlier is a quite generally accepted view. As we note in the Preface, however, the handbooks generally assert that this uniformity in stress assignment was achieved by subjecting an ever larger proportion of the borrowed vocabulary to the Initial Stress Rule (28). We cannot accept this view, for as shown in (48), for instance, there are numerous words in Levins' list that have noninitial stress and thus could not have been subject to rule (28):

(48) (a)   (b)   (c)   (d)

(a)	(b)	(c)	(d)
memórial	*oriéntal*	*divíne*	*lamént*
oríginal	*sacraméntal*	*debáte*	*stubbórn*
geométrical	*accidéntal*	*secúre*	*flagón*

It is obvious, on the other hand, that the words in (48) are readily accounted for by the Romance Stress Rule (34). In column (a) the stress is supplied by rule (34a); in column (b) by rule (34b); in columns (c) and (d) by rule (34c), where the examples in column (c) have no special markings but those in column (d) are marked as being exceptions to (34b). This suggests that we investigate whether the words of native origin which originally received their stress by the Initial Stress Rule will be correctly stressed by the Romance Stress Rule. There is no problem with monosyllabic words. Nor is there a problem with bisyllabic words that have a lax final vowel since rule (34b) will supply initial stress. Moreover, since most Germanic suffixes end with a weak cluster, there is no problem with most trisyllabic words either. Consider, in addition, the possibility that certain inflectional affixes like *-ed*, *-es*, *-ing*, and *-est* are handled as being neutral with regard to stress, that is, the addition of these affixes does not change stress location, just as in the modern language.[15] We can indicate stress neutrality by introducing the boundary # before the appropriate affix. The effect will be to block the application of the Romance Stress Rule on the last pass through the cycle, that is, the pass that includes the affix.

[15] See *Sound Pattern of English* (pp. 84–86) for discussion.

While it is hard to estimate accurately what percentage of words fails to be handled properly by the Romance Stress Rule in place of the Initial Stress Rule, there is little doubt that the number is relatively small. But this is really all that we need to establish, namely, that a person learning the language in the sixteenth century could deal effectively with a great portion of the vocabulary without recourse to the Initial Stress Rule but that it would be impossible for him to do so without recourse to the Romance Stress Rule.

In addition to examples such as those cited in (48), Levins' dictionary gives the words in (49):

(49) (a)   (b)
      óutlaw   *cánonise*
      óutrage   *délectable*
      óversight   *dívisible*
      fóresight   *téstamentary*
      súrname   *défensory*
                            églantine
                            ínstitute

The nouns in (49a) are obvious instances of the operation of the Stress Retraction Rule (17), which, as shown in the preceding sections, was in the grammar of Old English and was carried through into Chaucer's grammar as well. The effect of this rule is to retract stress to the initial syllable in certain forms which by a prior rule have received stress on a later syllable. With this fact in mind we turn to the examples in (49b). If the Romance Stress Rule were to apply to these words, they would receive stress on the last or on the penultimate syllable since one or the other of these syllables contains a tense vowel: *canonĩse*, *delectãble*, *testamentãry*, etc. According to Levins' testimony, however, the main stress in each of these words is instead on the first syllable. In Chaucer's dialect such words could have been handled by being assigned the lexical feature that would make them subject to the Initial Stress Rule. This account is ruled out here, however, since we explained the absence of stress doublets in Levins by assuming that the Initial Stress Rule as well as the concomitant lexical subcategorization had been eliminated. We propose, therefore, that in Levins' dialect the Stress Retraction Rule applied to a wider range of cases than it did earlier. In particular, we assume that after the Romance Stress Rule supplied the words in (49b) with final or penultimate stress, they were subject to a rule with the effect of the Stress Retraction Rule (17), that is, a rule which retracted stress from a later syllable in the word to the initial syllable. To bring this about, we need generalize (17) only slightly, as in (50):

(50) STRESS RETRACTION RULE (Levins)

$$V \rightarrow [\text{1stress}] \ / \ [C_0 \text{——} X(\#)_a C_0 \begin{bmatrix} \text{1stress} \\ V \end{bmatrix} C_0(+y)]_{(N)_b}$$

CONDITION: if a, then b

A comparison of (50) with the Old English Stress Retraction Rule (17) shows that the changes instituted are quite moderate. The syntactic restriction is weakened: all categories of words are now subject to retraction provided that they do not have a prefix which is separated from the stressed syllable by a $\#$ boundary (e.g., *over*$\#$*throw*); where such a boundary appears, retraction is limited to nouns.[16] Moreover, there is a modification in the phonetic nature of the optional post-tonic syllable, due in part to the loss of Old English declensional and conjugational endings. Since most of the actual examples that we have from this period of optional post-tonic syllables are of the suffix represented in the orthography as *-y*, we substitute the cover symbol $+y$ in (50) for the optional sequence $C_0[V, +B]C_0$ which appeared in (17).

The formula (50) abbreviates, among others, the three subrules in (51):[17]

(51) (a) $V \rightarrow [\text{1stress}] \ / \ [C_0 \text{——} X \# C_0 \begin{bmatrix} \text{1stress} \\ V \end{bmatrix} C_0]_N$

(b) $V \rightarrow [\text{1stress}] \ / \ [C_0 \text{——} X C_0 \begin{bmatrix} \text{1stress} \\ V \end{bmatrix} C_0 + y]$

---

[16] Somewhat surprisingly, the generalization of the Stress Retraction Rule did not at first extend to verb-noun pairs of the *permit* type (see (59)), which in present day English show final stress in the verb form but retracted stress in the noun (as discussed in Section 7 of Chapter 1). As will be noted (in the discussion preceding rule (66)), it is not until 1634 that we have reliable evidence of stress retraction in the nouns of this class. H. Sweet's (1891) well-known remark therefore applies to a later dialect than Levins': "in many cases where the same foreign word is used both as a noun and a verb in English, it keeps its end-stress when used as a verb by the analogy of the native verbs which have the same stress, while the corresponding noun- or adjective-form takes the stress on the first syllable, so that the distinction between such words as the noun ·*accent* and the verb *to ac·cent* is really ultimately due to the analogy of the OE pairs ·forwyrd, for·weorþan etc., which analogy was greatly aided by the fact that many verbs of French and Latin origin also threw forward their stress . . ." (§887).

[17] Strictly speaking, the following subrules should also appear in (51):

$$V \rightarrow [\text{1stress}] \ / \ [C \text{——} X \# C_0 \begin{bmatrix} \text{1stress} \\ V \end{bmatrix} C_0 + y]_N$$

$$V \rightarrow [\text{1stress}] \ / \ [C_0 \text{——} X C_0 \begin{bmatrix} \text{1stress} \\ V \end{bmatrix} C_0]_N$$

The first of these accounts for certain irregular retractions (see note 19 of Chapter 1). The second is just a special case of (51c). We shall therefore disregard these subrules in subsequent discussion.

(c) $\text{V} \rightarrow [1\text{stress}] \ / \ [\text{C}_0\text{------}X\text{C}_0\begin{bmatrix}1\text{stress}\\ \text{V}\end{bmatrix}\text{C}_0]$

Rule (51a) is nothing but a slightly modified version of the Stress Retraction Rule (17) and will handle all cases previously subject to that rule, such as those cited in (49a), in addition to some others. Rule (51c) will account for all the cases cited in (49b) except for *téstamentary* and *défensory*. To illustrate, the verb *canonīse* will receive final stress by the Romance Stress Rule (34c) since its last vowel is tense. It will then be subject to (51c) and hence will appear in the output with initial stress. The words *testamentary* and *defensory*, on the other hand, will receive stress on the tense penultimate syllable by case (b) of the Romance Stress Rule (34). They will therefore be subject to rule (51b), which will correctly assign initial stress.

In (52) we give a longer list of words culled from Levins which are stressed in accordance with the principles just outlined:

(52)

(a)	(b)	(c)	
éxorcise	*délectable*	*cómmentary*	
	éxcusable	*mómentary*	
	lámentable	*sécondary*	
	cómparable	*prébendary*	
	réparable	*áccessary*	
	éxplicable	*ádversary*	
	hóspitable		

(d)	(e)	(f)	(g)
ínventory	*cóncubine*	*cóntribute*	*nóminative*
sátisfactory	*célandine*	*réstitute*	*pérspective*
própitiatory	*túrpentine*	*ínstitute*	*défective*
défensory		*dístribute*	

All but the words in (52g) are readily handled in a fashion parallel to the examples of (49b). The words in column (g) reflect an interesting peculiarity that has been preserved fragmentarily in contemporary English, namely, the suffix *-ive* is treated as if it contained a tense vowel. This tense vowel appears in the output when the suffix is nonfinal: *nominatival, adjectival, substantival*. When the suffix *-ive* is final, a very special rule, operating after the rules of stress assignment, deletes the stress on the last syllable. The last syllable, however, must first receive stress by the Romance Stress Rule (case (34c)); otherwise, the Stress Retraction Rule (50) (or its contemporary counterpart) will have no way of applying and the initial stress exhibited by these forms in Levins will remain unaccounted for. We therefore assume that the words in (52g) have derivations such as in (53):

(53) perspect $+$ īve

	1	ROMANCE STRESS (34c)
1	2	STRESS RETRACTION (51c)
1		SPECIAL

Significantly, much as in contemporary English, not all occurrences of *-ive* found in Levins can be assumed to have a tense vowel. For example, if we suppose that the vowel in *-ive* is lax in the words in (54), the stress on the strong noninitial cluster can readily be accounted for by case (34b) of the Romance Stress Rule. If the affix were instead assumed to have a tense vowel here, rule (34c) would supply final stress and rule (50) would retract the stress to the initial syllable.[18]

(54) *defénsive*
demónstrative
inféctive

It appears to us that a suffix with a lax vowel must also be postulated to account for the stress in (55a) and (55b), which contrast with (52a) and (52b):

(55) (a)   (b)
recógnise   *agréeable*
solémnise   *remédiable*
                 defínable

We propose, moreover, that the differential treatment of the suffixes *-ity* and *-ry* illustrated in (56a) and (56b) may be accounted for in a parallel fashion:

(56) (a)   (b)
príncipality   *antíquity*
Máhumetry   *fratérnity*
prósperity   *dextérity*
húmidity   *infírmity*
bárbarity
própriety

We shall assume that *-y* represents a tense vowel in (56a). These forms are therefore subject first to the Romance Stress Rule and then to the Stress

---

[18] There is a question whether in *demónstrative* the suffix *-at* contains a tense or a lax vowel. If the vowel is assumed to be lax, the stress assignment is the result of the automatic application of (34a) of the Romance Stress Rule; if, instead, *-at* does not have a lax vowel, the Romance Stress Rule would have to be modified along the lines of modern English (see (85) and rule (100a) in Chapter 1). Since we lack sufficient evidence to settle this issue for Levins' dialect, we adopt the solution that requires no alteration of the proposed rules. See also note 19.

Retraction Rule (51c). On the other hand, the forms in (56b) are assumed to end with a lax vowel and hence will receive antepenultimate stress by case (34a) of the Romance Stress Rule. Alternatively, it is possible to claim that all but the last example in (56a) are formed with a "stress-neutral" suffix, that is, a suffix that does not affect the position of stress. The words would then be assumed to have a structure such as $[[mahumet]_N \#ry]_N$. This explanation, however, is difficult to justify for *propriety* and perhaps also for *barbarity*. We therefore adopt here the alternative outlined first.

There are other examples in Levins which can be accounted for in terms of an alternation between a tense and a lax vowel in a suffix. Thus in the forms *divúlgate*, *adúmbrate*, *incúlcate*, and *pertúrbate*, the assumption of a lax vowel in *-ate* will yield penultimate stress by the Romance Stress Rule (34b). The form *précipitate*, however, must have a tense vowel in *-ate* so that the Romance Stress Rule (34c) will assign final stress and rule (51c) will shift the stress onto the initial syllable.[19]

---

[19] There is a certain amount of evidence which points toward a lax vowel in the suffix *-ate*. Thus Sundby (1954), in his comments to Cooper's *English Teacher*, 1687, notes: "To judge from the numerous spellings with *-at* which turn up especially in E, the weakly stressed ending of verbs modelled on the Latin first conjugation was pronounced [æt] against ModE [eit]: *accèlerat* (E 54.21), *aggravat*, *agitat* (E 62.23,29), *celebrat* (A 61), *coagulat* (E 48.23), *commiserat* (A 63), *dècimat* (E 54.23), *delineat* (E 48.29), *dilàcerat* (E 54.30) . . ." (p. LVI).

Ekwall ((1907) *John Jones*, 1701) observes: "*-ate* in words like animate, intimate, ruminate, according to p. 28 (*at–ate*), is often sounded short [at], though 'it may be sounded *ate*' [āt] . . . Probably both pronunciations were used in Jones' time . . . The Present E. distinction between *ate* in adjectives and verbs is not to be traced in Jones' book" (§470).

Kökeritz ((1944) *Mather Flint*, 1740) says: ". . . Flint seems to follow Miège (§420) and make no distinction between adjectives and verbs in *-ate*; with the possible exception of *reiterate* 27, which is transcribed with [aite] . . . the remaining instances of *-ate* are transcribed [ett], viz. *desperate* 14, *operate* 20, *ingratiate* 43" (p. 130).

This evidence lends support to the hypothesis that *-ate* in Levins exhibited both tense and lax vowel variants. There is, however, another hypothesis which must be considered. As we shall see when we come to discuss later sources, two principles of stress retraction were operative in the language: one retracted stress to the initial syllable; the other retracted stress in accordance with the Romance Stress Rule. Without going into details here, we note that in a word like *confiscate*, assuming a tense vowel in the suffix, the first principle will yield *confiscate*; the second, *confiscate*. Thus it is conceivable that Levins' *altercate* and *alternate* versus *divulgate* and *adumbrate* constitute evidence that his dialect, like that of Walker's (an eighteenth-century writer whom we discuss in the next section), was subject to two different rules of stress retraction and that his lexicon, again like Walker's, was arbitrarily subcategorized as to which lexical item would be subject to which retraction rule. The evidence for this is unequivocal in Walker. In Levins, on the other hand, since tense-lax variants will account for the stress contours and since there is independent evidence from later orthoepists that supports such variants, we shall assume variation in the tenseness of *-ate* rather than the existence of two stress retraction rules. Nonetheless, we cannot totally exclude the possibility that the situation described in Walker is, in fact, true of a much earlier stage of the language.

A comment by Dobson (1968) is apposite here:

> Secondary stress in trisyllables was more common than in disyllables and survived rather longer, though less long than in words of more syllables than three. It is perhaps implied by Levins's accent-marking *dístribute*, *énrolment*, and *préferment*, for the main stress would hardly be retained on the first syllable without secondary stress on the third; and it is shown by Robinson's accent-markings, with the consequence that the diphthong descended from ME *ī* remains in words like *prezentleĭ*. But the shortened [ɪ] is of early occurrence in such words; it develops when the syllable is unstressed. Robinson, it should be remembered, was transcribing poetry; Gill expressly says that the retention of a secondary stress in trisyllables was characteristic of poetry and not of ordinary speech. But Coles shows secondary stress in *capitál* and *copióus* and J. Smith has (as a variant) *horisón*; it would seem, therefore, that secondary stress occasionally survived even in trisyllables until the second half of the seventeenth century (p. 445).

In terms of the framework described thus far, we account for initial stress in *observance* and *convenient* by supposing that these forms are marked as exceptions to case (b) of the Romance Stress Rule (34) and first receive primary stress on the vowel in the final syllable by case (c). Subsequently the stress is retracted to the initial syllable by (50), thereby lowering the stress on the final syllable. This would yield *óbservànce*, *cónveniènt*, which exhibit the contour that Dobson supposes in *enrolment* and *preferment*.

It is rather interesting to compare the stress of words found in Shakespeare, (57), with that in Levins, (52), since the writers were roughly contemporaries, *Manipulus vocabulorum* (1570) having been published six years after Shakespeare's birth.

(57) (a)	(b)	(c)	
sólemnize	*délectable*	*áccessary*	
	ácceptable		
	démonstrable		
	détestable		
	divídable		
	pérdurable		
	súpportable		

(d)	(e)	(f)	(g)
ínventory	*cóncubine*	*áttribute*	*pérspective*
péremptory	*cólumbine*		*córrosive*
cónsistory			*súccessive*

The fact that the two sets of forms show precise parallels is hardly surprising in view of their respective dates. Furthermore, many of Levins' forms cited in (54)–(56) are also found in Shakespeare. Thus, parallel to the words like *defénsive* in (54), Shakespeare has the noninitially stressed forms *deféctive, attráctive*; parallel to the words like *recógnise* in (55a), there are *advértize, authórize, canónize*, and *solémnize*; and parallel to the words like *defínable* in (55b), there are in Shakespeare *comméndable* and *excúsable*. However, there are no examples in Shakespeare corresponding to Levins' forms in (56a), that is, no forms such as *prósperity*; rather, all words ending in *-ity* are of the (56b) variety, that is, they all have antepenultimate stress. This therefore constitutes a minor difference between Levins and Shakespeare. In a similar vein, Shakespeare has noninitial *perémptory* and *invéntory* whereas Levins has no clear example of a word ending in *-ory* without initial stress. (The one relevant example is the nominal *propítiatorie*, but this is rendered doubtful by the corresponding adjectival *própitiatory*.)

Finally, as shown in (58), we find in Shakespeare precisely the same type of variants with respect to *-ate* as in Levins:

(58) (a)   (b)
   cónfiscate   *confíscate*
                         illústrate
                         extírpate
   démonstrate   *demónstrate*
   óbdurate   *obdúrate*

We may account for all the doublets just cited, as before, by supposing a tense-lax variation in the vowel of the suffix. Thus Shakespeare, like Levins, must be assumed to have had *-īve* alternating with *-ĭve*, at least in certain words, and a similar alternation in the suffixes *-ize* and *-able*. The evidence further suggests that Shakespeare had *-ōry* as well as *-ŏry*, whereas Levins had only the former. Conversely, Levins had both *-itȳ* and *-itȳ̆*, while Shakespeare had only the latter. Finally, both had *-āt* beside *-ăt*. (However, see note 19 for another possible explanation.)

Returning now to Levins' dialect, we note that the stress rules as described up to this point do not admit final stress in trisyllabic or longer words. When words of this type receive final stress by case (34c) of the Romance Stress Rule, they will automatically undergo stress retraction by (50) and therefore appear in the output with initial stress.[20] Notice, however,

---

[20] Note that while the rules exclude words with final stress, they allow words with noninitial stress on all but the final syllable.

that bisyllabic words do allow final stress. We have already seen this in the words in columns (c) and (d) of (48), and to these examples we may add the nouns in (59a) and verbs in (59b):

(59) (a)   (b)

contráct   *suspéct*   *bequést*   *depúte*
distráct   *prospéct* *efféct*   *recórd*
extráct   *decrée*   *afféct*   *rebél*
retráct   *rewárd*   *abúse*   *quarrél*
dischárge *regárd*

Most of the forms in (59a) are of the prefix + stem type discussed in Chapter 1, Section 7, and we shall analyze them as in modern English: *con=tract*, *sus=pect*. The effect of the = boundary is to block cases (34a,b) of the Romance Stress Rule and therefore allow case (c) to supply final stress. As we have formulated the Stress Retraction Rule (50), however, all of the forms in (a) and (b) of (59), as well as those in columns (c) and (d) of (48), have to be marked as exceptions. But this misses the obvious generalization that all of the examples in question that do not undergo stress retraction by (50) are bisyllabic. We can correct this if we simply reformulate rule (50), as in (60), so that it does not apply to bisyllabic words:

(60) STRESS RETRACTION RULE (Levins)

$$V \rightarrow [1\text{stress}] \ / \ [C_0 \text{---} X \left\{ \begin{matrix} (\#)_a \\ V \end{matrix} \right\} C_0 \begin{bmatrix} 1\text{stress} \\ V \end{bmatrix} C_0(+y)]_{(N)_b}$$

CONDITION: if *a*, then *b*

The examples in (59a) bring out an essential difference between Levins' speech and contemporary English: in the earlier stage of the language, verb-noun stress doublets did not occur in the Romance portion of the vocabulary but were restricted to the Germanic portion.[21] Formally this is reflected in the presence of the # boundary in the Stress Retraction Rule (60). We show the operation of the present set of rules in the derivations in (61), where, of the four forms given, only the deverbal noun *outlaw* (see (49)) is subject to (60):

---

[21] This view follows closely traditional treatments. Thus, Levins' editor Wheatley comments: "The substantive *contráct* (6.18) has the same accent as the verb *contráct* (6.22). It is generally supposed that the distinction now made between the substantive and the verb in these and other words is of late adoption, but we find in this dictionary *a récorde* (171.18) and *to recórde* (171.21), but the accent on the substantive may be misplaced" (p. vi).

(61) (a) [sus=pect]$_V$ [[sus=pect]$_V$]$_N$

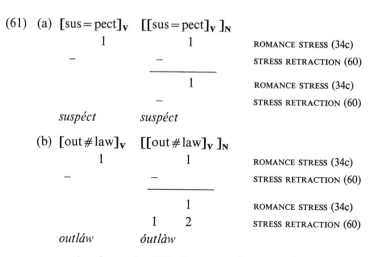

     1   1   ROMANCE STRESS (34c)

     –   –   STRESS RETRACTION (60)

           1   ROMANCE STRESS (34c)

           –   STRESS RETRACTION (60)

   suspéct   *suspéct*

  (b) [out≠law]$_V$ [[out≠law]$_V$]$_N$

     1   1   ROMANCE STRESS (34c)

     –   –   STRESS RETRACTION (60)

           1   ROMANCE STRESS (34c)

         1 2   STRESS RETRACTION (60)

   outláw   *óutlàw*

As shown in (62), however, there are four nouns with initial stress which correspond to the verbs cited in (59b):

(62) *députe*
   récord
   rébel
   quárrel

   Levins' editor suggests that one of these, *récord*, may be a mistake (see note 21). But it is not likely that all are printers' errors, and we shall have to account for them in some fashion. To begin with, the unanalyzed verbs in (59b) must be marked as exceptions to case (34b) of the Romance Stress Rule in order to account for their final stress. The most straightforward way to treat the nouns, then, is as separate lexical entries, not derived directly from the verbs in (59b). Assuming a lax final vowel, the nouns in (62) would then receive initial stress regularly by (34b).

   It is not surprising to find that Shakespeare shares with Levins the absence of noun-verb pairs differentiated by stress. Thus, Kökeritz (1953) comments:

> The functional or phonemic use of stress, illustrated in modern English by *éxtract* (n.) versus *extráct* (vb.), is not yet fully established or fixed. There is, e.g., no clear distinction between *tórment* (n.) and *tormént* (vb.), except perhaps in Cy 5.5.142: *Which torments me to conceal, By villany;* if however, we assume a disyllabic thesis in the first foot, we obtain normal stressing of *torments* and *conceal.* Other words of this category fluctuate a great deal. Thus *contract* (vb) is end-stressed, but the noun vacillates between - ́ and ́ -, with preference for the former accentuation. . . (p. 335).

We can assume, then, that the noun-verb distinction was still marginal in Shakespeare, as in Levins, and that the retraction rule in Shakespeare was precisely that in Levins, namely, (60). Certain consequences follow from this. According to Kökeritz (1953, p. 335), in the bisyllabic words in (63), Shakespeare has final stress only:

(63) *aspéct*   *impórt*   *turmóil*
      commérce   *instínct*   *abjéct*
      conjúnct   *portén\t*   *conflúx*
      contént   *pretéxt*   *intrínse*
      convérse   *protést*   *precínct*
      explóit   *survéy*   *refléx*

One of these, *turmóil*, is monomorphemic and contains a tense final vowel; here final stress is perfectly regular. The remainder of the examples are formed from a prefix + stem. Assuming a structure of the form *as＝spect*, *com＝merce*, final stress is again regular since the presence of the internal ＝ boundary is sufficient to block cases (a) and (b) of the Romance Stress Rule, and the Stress Retraction Rule (60) cannot apply to bisyllabic words.[22] (We shall see toward the end of this section that Cooper, about a century later, differed from Levins and Shakespeare in extending retraction to nouns of the *suspect* type, as in modern English.)

---

[22] Kökeritz (1953, p. 335) also notes that in certain words Shakespeare vacillates between stress contours with main stress on the last syllable and main stress on the first syllable. The examples he cites may be divided into four categories:

(a) *access, adverse, conquest, consort, precept, relapse*
(b) *comrade, divers*
(c) *outrage* (n.)
(d) *chastise*

The forms in (a) are of the structure *ac＝cess*, *ad＝verse*, etc., so that final stress is regular. To account for initial stress, we shall suppose an alternate structure of the form *ac+cess*, *ad+verse*, etc., to which the Romance Stress Rule (34b) will assign stress in the appropriate position. It is conceivable that these forms were actually *áccèss*. There is, however, no evidence in the sixteenth century with respect to nonprimary stress in bisyllables and the question must remain open.

The forms in (b) are monomorphemic. To achieve final stress, then, it is necessary to treat them as exceptions to cases (34a,b) of the Romance Stress Rule so that case (c) can supply final stress. To account for the initial-stressed variant, on the other hand, we suppose that these forms are not marked as exceptions to cases (a,b). This assumes that the stress contour of the initial-stressed variant is *cómrăde*, in which case the word is perfectly regular: it would receive initial stress by (34b) of the Romance Stress Rule and rule (60) would simply not apply.

The noun in (c) has the structure *out＃rage*. In the normal case rule (60) will apply to give *óutràge*. The end-stressed variant, then, is due to (60) being optional for this form.

The example in (d) is accounted for by assuming a tense-lax alternation in *-ise*. The initial stress would be derived from the lax alternate by the Romance Stress Rule (34b); the end-stressed form from the tense alternate by (34c).

As we have already noted (see (36) and the accompanying discussion), we can account for the fact that in Chaucer's dialect some borrowed words (e.g., *nature, bacon, banner*) shifted stress to the initial syllable by assuming that they were treated by English speakers as "native" words and hence were subject to the Initial Stress Rule (28). We also remarked that the unstressed vowels in these words were subject to reduction and elision (see note 11). Stress shifts of quite parallel character can be observed in words borrowed in Levins' time and later. A small sample of such words, with their attested dates, is given in (64):

(64)   *gallop*   (1523)   *credit*   (1542)   *model*   (1575)

        cannon (1525)   *carob*   (1548)   *frigate*   (1585)

        ribbon   (1527)   *prelude* (1561)   *cutlass*   (1594)

        method (1541)   *cavil*   (1570)   *carnage* (1600)

Since by Levins' time the Initial Stress Rule was no longer in the language, the stress shifts in (64) must be explained in a different fashion. We assume that words such as those in question were borrowed into the language with a lax vowel in the final syllable. In order to retain final stress—in keeping with the placement of stress in the source language, Old French—such forms therefore had to be marked as exceptions to cases (34a,b) of the Romance Stress Rule. To achieve initial stress in these words, on the other hand, it is necessary to assume only that this special marking was deleted from the lexical entries of the forms, thereby making them subject to (34b). This is consistent with the results of Chapter 1, where it was seen that bisyllabic words with lax last vowels normally exhibit initial stress while those with tense last vowels normally exhibit final stress.

The possibility that Levins had words with stress contours paralleling modern English $\overset{1}{alco}\overset{3}{ve}$ or $\overset{1}{arg}\overset{3}{yle}$ cannot be excluded. In view of the fact that we have almost no information about nonprimary stresses in words, however, we have assumed that such stress contours in bisyllabic words did not exist in Levins' time.

We have proposed here that the evolution of the stress pattern from Chaucer to Levins be attributed, on the one hand, to the elimination of the Initial Stress Rule (28) and of the lexical subcategorization presupposed by the coexistence in the language of two distinct main stress rules, and, on the other hand, to the generalization of the Stress Retraction Rule (17) which is given in (60). These two modifications are not independent of each other, however. Without the generalization of the Stress Retraction Rule, the abolition of the Initial Stress Rule would have resulted in a large number of words with noninitial stress. Instead, the extended Stress Retraction Rule considerably reduced the number of words with noninitial stress and the surface form of the language preserved much of its original character.

As noted in the beginning of this section, there is no indication in Levins' dictionary of stress other than primary.[23] Our treatment, however, has throughout assumed that in Levins' dialect, just as in contemporary English, some words had secondary or tertiary stress in addition to a primary stress. To our knowledge, the earliest statement referring directly to the existence of syllables with nonprimary stress in English words is to be found in Christopher Cooper's *Grammatica linguae Anglicanae* (1685).[24] It is significant that the syllables shown by Cooper to have nonprimary stress correspond precisely to those that are required by our rules. Thus we read in Cooper's book:

> Rule 4
> Some which end in *y* for *e* short, the most rapid of the vowels; and *ble*, which is sounded without a Vowel, have two Accents; one in the fourth or fifth syllable, another fainter than the former, in the last but one; as *àcadèmy*, *àccessòry*, *àcrimòny*, *àdmiràble*, *àdversàry*, *àlimòny*, *àllegòry*, *àmbulatòry*, *àmiàble*, *àmicàble*, *ànniversàry*, *àntimòny*, *àntiquàted*, *àpoplèxy*, *àrbitràry*, *àuditòry*, *àuxiliàry*, *hàbitàble*, *hìeràrchy*, *nècessàry*, *nècromàncy*, *rèfractòry*, *sèdentàry*, *sèptenàry*, *tèmperàment*, **spìrituality**, And all words of four or more syllables in *ness* (p. 113).

While there are few shared examples between Cooper and Levins, there are obviously comparable forms, as shown in (65):[25]

(65) | COOPER | LEVINS |
|---|---|
| *àccessòry* | *áccessary* |
| *àdversàry* | *ádversary* |
| *ànniversàry* | *téstamentary* |
| *àntimòny* | *mómentary* |
| *rèfractòry* | *sátisfactóry* |

Cooper's dialect differs in one respect from that of Levins. While in the earlier dialect the noun-verb stress distinction is barely if at all present, it is very much in evidence by the beginning of the seventeenth century. Charles Butler, in *English Grammar* (1634), gives several examples of such pairs, including *óverthrow–overthrów* and *cóncord–concórd*. And, again, Cooper (1687) is very explicit:

---

[23] *Sátisfactóry* is the only word in the entire dictionary with more than one stress marked, and the stress on *-ory* is most likely a misprint.

[24] All quotations are from Cooper's *English Teacher* (1687), which is an expanded and improved English version of the *Grammatica*. Rule 4, to follow, appears in both versions.

[25] See note 23 with regard to *satisfactory* here.

Rule 3

Some Nouns by translating the Accent are changed into Verbs; as *àbsent*, to *absènt*; *còllects*, to *collèct*; *cònfines*, he *confìnes*; *cònflict*, to *conflìct*; *cònsort*, to *consòrt*; *ìncense*, to *incènse*; an *òutcast*, to *outcàst*; *prèmises*, he *premìses*; *pròject*, to *projèct*; *rèfuse*, to *refùse*; *unit*, to *unìte*; *fèrment*, to *fermènt*; *cònvert*, to *convèrt*; *a tòward boy*, *towárds*; *prèsent*, to *presènt*; an *object*, to *objèct*; a *subject*, to *subjèct*; a *còntest*, to *contèst*; *rècords*, to *recòrd*; *tòrment*, to *tormènt* . . . (p. 113).

In view of the fact that in Cooper's dialect verb-noun stress doublets were common, it is necessary to assume slightly different stress rules from those of Levins'. In fact, the difference is in the Stress Retraction Rule: in place of (60), Cooper's dialect had (66):

(66) STRESS RETRACTION RULE (Cooper)

$$V \rightarrow [\text{1stress}] \quad / \quad [C_0\text{———}X\left\{(\left\{\begin{matrix}\#\\=\end{matrix}\right\})_a\\V\right\} C_0\begin{bmatrix}\text{1stress}\\V\end{bmatrix}C_0(+y)]_{(N)_b}$$

CONDITION: if *a*, then *b*

The most important subrules of (66) are given in (67) and (68):

(67) $V \rightarrow [\text{1stress}] \quad / \quad [C_0\text{———}X\left\{\begin{matrix}\#\\=\end{matrix}\right\}C_0\begin{bmatrix}\text{1stress}\\V\end{bmatrix}C_0]_N$

(68) $V \rightarrow [\text{1stress}] \quad / \quad [C_0\text{———}XVC_0\begin{bmatrix}\text{1stress}\\V\end{bmatrix}C_0(+y)]$

It is evident that (66) is more general than (60) since it applies to nouns such as *sus=pect* as well as to nouns such as *out#law* (cf. (61)).[26] This generalization of the Stress Retraction Rule appears to be the major difference between Levins' stress system of 1570 and that of Cooper, who lived about a century later.

The Eighteenth Century (Walker, Nares)

As discussed in the preceding section, in the seventeenth century and earlier, the rule of stress retraction drew the main stress from the last (or, in some cases, from the penultimate) syllable to the first syllable of the word

---

[26] In the substring $\{\#, =\}$ in (67) the two boundary markers are represented in an informal fashion. A more formal description would instead utilize the feature complexes [−Morpheme Boundary, +Word Boundary] for $\#$, and [−Morpheme Boundary, −Word Boundary] for $=$. The conjunction $\{\#, =\}$ would therefore be represented by [−MB], and the generalization of the Stress Retraction Rule under discussion would consist of replacing the feature complex [−MB, +WB] by [−MB], which, in effect, increases the conciseness of the rule by one feature.

without regard for the nature and number of intervening syllables. In the eighteenth century this situation changes, and we find clear examples of stress retraction based on different principles. The relevant words appear to belong almost exclusively to the learned stratum of the vocabulary, to the portion of the vocabulary where, because of his relative unfamiliarity with the words, the average native speaker has the least clear intuitions. We mention this fact here because it seems to us that the change under discussion differs from most ordinary sound changes by being "imposed from above," as it were, that is, by being the result of suggestions made by professional guardians of "correct usage." Normally such suggestions have little influence on the evolution of language. In the instance under discussion, however, it does appear to be likely that the suggestions of the orthoepists and lexicographers of the eighteenth century exercised some influence over pronunciation.

It is a striking fact that in the eighteenth century there was a great deal of uncertainty about the stress contours of certain learned words, and this uncertainty is directly reflected in the discussions of the orthoepists. Symptomatic of the situation are the lists of stress doublets in (69) from Solomon Lowe's *The Critical Spelling Book* (1755), where the author places his seal of approval on some forms and disapproval on others:

(69) RECOMMENDED   "INCORRECT"
      ácademy   *acádemy*
      ácceptable   *accéptable*
      ádmirable   *admírable*
      ávenue   *avénue*
      chástisement   *chastísement*
      cónfessor   *conféssor*
      cónventicle   *convénticle*
      cónversant   *convérsant*
      córrosive   *corrósive*
      córruptible   *corrúptible*
      délectable   *deléctable*
      réceptacle   *recéptacle*
      réfractory   *refráctory*

Lowe's data not only suggest that a second principle of retraction was operative in the language, but also that there was uncertainty as to which principle was the preferred one. Lowe himself considers the "incorrect" alternates to be cases in which "custom is uncertain or against reason."[27]

[27] We are indebted to Marsha Jospe for bringing to our attention the data from Lowe.

The same uncertainty regarding the accentuation of words is found in many of the other writers of the period. It is reflected most clearly, perhaps, in the work of John Walker, who was one of the most influential orthoepists of the time. The most useful evidence about the pronunciations of interest to us is to be found in articles appended to key words in his *A Critical Pronouncing Dictionary, and Expositor of the English Language* (1791). Under the entry for *receptory*, for example, Walker makes the following observations:

> Dr. Johnson and Mr. Sheridan place the accent on the first syllable of this word, and on the second of *Deceptory*, but as these words are both of the same form, till some reason can be given for accenting them differently, I shall consider them both as accented on the first syllable, as that accentuation appears to be not only most agreeable to polite usage, but to the general analogy of words of this termination . . .

A view of the diversity of accentuation among our orthoepists will enable the inspector to judge of the propriety of that which I have adopted:

Rec'eptary, Mr. Sheridan, Dr. Johnson, folio and quarto, and Barclay.

Recep'tary, Dr. Ash, Mr. Scott, Scott's Bailey, Mr. Perry, Fenning and Entick.

Rec'eptory, Dr. Johnson, folio, Mr. Sheridan, Mr. Smith and Barclay.

Recep'tory, Dr. Johnson, quarto, Dr. Ash, Mr. Perry, Barclay, Fenning, Scott's Bailey and Entick.

Dec'eptory,

Decep'tory, Mr. Sheridan, Dr. Johnson, Dr. Ash, Mr. Perry, Barclay, Scott's Bailey and Fenning.

Under the entry for *refectory*:

> Almost all the dictionaries I have consulted, except Mr. Sheridan's, place the accent on the second syllable of this word; and yet, so prevalent has the latter accentuation [initial stress] been of late years, that Mr. Nares is reduced to hope it is not fixed beyond recovery. There is, indeed, one reason why this word ought not to have the accent on the first syllable, and that is, the two mutes in the second and third, which are not so easily pronounced when the accent is removed from them, as the mutes and liquids in *accessory, consistory, desultory,* etc.; and there I am decidedly in favour of the accentuation on the second syllable, which is adopted by Dr. Johnson, Dr. Ash, Dr. Kenrick, W. Johnston, Mr. Nares, Buchanan, Perry, Scott, Bailey, Barclay and Entick, as all words of this termination have the accent on the same syllable.... See *Refractory, Peremptory, Corruptible,* and *Irrefragable.*

Under the entry for *peremptory*:

> If we consult our orthoepists, there can scarcely be any two pronunciations [initial and antepenultimate] more equally balanced than those that are given for this word.

Under the entry for *perfunctory*:

> I have differed from Mr. Sheridan and W. Johnston who accent this word on the first syllable; but have Dr. Johnson, Dr. Ash, Mr. Nares, Barclay, Fenning, Bailey, Buchanan and Entick, on my side for accenting the second: and this pronunciation without any authority would be more eligible than the other; from the difficulty of pronouncing the uncombinable consonants in the last syllables without the assistance of accent, especially when we consider that the adverb *perfunctorily*, and the possible abstract noun *perfunctoriness*, must necessarily have the same accent as the adjective.

It is clear from the preceding quotations that there were two modes of accentuation in the last half of the eighteenth century. One of these, which is responsible for initial stress in words like *réceptory*, *réceptary*, *déceptory*, *réfectory*, *péremptory*, and *pérfunctory* cited in Walker's articles (the number of such examples can, of course, be greatly increased), is a direct continuation of the stress systems of Levins and Cooper. As we have already seen, Walker generally shies away from this pronunciation, though not consistently, as his *réceptory* comments attest. The principle of stress retraction preferred by Walker was most succinctly formulated by one of his contemporaries, R. Nares, in *The Elements of Orthoepy* (1784). In commenting, first, on the initial stress pattern, Nares observes:

> It has generally been said and believed, that it is conformable to the genius of English pronunciation, to throw back the accent as far as possible from the end of a polysyllable. This supposition has, at times, corrupted our speech with many barbarous and unpleasing sounds, which are in reality repugnant to its analogy: such as *ácademy*, *réfractory*, *pérfunctory*, *réceptacle*, *súsceptible*, etc. which no ear can hear without being offended. It is high time, then, that this false notion should be controverted and the further ill effects of it be prevented... (p. 185).

Instead of drawing stress back to the first syllable of the word, Nares proposes that at least in some types of words the stress should be retracted in accordance with a different principle:

> But these terminations, *-ble*, [*-cle*, *-ary*, *-ory*], etc. when not derivative, have still a tendency to throw back the accent to the fourth syllable; as in *inéxorable*, *inévitable*, *séminary*, *lúminary*, *péllitory*; except there be in any part of the word the concurrence of two consonants; in which case the accent is disposed to rest wherever the two consonants meet, as in *combústible*, *satisfáctory*, *contradíctory*. We ought therefore analogously to say, *recéptacle*, *suscéptible*, *refráctory*, *perfúnctory*; and the more especially as the other accentuation produces so barbarous a cacophany (p. 188).

Nares advocates here the same principle as that implicit in Walker's examples, that is, stress is to be retracted not to the initial syllable but rather in accordance with the weak cluster principle of the Romance Stress Rule. The examples in (70) bring out clearly the difference between the stress pattern of Walker and Nares and that of their predecessors in the sixteenth and seventeenth centuries:

(70) LEVINS-COOPER   WALKER-NARES

    (a)   (b)   (c)

réfractory	*refráctory*	
pérfunctory	*perfúnctory*	
péremptory	*perémptory*	
réfectory	*reféctory*	
ánniversary	*annivérsary*	
áuxiliary	*auxíliary*	
ádversary		*ádversary*
cónsistory		*cónsistory*
sédentary		*sédentary*
cápillary		*cápillary*
áccessory		*áccessory*
		réceptory

The examples of column (a) of (70), as we have already seen, are subject to case (b) of the Romance Stress Rule, which supplies stress on the tense penultimate vowel. Subsequently, stress retraction to the initial syllable takes place by the operation of the Stress Retraction Rule (66). When we come to Walker and Nares, however, we find two sets of examples. Those in column (c) are precisely like those in column (a) and can be handled identically. What is new is the intrusion into Walker's dialect of yet another principle of stress retraction, illustrated in column (b) of (70). As suggested by Nares, stress is retracted in these examples on the basis of the principle of the Romance Stress Rule: in every case, stress is shifted to a syllable ending with a strong cluster immediately to the left of the stressed syllable *-ary/-ory*; or, if the syllable immediately to the left does not end with a strong cluster, stress is shifted to the second syllable to the left of the stressed syllable.

What is of special interest in Walker's dialect, then, is not the fact that it exhibits stressed forms which demonstrate a continuity with past stages of the language, but rather that it illustrates a new kind of stress retraction which requires that a special rule be added to the grammar. This rule, which handles forms with noninitial stress, supplements rather than supersedes the Stress Retraction Rule (66): some words are subject to the new rule; others retract stress by the old rule. There is, however, no way to predict which words of the learned portion of Walker's vocabulary will be subject to which rule, as is clear from the fact that Walker prefers *reféctory* but *réceptory*. Since these forms are perfectly parallel in structure, the only way in which we can deal with them is by assuming that the two stress retraction rules apply totally idiosyncratically; that is, each item of the learned vocabulary is lexically marked as to which rule of stress retraction it will undergo. We are forced to say, then, that all of the words in column (b) of (70) are lexically marked as being subject to the new rule of stress retraction, based on the weak cluster principle, which has been added to Walker's grammar, while all the forms in column (c) are lexically marked as undergoing the old rule of stress retraction, based on the initial stress principle, which Walker inherited from Levins-Cooper.

Before we state the new stress retraction rule, it is worth remarking that this sort of arbitrary division of the lexicon might be expected in a dialect like Walker's, namely, an artificial dialect which he is trying to impose rather than a natural one which he has encountered and is attempting to describe. The data in Walker's dictionary thus exhibit traits that are not surprising in the dialect of one who has adopted a new principle of stress placement and is applying it somewhat uncertainly or inconsistently to a fixed portion of his vocabulary. It is not without interest that Walker and his fellow orthoepists are able to do this only because tinkering with so limited and well-defined a portion of English has few repercussions elsewhere in the grammar.

We now give in (71) the new stress retraction rule which supplemented rule (66) in Walker's dialect:

(71) NEW STRESS RETRACTION RULE (Walker)

$$V \rightarrow [\text{1stress}] \ / \ [X\text{---}C_0(\begin{bmatrix} -\text{tense} \\ V \end{bmatrix}C_0^1)\begin{bmatrix} \text{1stress} \\ V \end{bmatrix}C_0(+y)]$$

We observe that subrule (68) of (66) and rule (71) may affect precisely the same types of strings but with differing results. For example, whereas (68) yields *réfectòry* and *cónfiscàte*, (71) produces *reféctory* and *confíscate*. Thus, as we noted with regard to the examples in (70), in Walker's dialect the question of whether a word was subject to retraction by (71) or by (68) was a purely idiosyncratic matter, a fact that was reflected by special markers in the lexicon. There is considerable evidence in addition to (70) in favor of this view. The words in (72), for example, must have their stress retracted in accordance with rule (68):

(72) *ánecdote*
      tábernacle
      cávalcade
      brígantine
      túrpentine

On the other hand, verbs ending in *-ate* retract stress in accordance with rule (71), as illustrated in (73):

(73)

(a)	(b)	(c)	(d)
própagate	*discríminate*	*confíscate*	*vácate*
súpplicate	*invéstigate*	*contémplate*	*díctate*
ábdicate	*exággerate*	*demónstrate*	*víbrate*
éxplicate	*eláborate*	*enérvate*	*stágnate*
cástigate	*anníhilate*	*extírpate*	*trúncate*
	intérrogate	*illústrate*	

Let us now examine the relationship between the rules that retract stress and the rule that assigns stress, namely, the Romance Stress Rule (35), which, for convenience of reference, we restate here as (74):

(74) (a,b) $V \rightarrow$ [1stress] $/ \ [X\text{---}C_0(\begin{bmatrix} -\text{tense} \\ V \end{bmatrix} C_0^1) \begin{bmatrix} -\text{tense} \\ V \end{bmatrix} C_0]$

(c) $V \rightarrow$ [1stress] $/ \ [X\text{---}C_0]$

The two retraction rules (66) and (71) require for their application that a word have stress on the last or, in certain cases, on the penultimate syllable. Since words are in general entered in the lexicon without stress indication and receive stress only by the Romance Stress Rule, any word that is to undergo retraction must first undergo the Romance Stress Rule (74). In particular, the examples cited in columns (b) and (c) of (70) show that case (74b) of the Romance Stress Rule must apply to words ending with *-ory* before one or the other of the two retraction rules can apply. Furthermore, the words ending with *-ate* cited in (73) receive stress by case (74c), and only then are they subject to stress retraction by (71). On the other hand, the examples such as *anecdote* in (72) also receive stress by case (74c), but they are then subject to stress retraction by (66). Thus, there is good motivation for ordering cases (b) and (c) of the Romance Stress Rule (74) before both retraction rules. And, while the examples under discussion here provide no argument for the relative ordering of case (74a), it was seen in previous sections that this subrule must precede both (74b) and (74c). We therefore conclude that all three subrules of the Romance Stress Rule (74) must precede the two retraction rules (66) and (71). This ordering, however, is somewhat problematical.

It is readily seen that the new Stress Retraction Rule (71) is partially identical with (74a,b). Both include the substring (75), which expresses the weak cluster principle of the Romance Stress Rule:

(75) $V \rightarrow$ [1stress] $/ \ [X\text{---}C_0(\begin{bmatrix} -\text{tense} \\ V \end{bmatrix} C_0^1)\ldots$

This partial identity, however, is not explicitly taken into account in a grammar in which all three cases of the Romance Stress Rule (74) become applicable before the Stress Retraction Rule (71). As long as case (c) of the Romance Stress Rule (74) must precede rule (71), the substring (75) that the Stress Retraction Rule (71) shares with cases (a,b) of the Romance Stress Rule (74) cannot be factored out by the abbreviatory conventions that are available in the present theory of phonology. The grammar we postulate for Walker is therefore nonoptimal.

To summarize, Walker's dialect is assumed to have been subject to the Romance Stress Rule as stated in (74) and to the two Stress Retraction Rules (66) and (71), with the choice between these latter two being lexically determined. It should be remarked in this connection that the effect of the subrule (67) of (66), which accounts for stress retraction in prefixed nouns, can also be obtained by (76), which is partially identical with the new Stress Retraction Rule (71):

$$(76) \quad V \rightarrow [\text{1stress}] \ / \ [X\text{——}C_0(\begin{bmatrix} -\text{tense} \\ V \end{bmatrix} C_0^1) \begin{Bmatrix} \# \\ = \end{Bmatrix} C_0 \begin{bmatrix} \text{1stress} \\ V \end{bmatrix} C_0]_N$$

Whereas (67) retracted stress to the initial syllable without regard for the intervening syllables, (76) obeys the weak cluster principle. However, since English has no trisyllabic or longer prefixes and its bisyllabic prefixes invariably end with a weak cluster, the results of (67) are indistinguishable from those of (76). Because the following exposition is somewhat simpler if rule (76) rather than (67) figures in the grammar of Walker and his contemporaries, we shall assume that this change had indeed taken place and attribute to the end of the eighteenth century the stress retraction rules listed in (77):

$$(77) \quad (a) \quad V \rightarrow [\text{1stress}] \ / \ [X\text{——}C_0(\begin{bmatrix} -\text{tense} \\ V \end{bmatrix} C_0^1) \begin{bmatrix} \text{1stress} \\ V \end{bmatrix} C_0(+y)]$$

$$(b) \quad V \rightarrow [\text{1stress}] \ / \ [X\text{——}C_0(\begin{bmatrix} -\text{tense} \\ V \end{bmatrix} C_0^1) \begin{Bmatrix} \# \\ = \end{Bmatrix} C_0 \begin{bmatrix} \text{1stress} \\ V \end{bmatrix} C_0]_N$$

$$(c) \quad V \rightarrow [\text{1stress}] \ / \ [C_0\text{——}XVC_0 \begin{bmatrix} \text{1stress} \\ V \end{bmatrix} C_0(+y)]$$

It is obvious that (77a) and (77b) can be coalesced into (78):

$$(78) \quad V \rightarrow [\text{1stress}] \ / \ [X\text{——}C_0(\begin{bmatrix} -\text{tense} \\ V \end{bmatrix} C_0^1) (\begin{Bmatrix} \# \\ = \end{Bmatrix} C_0)_a \begin{bmatrix} \text{1stress} \\ V \end{bmatrix} C_0(+y)]_{(N)_b}$$

CONDITION: if a, then b

Rule (78) can in turn be coalesced with (77c) to yield (79):

$$(79) \quad V \rightarrow [1\text{stress}] \ / \ \begin{Bmatrix} [X\text{---}C_0\begin{bmatrix} -\text{tense} \\ V \end{bmatrix}C_0^1)(\begin{Bmatrix} \# \\ = \end{Bmatrix}C_0)_a \\ [C_0\text{---}XVC_0 \end{Bmatrix} \begin{bmatrix} 1\text{stress} \\ V \end{bmatrix}C_0(+y)]_{(N)_b}$$

CONDITION: if a, then b

We shall see the significance of this relationship among the rules in the next section.

The Nineteenth Century

In the preceding section it was found that the system of stress rules that was proposed to account for the pronunciation of the eighteenth-century orthoepist John Walker contained certain nonoptimal features. Thus, not only did two almost identical stress retraction rules, (77a) and (77c), have to be postulated, but, moreover, there was no principled way of deciding which of these rules applied in the case of a given word; instead, the choice of rule was an idiosyncratic fact of each individual lexical item which had to be specially marked in the dictionary representation. In addition, Walker's grammar was forced to have a nonoptimal order of rules which made it impossible to capture explicitly the fact that two of the stress rules—the Romance Stress Rule (74) and the Stress Retraction Rule (77a)—operated in accordance with the same weak cluster principle. An artificial grammar of this kind is plausible in the case of persons who have acquired their pronunciations not as children but rather as adults, after their speech habits have, in the main, been set. We know that the innovations advocated by Walker and his fellow orthoepists eventually became the norm for all speakers of the standard dialects. At some point in the nineteenth century, therefore, there must have been speakers who learned as children, in the normal course of growing up, a dialect that included these innovations. It is to be expected that the grammar of such "natural" speakers did not exhibit the nonoptimal features that we found in Walker.[28]

As discussed toward the end of the preceding section, one of the "imperfections" of Walker's grammar was a result of the impossibility of ordering the Stress Retraction Rule (77a,b) = (78) next to (74a,b) of the Romance Stress Rule. Since in an optimal grammar these two rules would be consecutively ordered, we shall assume that such a reordering did in fact take

---

[28] For further discussion see *Sound Pattern of English* (p. 251) and Halle (1962).

place in the nineteenth century and examine the consequences of this assumption.

Once case (74c) of the Romance Stress Rule is ordered after rule (77a,b) = (78), it is immediately possible to coalesce rules (74a,b) and (77a,b) = (78) so as to make explicit the fact that they share the substring (75). This is quite obvious when we examine the reordered set of stress rules (80):

$$(80) \quad \text{(a)} \quad V \rightarrow \text{[1stress]} \quad / \; [X\text{----}C_0(\begin{bmatrix} -\text{tense} \\ V \end{bmatrix}C_0^1)\begin{bmatrix} -\text{tense} \\ V \end{bmatrix}C_0] \qquad \text{(74a,b)}$$

$$\text{(b)} \quad V \rightarrow \text{[1stress]} \quad / \; [X\text{----}C_0(\begin{bmatrix} -\text{tense} \\ V \end{bmatrix}C_0^1)(\begin{Bmatrix} \# \\ = \end{Bmatrix}C_0)_a\begin{bmatrix} 1\text{stress} \\ V \end{bmatrix}C_0(+y)]_{(N)_b}$$
$$\text{(77a,b)} = (78)$$

CONDITION: if *a*, then *b*

$$\text{(c)} \quad V \rightarrow \text{[1stress]} \quad / \; [X\text{----}C_0] \qquad \text{(74c)}$$

$$\text{(d)} \quad V \rightarrow \text{[1stress]} \quad / \; [C_0\text{----}XVC_0\begin{bmatrix} 1\text{stress} \\ V \end{bmatrix}C_0(+y)] \qquad \text{(77c)}$$

Given the set of rules in (80), (a)–(c) must be formally coalesced as in (81). (We return to (80d) directly.)

$$(81) \quad V \rightarrow \text{[1stress]} \quad / \; [X\text{----}C_0((\begin{bmatrix} -\text{tense} \\ V \end{bmatrix}C_0^1)\begin{Bmatrix} \begin{bmatrix} -\text{tense} \\ V \end{bmatrix}C_0] \\ (\begin{Bmatrix} \# \\ = \end{Bmatrix}C_0)_a\begin{bmatrix} 1\text{stress} \\ V \end{bmatrix}C_0(+y)]_{(N)_b} \end{Bmatrix})$$

CONDITION: if *a*, then *b*

It should be noted that (81) expresses not only the fact that (80a) and (80b) have a substring in common, but also that both are in turn special cases of (80c). Hence, by the principle of disjunctive ordering, the same string may undergo (80a) and (80b), but once a string is subject to one or both of these subrules, it cannot also undergo (80c). In terms of the empirical consequences, then, forms that receive their stress by (80c) cannot now have their stress retracted by (80b). Rather, if a word receives stress by (80c), the only rule which can retract the stress is (80d). Rules (80) will thus assign to some words quite different stress contours than will the rules postulated for Walker. We shall now show that these differences are indeed what distinguishes Walker's speech from that of the nineteenth century.

First, words such as those listed in column (c) of (73), namely, *confiscate, contemplate, demonstrate, enervate, extirpate,* and *illustrate,* can no longer receive penultimate stress as they did in Walker's dialect. Since the final vowel is tense, primary stress is assigned by (80c). But (80b) cannot now apply to retract the stress since this rule has already been passed in the order. The remaining rule of stress retraction is (80d), which will provide initial primary stress: *cónfiscàte, cóntemplàte, démonstràte*, etc. This change in pronunciation did in fact take place in the nineteenth century. In the *Oxford English Dictionary* (OED), the materials for which were collected during the nineteenth century, it is specifically noted that verbs ending in *-ate* were under-going stress shift, so that the younger generation knew only *cónfiscàte* while *confíscate* was known to "middle-aged men" and was acquiring the "flavour of age."[29]

Observe that with the stress rules reordered as in (80), if a word receives stress by (80a), retraction must now take place by (80b) and not by (80d). This means that words that were stressed *réceptòry* and *cónsistòry* by (80a,d) in Walker's time must now receive stress by (80a,b), yielding *recéptory* and *consístory*. Moreover, initial stress in words like *auxiliary* would now consistently be *auxíliàry*. And, indeed, the latter pronunciation did replace the former in the nineteenth century, a direct consequence of the rule reordering in (80). (There is a special problem with regard to *sédentàry* and *ádversàry* as opposed to *eleméntary* and *annivérsary*. See Chapter 1, Section 8.)

Typical derivations are given in (82):

(82) refract$+$ōr$+$y   auxili$+$ār$+$y
           1   1   RULE (80a)
      1   2   1   2   RULE (80b)

Words ending with the suffixes *-ōry* and *-āry*, as in (82), are treated in the same way regardless of whether (80c) precedes or follows (80b). The

[29] The citation from the OED under the entry *contemplate* reads: " In a few rare cases (Shaks., Hudibras) stressed *co·ntemplate* in 16th–17th c.; also by Kenrick 1773, Webster 1828, among writers on pronunciation. Byron, Shelley, and Tennyson have both modes, but the orthoepists generally have *conte·mplate* down to third quarter of 19th c.; since that time *co·ntemplate* has more and more prevailed, and *conte·mplate* begins to have a flavour of age. This is the common tendency with all verbs in *-ate*. Of these, the antepenult stress is historical in all words in which the penult represents a short Latin syllable, as *acce·lerate, a·nimate, fa·scinate, ma·chinate, mi·litate*, or one prosodically short or long, as in *ce·lebrate, co·nsecrate, e·migrate*; regularly also when the penult has a vowel long in Latin, as *a·lienate, a·spirate, conca·tenate, de·nudate, ela·borate, i·ndurate, pe·rsonate, ru·inate* (L. *aliēno, aspiro*, etc.). But where the penult has two or three consonants giving positional length, the stress has historically been on the penult, and its shift to the antepenult is recent or still in progress, as in *acervate, adumbrate, alternate, compensate, concentrate, condensate, confiscate, conquassate, constellate, demonstrate, decussate, desiccate, enervate, exacerbate, exculpate, illustrate, inculcate, objurgate*, etc., all familiar with penult stress to middle-aged men . . ."

same is true of the deverbal nouns of the *permit* type, since in this case the stress assignment rule and the stress retraction rule apply on different cycles.[30]

Given the present ordering, words ending with *-y* will never be subject to retraction by (80d) since they will first undergo (80a,b). This fact allows us to simplify (80d) by deleting the string ($+$y), as in (83):

$$(83) \quad V \quad \rightarrow \quad [\text{1stress}] \quad / \quad [C_0 \text{——} XVC_0 \begin{bmatrix} \text{1stress} \\ V \end{bmatrix} C_0]$$

A further result of the reordering, aside from the very obvious generalization of the rules, is that the lexical subcategorization with regard to which the stress retraction rules were applied becomes unnecessary. Given the conventions with regard to rule order, the two stress rules can no longer be applicable to the same string: words that receive stress by (80a) retract stress by (80b); words that receive stress by (80c) retract stress by (80d) = (83). In particular, words in *-ory* and *-ary* retract stress by (80b); words in *-ate* and words like *ánecdòte, cávalcàde, brígantìne, túrpentìne, exácerbàte* (cf. (72)) retract stress by (83). Thus, the reordering of the rules in (80) also clears up the other "artificiality" noted in the grammar of Walker. Once the rules are reordered, the question as to which of the two stress retraction rules applies to a given word is no longer arbitrary but is fully motivated. And, as we have shown in Chapter 1, this ordering holds for the language in the twentieth century.

To complete the story, some brief remarks must be made about the second stress retraction rule, (83), which is still in need of some slight modification. We recall that the only cases where (83) applies are those which receive final stress by (80c), namely, words like *confiscate, anecdote*. If it were assumed that the nineteenth-century version of the second retraction rule, like its ancestor, drew the main stress back to the first syllable of the word, then such words would still be correctly stressed: *cónfiscàte, ánecdòte, brígantìne*. But the words listed in column (b) of (73)—*discriminate, investigate, exaggerate, elaborate, annihilate, interrogate*—would incorrectly receive stress on the initial syllable. If, on the other hand, the nineteenth-century version

---

[30] Recall that as noted in Chapter 1 (see (77) and (89)) these deverbal nouns have the underlying representation [## [*per* $=$ *mit*]$_V$ ##]$_N$. Hence, on the first pass through the stress rules, (80c) will assign stress to the last syllable since the $=$ boundary blocks (80a,b). This will yield the correct output for the verb: *permít*. On the second pass, (80b) = (76) will apply, retracting the stress to the first syllable of the word. Notice that the earlier distinction between the verb *outláw* and the noun *óutlàw* (see derivation (61b) in this chapter) has since been lost. A contemporary account might treat the verb *óutlàw* as denominal or handle the two forms as separate lexical items. We leave this question open.

of (83) were to retract stress not to the initial syllable but to the antepenultimate syllable, not only would it handle trisyllabic words like *confiscate*, *anecdote*, but it would also correctly account for the large number of longer words such as those in (73b).[31] We shall therefore assume that (83) was reformulated as in (84), which is basically identical with the Alternating Stress Rule of modern English (cf. (75) of Chapter 1):

$$(84) \quad V \quad \rightarrow \quad [\text{1stress}] \quad / \quad [X\text{——}C_0VC_0 \begin{bmatrix} \text{1stress} \\ V \end{bmatrix} C_0]$$

The more natural grammar that grew out of the quite artificial grammar of the eighteenth century, then, was the result of a reordering of rules which, in turn, made possible an abolition of the lexical subcategorization required by the earlier grammar. In other words, the later grammar seems to support the hypothesis that in "naturally acquired" grammars lexical subcategorization is less likely to be used than phonological conditions.

We arrive in the nineteenth century, then, with a grammar containing the Romance Stress Rule (81), followed by the Alternating Stress Rule (84). A comparison of these rules with the corresponding rules of the grammar of the contemporary language shows near identity. Our objective has therefore been achieved, for we have followed the evolution of the English stress system from the eleventh century to the present.

5. *Conclusion*

In our discussion of the stress rules of modern English in Chapter 1, we tried to show how the formal constraints which were required to deal with certain obvious phenomena of stress placement, subordination, and vowel reduction entailed other, more subtle and less obvious empirical consequences. The fact that the predicted consequences were actually found in English constitutes strong support for the theory described. Indeed, as we observed earlier, it is only in terms of the theory that these subtle facts of English acquire any meaning. Otherwise, they remain rather odd and unconnected properties of the language.

There is a strong parallel to this in the evolution of English stress. The formalism assumed for our rules requires that generalizations inherent in the rules be captured insofar as possible. This was accomplished by a

---

[31] For an account of the forms in column (d) of (73), namely, *vácate, díctate, víbrate, stágnate, trúncate,* see the discussion accompanying (137) and (138) in Chapter 1.

reordering of the stress rules in the nineteenth century, which resulted in the incorporation of the new stress retraction rule into the body of the Romance Stress Rule. However, this incorporation, required on purely formal grounds germane to the particular set of rules under consideration, entailed further empirical consequences, namely, that stress contours such as *confíscàte* and *réfectòry* were no longer possible. The fact that precisely these stress contours disappeared from the language during the nineteenth century constitutes strong corroboratory evidence for the theoretical framework within which our rules are formulated. Indeed, were this theory not available, the fact that speakers during the nineteenth century began to say *reféctory* and *cónfiscàte* and to avoid *réfectòry* and *confíscàte* would be just another bit of odd information of little interest to anyone save the compulsive collector of linguistic curiosa.

3

A Theory of Meter

3

What, then, exactly is Prosody? Our English word is not carried over from the Greek word with its uncertain and various meanings, but it must have come with the French word through the scholastic Latin; and like the French term it primarily denotes the rules for the treatment of syllables in verse, whether they are to be considered as long or short, accented or unaccented, elideable or not, etc., etc. The syllables, which are the units of rhythmic speech, are by nature of so indefinite a quality and capable of such different vocal expression, that apart from the desire which every artist must feel to have his work consistent in itself, his appeal to an audience would convince him that there is no chance of his elaborate rhythms being rightly interpreted unless his treatment of syllables is understood. Rules must, therefore, arise and be agreed upon for the treatment of syllables, and this is the first indispensable office of Prosody.

BRIDGES (1966)

1. Introduction

When a poet composes metrical verse, he imposes certain constraints upon his choice of words and phrases which ordinary language does not normally obey. The poet and his readers may not be able to formulate explicitly the nature of the constraints that are operative in a given poem; there is little doubt, however, that neither the poet nor the experienced reader would find great difficulty in distinguishing wildly unmetrical lines from lines that are straightforwardly metrical. Thus, few people familiar with the canon of metrical English verse from Chaucer to Yeats would disagree with the proposition that (1b) and (1c) are lawful embodiments of the iambic pentameter, whereas (1a) is not, even though (1a) has the same number of syllables as (1b) but (1c) has a different number:

(1) (a) *Ode to the West Wind by Percy Bysshe Shelley*
     (b) *O wild West Wind, thou breath of Autumn's being*
     (c) *The curfew tolls the knell of parting day*

In addition, readers of verse possess the ability to categorize metrical lines as more or less complex. Thus, most readers would no doubt judge (1b) to be a more complex iambic pentameter line than (1c).

We shall look upon these readily observable abilities of experienced poetry readers as crucial facts that must be accounted for by an adequate theory of prosody. Such a theory, however, should be expected to do more than this; it should also help us to understand the nature of metrical verse and illuminate the relationship between a speaker's everyday linguistic

139

competence and his ability to judge verses as metrical or unmetrical and as complex or simple.

We propose that the aforementioned ability of readers and poets to make judgments about verse lines is due to their knowledge of certain principles of verse construction. This knowledge, much like the average speaker's knowledge of his language, is in general tacit rather than explicit. When questioned, people may be unable to give a coherent statement of the principles that they employ in judging verse lines in terms of metricality and complexity. It is therefore the task of the metrist to provide a coherent and explicit account of this knowledge, just as it is the task of the grammarian to make explicit what is known by the fluent speaker of a language.

The Nature of Meter

We propose to view meter as the encoding of a simple abstract pattern into a sequence of words. This is achieved by establishing a correspondence between the elements constituting the pattern and specific phonetic (or phonological) properties of the word sequence. The study of meter must therefore be composed of two separate parts, namely, the study of abstract patterns and the study of the correspondence rules which enable a given string of words to be viewed as an instance of a particular abstract pattern.

To make clear our intention here, let us consider a very simple example. One of the most rudimentary metrical patterns is one which consists of entities of a single type repeated some number of times. Examples of such patterns are given in (2):

(2) XXX   XXXX   XXXXX
     XXX   XXXX   XXXXX
     XXX   XXXX   XXXXX

It is obvious that there is an infinity of arrangements of physical objects that can be said to realize one of these patterns—flowers in a flower bed, desks in a classroom, windows on the side of a house. A correspondence rule which said that each X was to be realized by a particular object (a flower, a desk, a window) would then tell us where to look for the patterns in (2). There is no need to instantiate the patterns by means of a static arrangement of objects, however; they could be equally well actualized by means of phenomena organized in a temporal sequence, as a series of drumbeats, a series of light flashes, a series of dance steps. All that would be required is that the correspondence rule be appropriately modified. When we choose to instantiate the pattern with a sequence of syllables, the result is a line of verse. Consider, in this regard, the verses in (3) by the Spanish poet Lope de Vega:

(3)   *Zagala divina,*
        bella labradora,
        boca de rubíes,
        ojos de paloma.

   Each of the lines in (3) contains six syllables.[1] Thus, we may say that the metrical scheme underlying this poem is

XXXXXX

and that the correspondence rule is one which establishes a one:one correspondence between syllables of the line and X's of the metrical pattern. That this is only a first approximation of the correct correspondence rule, however, becomes apparent when we look at the lines in (4), which immediately follow those in (3) in the poem:

(4)   *Santísima Virgen,*
        soberana aurora,
        arco de los cielos,
        y del sol corona.

   The second line of (4) has seven syllables rather than the expected six. But we note that in this line a word ending with a vowel is followed by a word beginning with a vowel. It is a well-known feature of Spanish verse that vowel sequences may count as the metrical equivalent of a single syllable, in which case they are said to exhibit "synalepha." This is purely a metrical convention. The commonly held idea that the vowel sequences in question are always slurred together in pronunciation is simply not true. Baehr (1962) observes that synalepha occurs in dramatic poetry even where the word ending with a vowel is spoken by one character and the word beginning with a vowel is spoken by a different character. As an example, he cites (p. 21) the line from Tirso de Molina:

Ay, Aurora hermosa. — Adiós

where the vowels joined by the tie are counted as a single metrical entity even though the words are assigned to different actors.

   The conditions under which the abstract pattern XXXXXX is realized can thus be expressed by means of the alternative correspondence rules (5a) and (5b):[2]

---

[1] We use the term "syllable" here as the equivalent of "sequence of speech sounds consisting of one syllabic sound (vowel) preceded and followed by any number of consecutive nonsyllabic sounds (consonants)." In particular, we do not take a position on the vexing question of whether or not utterances can be uniformly segmented into syllables.

[2] Needless to say, the analysis presented here is not intended to do justice to the intricacies of Spanish syllable-counting verse but serves merely as an expedient example with which to begin our discussion of metrical theory.

) (a) Each element X of the abstract metrical pattern corresponds to a single vowel in the verse line

OR

(b) Each element X of the abstract metrical pattern corresponds to one or more consecutive vowels in the verse line

The second line of (4) is metrical by virtue of rule (5b), whereas all the other lines in (4), as well as those in (3), are metrical by virtue of (5a).

Metrical Complexity or Tension

We mentioned earlier that readers of poetry are capable of distinguishing not only metrical from unmetrical lines but also more complex metrical lines from less complex lines. Thus, it seems correct to say that while all the lines in (3) and (4) are metrical, the second line of (4) is more complex than the other lines. The order of the alternatives in (5) is significant in this respect, for it is an order of increasing complexity: (5a) admits as metrical only lines where each vowel is matched up with an X of the abstract metrical pattern; the second alternative, (5b), enlarges the class of lines admitted as metrical by allowing us also to match up any number of consecutive vowels in the line with a single X.

We shall assume here and henceforth that correspondence rules are composed of alternatives which can be arranged in such a fashion that later ones subsume—and hence are generalizations of—earlier ones. In effect each subsequent alternative allows more lines to be deemed metrical than the earlier alternatives. But this means that by invoking a more general correspondence rule, we make the line more, not less, complex: if the means whereby a given abstract pattern is actualized are narrowly restricted, the pattern is readily perceived as being present in the data; on the other hand, if the means whereby a pattern is actualized are allowed to be of a great variety, it becomes correspondingly difficult to discern that the pattern is encoded in a given sequence of words. Thus, while the iambic pentameter pattern in (1c) is immediately obvious, considerable sophistication is required to see that the same pattern is present in (1b). We are proposing, therefore, that a line in which later alternatives of the correspondence rules must be invoked is metrically more complex than one in which earlier alternatives are invoked. The complexity of a line increases also with the number of instances in the line where later alternatives are invoked. The order of the alternatives in the correspondence rules is thus our formal device for capturing the important concept of metrical complexity, or "tension," which plays such a large role in contemporary discussions of meter.

The increased difficulty in perception of the pattern which results from utilizing more complex alternatives of the correspondence rules explains why one does not find lines in which all and only the most complex correspondence rules are utilized. Such lines would exceed the threshold of the reader's ability to perceive the pattern. We shall see later ((69) and the accompanying discussion) how this holds true of iambic pentameter verse. The same increased difficulty in perception no doubt explains why one would not expect to find lines in Spanish verse which realize the abstract metrical pattern XXXXXX in a way that would make it necessary to invoke (5b) six times in the same line.

We shall now scan some lines of Spanish verse which are more complicated than those in (3) and (4). When a vowel can be shown to actualize an X by virtue of the first alternative (5a), we shall leave that vowel unmarked; when the alternative (5b) has to be invoked because a vowel sequence actualizes an X, we shall underline the sequence. The X enclosed in parentheses at the end of certain lines represents the so-called "feminine close" (*verso llano*) which is an optional variant of every Spanish meter.

Yo sueño que estoy aquí
X XX X X X X

destas prisiones cargado,
X X XXX X X(X)

y soñé que en otro estado
X XX X X X X(X)

más lisonjero me vi.
X XX XX X X

¿Qué es la vida? Un frenesí.
X X X X XXX

¿Qué es la vida? Una ilusión,
X X X X XXX

una sombra, una ficción
XX X X XX X

y el mayor bien es pequeño;
X XX X X X X(X)

que toda la vida es sueño,
X XX X X X(X)

y los sueños, sueños son.　　　　　(CALDERÓN DE LA BARCA, *La vida es sueño*)
X X XX XX X

For purposes of discussion we may assume that each underline increases the complexity of the verse by one. Thus, for example, the sixth line of the verse above has a complexity of 3, whereas the first line has a complexity of 1 and the last line a complexity of 0. (We return to the question of measuring the complexity of a line in our discussion of the iambic pentameter.)

Different Correspondence Rules for the Same Abstract Pattern

Since metrical patterns are separate from the rules that map these patterns onto actual lines of verse, we must expect to find cases where, by virtue of different correspondence rules, the same metrical pattern is exhibited by totally different verbal material. Compare, from this point of view, the lines from Iriarte's *Los gustos estragados* given in (6a) and the English nursery rime in (6b):

(6) (a) *Que corren,*
        X X (X)
      Que saltan,
        X X (X)
      Que ríen,
        X X(X)
      Que parlan,
        X X (X)
      Que tocan,
        X X(X)
      Que bailan,
        X X (X)
      Que enredan,
        X̲ X(X)
      Que cantan;
        X X (X)

  (b) *A swárm of bées in Máy*
        X   X   X
      is wórth a lóad of háy;
        X   X   X
      A swárm of bées in Júne
        X   X   X
      is wórth a sílver spóon;
        X   X   X
      A swárm of bées in Julý
        X   X   X
      ís not wórth a flý.
      X   X   X

In these two poems the abstract metrical patterns are identical, namely, XXX, but the correspondence rules are not. For (6a) the correspondence rule is (5); for (6b), on the other hand, the correspondence rule is (7a):

(7)   (a) Each element X of the meter corresponds to a fully stressed vowel[3]
        OR
      (b) to a subsequence consisting of one or two fully stressed vowels within the same syntactic constituent, provided that no other vowel appears between them

The rime in (8) is scanned by means of the correspondence rule (7a):

(8)   *Ráin, ráin, gó awáy*
        X   X   X   X
      Cóme agáin anóther dáy
        X   X   X   X
      Líttle Jóhnny wánts to pláy.
        X   X   X   X

Consider, now, the rime in (9):

(9)   *Ríde a cóck-hórse to Bánbury Cróss*
        X   X̄   X   X
      To sée a fíne lády upón a whíte hórse
          X   X̄   X   X̄
      Ríngs on her fíngers, bélls on her tóes
        X   X   X   X
      Shé shall have músic wheréver she góes.
        X   X   X   X

The last two lines of (9) show four fully stressed vowels and are readily seen to correspond to a four-unit meter by virtue of (7a). Notice, however, that the first and second lines contain five and six fully stressed vowels, respectively. In order to assign these lines to a four-unit meter, it is necessary to resort to the second alternative of (7), according to which two fully stressed

---

[3] By "fully stressed vowel" we mean the vowel that has the main stress in the word; all other vowels in the word are subsumed under the term "unstressed." Thus, in the word *instrumentality*, for example, the antepenult will be viewed as "stressed" and all other vowels lumped together as "unstressed." Vowels with subordinate stress in compounds are fully stressed since they bear the main stress of the word in which they occur, e.g., *horse* in *cóck-hòrse* and *Banbury* in *Bànbury Cróss* in (9). Also, the verbal particle, as well as the verb, is fully stressed in constructions such as *eat up*. But clitics such as articles, conjunctions, prepositions, clitic adverbs, and verbal auxiliaries do not contain fully stressed vowels.

vowels in the same syntactic constituent with no vowel intervening may correspond to a single metrical element. In the first line the sequence *cóck-hórse* and in the second line the sequences *fíne lády* and *whíte hórse* may be assigned to a single X by (7b). Therefore the first two lines may also be seen to correspond to a four-unit metrical pattern, though less directly.

The correspondence rule (7), then, not only allows all of the lines in (9) to be adjudged metrical, but it also assigns to them a relative order of complexity. The last two lines are the most neutral realizations of the abstract metrical pattern XXXX since only rule (7a) is utilized; the first line is the next complex, with (7b) invoked once; the second is the most complex, with (7b) used twice. This assignment appears to us to be intuitively correct.

The meters of English nursery rimes commonly allow one optional X. Thus, we may also have patterns such as (10) and (11):[4]

(10) XX(X)

Thrée wíse mén of Gótham
  X   X   X

Wént to séa in a bówl
  X   X   X

If the bówl had been strónger
     X   X

My sóng had been lónger.
   X   X

(11) XXX(X)

Thírty dáys hath Septémber
  X   X   X

Ápril, Júne and Novémber;
  X   X   X

Fébruary has twénty-éight alóne
  X   X   X   X

Áll the rést have thírty-óne,
  X   X   X   X

Excépting léap yéar, thát's the tíme
   X   X   X   X

When Fébruary's dáys are twénty-níne.
   X   X   X   X

---

[4] This is reminiscent of Old English meter, which we discuss in the next section. Indeed, there are other obvious parallels between nursery rimes such as those scanned here and Old English poetry. For a discussion of the relationship among nursery rimes, Old English meter, and Middle English alliterative verse as exemplified in *Gawain and the Green Knight*, see Keyser (1969a) and references there.

2. *Old English Alliterative Verse*

The verse form which is exemplified in the Old English epic poem *Beowulf* shares certain fundamental properties with the English nursery rimes just examined. It is, however, far more complicated, as is to be expected of a sophisticated art form. The Old English alliterative verse line had a specified number of vowels with primary stress but, unlike the nursery rimes, the Old English verse required, in addition, that the consonant clusters preceding certain stressed vowels in the line alliterate. As a typical example consider (12):

(12) *bát under béorge. Béornas géarwe* *(B.211)*
boat beneath the sea-cliffs. Warriors eagerly

This line has four vowels with primary stress, the first three of which alliterate, that is, are preceded by identical consonants (indicated in boldface type). In order to capture these facts in our metrical theory, we postulate two sorts of abstract metrical entities, S and W, arrayed in the pattern (13), and the correspondence rule (14):

(13) SSSW

(14) (a) Each abstract entity of the verse, that is, each S or W, corresponds to a single syllable bearing primary stress

   DEFINITION: If in two or more stressed syllables the zero or more consonants which precede the vowel are identical or begin with an identical consonant or *s*-cluster, the syllables alliterate[5]

   (b) Syllables in S positions alliterate; syllables in W positions do not alliterate

In accordance with (13) and (14), we would scan (12) as in (15):

(15) *bát under béorge. Béornas géarwe*
     S   S   S   W

---

[5] In other words, all syllables that begin with a stressed vowel (that is, all syllables with zero consonants before the stressed vowel) alliterate, as do syllables where the stressed vowel is preceded by the same single consonant. A stressed syllable beginning with more than one consonant alliterates with a stressed syllable which begins with any number of consonants as long as the first consonant of the respective syllables is the same. However, stressed syllables beginning with an *s*-cluster alliterate only if the obstruent following the *s* is the same.

Certain exceptional alliterations have been omitted from the definition. Thus [k] and [č] alliterate with each other, as do [g] and [y]. Bliss (1958, p. 11) suggests that the rules of alliteration had become traditional. However, it is conceivable that alliteration was defined on an abstract level where [k] and [č] were identical segments, as were [g] and [y].

Other lines which are similarly scanned are given in (16):

(16) (a) *mónegum mǽgþum méodoseṭla oftéah*   *(B.5)*
          S   S   S   W
        wrested the mead-seat from many tribes

     (b) *lífde æfter láþum, lánge þráge*   *(B.1257)*
          S   S   S   W
        lived after the hateful foe for a long while

     (c) *Hē geféng þā fételhilt, fréca Scýldinga*   *(B.1563)*
             S   S   W
        He, warrior of the Scyldings, seized the linked hilt

A rather interesting set of verses of this type appears in (17):

(17) (a) *dríhtsele dréorfāh, þonne dǽg líxte*   *(B.485)*
          S   S   S W
        the splendid hall stained with blood, when day dawned

     (b) *wréoþenhilt ond wýrmfāh. Đā se wísa sprǽc*   *(B.1698)*
          S   S   S   W
        with twisted hilt and serpentine ornamentation. Then the wise one spoke

In each of these lines we find compound words: *dríhtsele* and *dréorfāh* in (17a) and *wréoþenhilt* and *wýrmfāh* in (17b). We have seen in our discussion of Old English stress that the second element of such words contains non-primary stress. The scansions indicated in (17), then, are based upon the premise that in compound words subsidiary stress is not metrically significant. This assumption is borne out by the fact that second elements of compound words never alliterate. Thus, in the discussion which follows, we assume that only primary-stressed syllables may actualize S's and W's. These syllables are generally to be found only in major lexical items—nouns, verbs, adjectives, nonclitic adverbs, and the first element of compound words. In addition, we assume as a special convention that adjectives always contain primary-stressed vowels, even when they modify nouns. There are occasional lines in which prepositions and personal and demonstrative pronouns actualize S positions. (See note 7 for further details.)

    A cursory inspection of the verses in *Beowulf* reveals that approximately thirty percent of the lines are of the pattern shown in (15), (16), and (17). But what of the remaining lines? There are several other verses which indicate that while the pattern in (13) and the rule in (14) are basic to *Beowulf* prosody, certain modifications are needed in order to account for the full variety of lines in the poem. Consider, to begin with, the lines in (18):

(18) (a) *éaforum Écgwelan, Ár-Scyldingum*   *(B.1710)*
          S   S   S
        the offspring of Ecgwela, the glorious Scyldings

(b) *sē for ándrysnum éalle bewéotede*   *(B.1796)*
    S   S   W
who in courtesy watched over all

In (18a) there is no W position since all the syllables with primary stress begin with an alliterating segment. This suggests that the abstract metrical pattern (13) be modified so as to allow the final W to be optional. Furthermore, the initial S of the abstract metrical pattern is optional as well since (18b) exhibits only two syllables which are assignable to S positions in accordance with rule (14). We have already seen in (10) and (11) that an optional abstract metrical entity is characteristic of the meter of English nursery rimes, and Old English poetry shares this feature. Because lines in which the optional entities are filled are much more common than those in which the optional entities are absent, we shall introduce an asterisk notation to represent the fact that omission of the optional entity makes the line more complex. We therefore modify (13) as in (19) but leave the correspondence rule (14) as it is:

(19)   (S)*SS(W)*

Notice, however, that the abstract pattern (19) now makes the prediction that one ought to find lines in *Beowulf* corresponding to the metrical pattern SS and that this pattern ought to be found less frequently than any of the three meters mentioned earlier. (Recall that by starring the parentheses in (19) we indicate the fact that when the enclosed material is omitted the line is more rather than less complex.) These expectations are, in fact, borne out: there are lines of the type SS, as in (20), and they are less common than the lines discussed previously (see (30)):

(20) (a) *þone sélestan sǽcyninga*   *(B.2382)*
          S   S
     the best of sea-kings

    (b) *oþ þæt hē fǽringa fýrgenbēamas*   *(B.1414)*
             S   S
     until he suddenly mountain-trees

Although the modified pattern (19) allows us to handle all the lines cited thus far, it does not resolve all difficulties. Thus, lines such as those in (21) are ruled out, but they are clearly metrical:

(21) (a) SWWSW

    frǽan Scýldinga. Gewítaþ fórð béran   *(B.291)*
    S   W   W   S   W
    lord of the Scyldings. Go forth bearing

(Continued on p. 150)

21 (*Continued*)

(b) SWWS

> *mǽg Ælfheres; geséah his móndryhten*   (*B.2604*)
> S W   W   S
>
> kinsmen of Ælfhere; he beheld his lord

(c) SSWWSW

> *héard hǽr cúmen, sóhte hóldne wíne*   (*B.376*)
> S   S   W   W   S   W
>
> come boldly here, and visited a trusty friend

(d) SSSWW

> *Béowulf wæs brǽme—blǽd wíde spráng—*   (*B.18*)
> S   S   S   W   W
>
> Beowulf was renowned—his fame ranged afar—

In order to account for (21), it is necessary to allow the occurrence of more than one W between internal S positions. On the basis of the lines cited here, one might propose to permit two W positions to occur between the penultimate and ultimate S, giving the pattern in (22), where the unstarred parentheses enclose optional material that does not affect the complexity of the line:

(22)   (S)*S(W)(W)S(W)(W)*

However, even this modification is not sufficient since it excludes a line containing two or three S positions preceded by a W position. The existence of such verse types is illustrated in (23):

(23) (a) WSSWSW

> *gebád wíntra wórn, ǽr hē on wég hwúrfe*   (*B.264*)
> W S   S   W   S   W
>
> he lived to see many a winter before he turned away

(b) WSSSW

> *þæt hē hǽfde mód mícel, þēah þe hē his mágum nǽre*   (*B.1167*)
> W   S   S   S   W
>
> that he had much courage, though he might not have been with his kinsmen

(c) WSSS

> *hǽfde mǽre mǽgen. Þā hine on mórgentíd*   (*B.518*)
> W   S   S   S
>
> he had greater strength. Then him in the morning

(d) WSSW

> "*Ne frín þū æfter sǽlum! Sórh is geníwod*   (*B.1322*)
> W   S   S   W
>
> "Do not ask after happiness! Sorrow is renewed

(e) WSSWW

Gewíton him þā féran, — flóta stílle bád (*B.301*)
  W   S   S   W   W

Then they started out,—the ship remained still

(f) SWSSW

fíf níhta fýrst, oþ þæt unc flód tōdráf (*B.545*)
 S W   S   S   W

a space of five nights, until the flood separated us

There are no cases in *Beowulf* of two W positions before the initial S or of two W's after the initial S in a line containing three S positions. There are, moreover, no cases of a final S being followed by three W positions. Nor are there lines that have more than three nonalliterating stressed syllables. To capture these facts, as well as the facts of (23), in which a W position precedes two or three S positions, we modify the abstract underlying pattern (22) as in (24):

(24) (W)(S(W))*S(W)(W)S(W)(W)*

CONDITION: no verse can have more than three W positions

The condition that we have imposed rules out such nonexistent abstract patterns as SWSWWSWW, WSWWSW, and WSWSWSW.

While (24) is empirically adequate in that it makes no false predictions, it fails to provide true insights into the nature of the verse line in *Beowulf*. It also permits a great many more abstract patterns than are actually attested, as shown in (27), where we list systematically all patterns allowed by (24). To simplify the task of listing, we have divided the formula (24) into two halves: the first half subsumes all substrings allowed by the first three symbols; the second half subsumes the substrings allowed by the last six symbols. The first half thus allows for the six substrings in (25):

(25) ϕ WS
     W   SW
     S   WSW

The second half allows for the eight substrings in (26):

(26) SS   SWSW
     SWS   SWWSW
     SWWS   SSWW
     SSW   SWSWW

The ninth line-half SWWSWW is ruled out since it violates the condition that no line contain more than three W's.

A verse pattern is constituted by combining any of the six patterns in (25) with any of the eight patterns of (26) as shown in (27):

(27)

First Half	Second Half							
	SS	SWS	SWWS	SSW	SWSW	SWWSW	SSWW	SWSWW
φ	SS	SWS	SWWS	SSW	SWSW	SWWSW	SSWW	SWSWW
W	WSS	WSWS	~~WSWWS~~	WSSW	WSWSW	—	WSSWW	—
S	SSS	SSWS	SSWWS	SSSW	SSWSW	SSWWSW	SSSWW	SSWSWW
WS	WSSS	~~WSSWS~~	~~WSSWWS~~	WSSSW	~~WSSWSW~~	—	~~WSSSWW~~	—
SW	SWSS	~~SWSWS~~	~~SWSWWS~~	SWSSW	~~SWSWSW~~	—	~~SWSSWW~~	—
WSW	~~WSWSS~~	~~WSWSWS~~	—	~~WSWSSW~~	—	—	—	—

The patterns represented by dashes in (27) are ruled out by the constraint limiting the number of W positions to three or less. The patterns with lines drawn through them, on the other hand, are allowed by (24) but are not found in the poetry. Out of 37 patterns permitted by (24), twelve are unattested. This is a rather large number and suggests that the theory developed here does not adequately represent the data.

Up until now we have operated on the assumption that the verse in *Beowulf* has a purely linear structure, as indicated in the abstract pattern (24). In this respect the discussion here has departed from most traditional treatments of Old English meter, which assume that between the line and the sequences of S and W there intervenes another theoretical entity, the half-line. We shall show directly that with this new entity a greatly improved account of the *Beowulf* meter can be obtained.[6]

It must be noted at the outset that the half-line is a metrical construct, not a syntactic or phonetic entity. Although this view is implicit in many discussions of the half-line, it is commonly somewhat obscured by the insistence of metrists on various secondary phenomena that are correlated with the half-line but cannot be taken as defining characteristics. Typical of the way the half-line is usually presented is the following remark by Bliss (1962):

> The lines of OE poetry are divided by a pause (one of the natural breath-pauses we have already discussed) into two half-lines or *verses*; this pause is usually marked in printed texts by a wider space and in the MSS by a point. The first verse in each line is known as the *a*-verse, the second as *b*-verse. The *metrical unit* in OE is not, as in MnE, the line, but the verse; that is, although the structure of the verse is very strictly governed by elaborate rules, the combination of the verses into lines is free—the structure of the *b*-verse bears no special relationship to that of the *a*-verse (pp. 11–12).

[6] It should be noted that the splitting of the lines into two halves to facilitate the listing of the abstract patterns in (27) was a purely expository step without theoretical significance. The line-halves of (27) are therefore not to be identified with the half-lines under discussion here.

Taken at face value Bliss's assertion that the half-line is a phonetic entity defined by a pause is false, for there are lines such as those in (28) where no pause marks the division into half-lines:

(28) (a) *hú ðā ǽþelingas éllen frémedon*   *(B.3)*
      W S   S   W
     how those nobles performed valorous deeds

    (b) *Sétton sǽmēþe síde scýldas*   *(B.325)*
       S   S   S   W
     seaweary, they set down the wide shields

As a matter of fact, Bliss himself appears to realize that the presence of a major syntactic boundary cannot be a defining property of the half-line, for he tells us that "every editorial punctuation mark in printed OE texts must correspond to a cæsura; but the cæsura is often unmarked. In Anglo-Saxon MSS the cæsura is sometimes marked by a point, *even when no punctuation would now be considered appropriate*" [emphasis ours] (p. 10). A cæsura may thus occur whether or not it is syntactically justified by the text. The sequence delimited by the cæsura, then, is not a syntactic entity; it is primarily a metrical entity postulated for purely metrical reasons. This does not mean, of course, that the high degree of coincidence between half-line and major syntactic entity is of small importance. On the contrary, it is a fact of great significance, but the coincidence cannot be a defining feature of the half-line. The situation under discussion is quite similar to that in artistic (as opposed to popular) verse, where although in the overwhelming majority of cases verse boundaries coincide with major syntactic boundaries, the fact that enjambment is allowed proves that syntactic boundaries cannot be used to define the line.

While we basically agree with the traditional theory that the Old English line is composed of two half-lines, we are unable to accept proposals concerning the composition of the half-line, especially those advanced by E. Sievers (e.g., (1885)). We reject these theories for reasons that were detailed in Keyser (1969a) and will not be repeated here.

The metrical theory that we propose to account for the verse of *Beowulf* is given in (29):

(29) (a) ABSTRACT METRICAL PATTERN RULES

     (i) A verse line is composed of a first and second half-line
     (ii) The first half-line is composed of (X)*X
     (iii) The second half-line is composed of X(W)*

(Continued on p. 154)

29 (*Continued*)

(b) CORRESPONDENCE RULES

(i) Each X corresponds to a single S

OR

One X in a half-line may correspond to an S and a W in either order

DEFINITION: If in two or more stressed syllables the zero or more consonants that precede the vowel are identical or begin with an identical consonant or *s*-cluster, the syllables alliterate

(ii) Syllables in S positions alliterate; syllables in W positions do not alliterate

(c) CONDITIONS

(i) No half-line is shorter than two syllables
(ii) If a line contains a line-internal clause or sentence boundary, the boundary must coincide with that of the half-line

Given these rules, the first half-line in *Beowulf* may have any of the seven abstract patterns shown in the left-hand column of (30), whereas the second half-line may assume any of the five patterns shown along the top of (30). Since any of the seven first half-lines can be followed by any of the five second half-lines, we expect to obtain 35 distinct abstract patterns, as illustrated.

(30)

First Half-Line	Second Half-Line				
	SW	S	SWW	WSW	WS
SS	SSSW 999	SSS 277	SSSWW 77	SSWSW 67	SSWS 17
S	SSW 665	SS 200	SSWW 21	SWSW 25	SWS 9
SW	SWSW 405	SWS 95	SWSWW 27	SWWSW 17	SWWS 2
WS	WSSW 137	WSS 33	WSSWW 1	WSWSW 19	WSWS 3
SSW	SSWSW 38	SSWS 8	SSWSWW 4	SSWWSW 3	SSWWS 1
WSS	WSSSW 13	WSSS 6	WSSSWW 0	WSSWSW 0	WSSWS 0
SWS	SWSSW 6	SWSS 1	SWSSWW 0	SWSWSW 0	SWSWS 0

The theory outlined in (29) specifies the 35 line types shown in (30), of which only six are unattested (namely, those accompanied by the numeral "0"). This is clearly an improvement over the theory postulated in (24), where twelve of 37 patterns postulated were unattested. The numbers beneath the metrical types listed in (30) refer to the number of lines in *Beowulf* which exhibit the associated metrical sequence. The scansions on which these statistics are based are the work of Ann Reed.[7] In making the scansions, the eleven so-called "hypermetrical" lines (see Sievers (1905, §23)) were included among the regular lines, and six lines were omitted because of a corrupt manuscript.

Among the line types listed in (30) there are a number of duplicates: SWS, SSWS, SWSW, and SSWSW appear twice. In each pair, however, the metrical boundary between the first and the second half-line is in a different place. For example, in the second column SWS represents a sequence with the boundary after the W, i.e., SW/S, while in the last column the boundary occurs before the W, i.e., S/WS. In view of the condition (29cii), these are not true duplicates for they allow different placement of the line-internal clause or sentence boundary, and the poet takes advantage of this freedom. We summarize the statistics of these pairs of metrical patterns in (31) on the next page.

In the case of the metrically ambiguous lines listed in (31), it was necessary to make a certain numerical adjustment. Consider, for example, the sequence SWSW. As indicated in (31), 198 lines in *Beowulf* correspond to the

---

[7] Mrs. Reed's study of Old English prosody is still in progress. We are grateful to her for allowing us to summarize her initial findings, and we are looking forward to a publication of her complete study in the not too distant future.

The scansions upon which the numerical data in (30) are based proceeded under the following assumptions. Mrs. Reed supposes primary stress for all adjectives, nouns, and verbs. However, *eom*, *bēon*, and *wesan* are unstressed except when they appear in the imperative mood and, in one case, in the subjunctive mood (see *wǣre B.3180*). In addition, the preterite present verb *sculan* is treated as unstressed throughout, while the verbs *magan* and *āgan* are sometimes stressed and sometimes not.

Nonclitic adverbs are generally stressed. Clitic adverbs such as *swā*, *þā*, *þonne*, and *ne* are never stressed, nor is *tō* as an intensifier. In addition, the nonclitic adverbs *hū*, *hūru*, and *swylce* are treated as unstressed. Finally, the following adverbs exhibit variable behavior, sometimes requiring stress and sometimes not: *nō*, *nū*, *þǣr*, and *giō*.

An apparent regularity appears in adverb pairs such as *þǣr on*, *þǣr inne*, *elles hwergen*, *þā gēn*, namely, when two such adverbs occur adjacent to each other and in close construction, only one (usually the second) bears a primary stress. In other words, these adverbs seem to behave precisely like modern English *wherefore, however, therein, thereupon*, etc.

Personal pronouns are generally unstressed although occasionally they too exhibit primary stress, presumably under emphatic stress. The substantive pronouns *selfa*, *ǣghwylc*, *ǣghwæðer*, *gehwæðer*, and *welhwylc* are treated as bearing primary stress in more than half of their occurrences.

(31)

VERSE TYPE	NUMBER OF LINES WITH VERSE-INTERNAL CLAUSE OR SENTENCE BOUNDARY
SW/S	54
S/WS	5
SS/WS	16
SSW/S	7
SW/SW	198
S/WSW	12
SS/WSW	53
SSW/SW	30

line type SW/SW and 12 lines correspond to S/WSW, for a total of 210 lines with internal clause or sentence boundary. However, an additional 220 lines exhibit the metrical sequence SWSW without an internal boundary to indicate whether the line is an example of SW/SW or S/WSW. To resolve this unclarity, we have assigned the ambiguous lines to the categories in question in proportion to their occurrences in the clear cases. Thus, of the 210 SWSW lines with clear internal boundaries, 198 lines or 94 percent are of the type SW/SW while 6 percent are of the S/WSW variety. We therefore counted 207 (or 94 percent) of the 220 unclear lines as belonging to the SW/SW pattern and the remaining 13 (or 6 percent) as belonging to the S/WSW pattern, thereby arriving at the respective totals of 405 and 25 shown in (30). Similar calculations were carried out for the other duplicate metrical patterns which are listed in (31).

Differences in the location of the syntactic boundary are practically unattested in the remaining metrical patterns. There are eight lines in *Beowulf* where the verse-internal syntactic boundary does not coincide with the boundary between half-lines, thereby violating condition (29cii). Since there are about 1500 lines with verse-internal syntactic boundaries, these eight lines, which we list in (32), constitute a small residue of metrically deviant verses:

(32) (a) *æt fótum sǽt frǽan Scýldinga; gehwylc hiora his férhþe tréowde*   (*B.1166*)
         S   W   S   W   S   W
       at the foot of the lord of the Scyldings; each of them trusted in his spirit

     (b) *Flód blóde wéol—fólc tō sǽgon—*   (*B.1422*)
         S   W   W   S   W
       The water surged with blood—the people gazed—

fficient children's librarians?

(c) "*Gepénc nū, se mǽra mága Héalfdenes*   (*B.1474*)
      W   S   S   W

"Remember now, O famous son of Healfdene

(d) *Đā cóm nón dǽges. Nǽs ofgéafon*   (*B.1600*)
   W   S   W   S   W

Then came the ninth hour of the day. They quitted the headland

(e) *cwǽð, hē þone gúðwine gódne téalde*   (*B.1810*)
   W   S   S   W

he said he counted it a good battle friend

(f) *wésan, þénden ic wéalde wídan ríces*   (*B.1859*)
   S   W   S   S   W

there shall be while I rule this wide kingdom

(g) *éðbegéte þūm ðe ǽr his élne forléas*   (*B.2861*)
   S   S   S   W

easy to obtain for him who before lacked courage

(h) *cwǽð, hē on mérgenne méces écgum*   (*B.2939*)
   W   S   S   W

he said, he in the morning with the sword's edge

Recall that in our account of the metrical theory of *Beowulf* in (29), we have stated the abstract metrical pattern and correspondence rules in such a fashion that later alternatives subsume earlier alternatives, and we have adopted the convention that lines which are scanned by later alternatives of the metrical rules are to be considered more complex than lines scanned by earlier alternatives. We have also noted that the metrical complexity of a line type and its frequency of occurrence ought to be inversely related, that is:

(33)   The more complex the line in terms of (29), the less frequently it occurs.

This inverse relationship is quite plausible on the common sense grounds that, in general, people avail themselves of more complex means of expression less frequently than they utilize more simple means. However, it should be immediately noted that while the statement (33) will hold for very large bodies of data, deviations may be expected in restricted bodies of data. A poet may decide to write a poem which exhibits only the more complex actualizations of the pattern, and as a result the statistics of the poem may violate the inverse relationship that may be expected to hold in general. But this is a purely local deviation that does not vitiate the general principle.

Keeping these limitations in mind, we proceed to explore the statistics of (30) in some detail in order to obtain a clearer grasp of the extent to which (33) is valid. We consider first the second half-line, where we have assumed that $X(W)^* \rightarrow SW$ is the simplest actualization. Observe that in each row of

(30) the numbers in the first column are larger than those in the other columns. There is no logical reason why this should be the case; indeed, only the first two half-line types, SS and S, were considered when the order of complexity of second half-lines was established. The fact that, for any given actualization of the first half-line, the least complex actualization of the second half-line (i.e., SW) is also the most numerous is therefore important support for the validity of (33).

The second most frequent half-line type is S, which is generated by the second alternative of the abstract metrical pattern (29aiii) in conjunction with the first alternative of the correspondence rule (29bi). To generate the half-line type SWW, which heads the third column in (30), we must invoke the first alternative of the abstract metrical pattern (29aiii) but make use of the second alternative of the correspondence rule, namely, $X(W)^* \rightarrow SWW$. Since the numbers in the second column, headed by S, are larger than those in the third column, headed by SWW, we shall say that later alternatives in the abstract metrical pattern increase complexity less than do later alternatives in the correspondence rules. It is not clear from the statistical data whether the second half-line SWW is more complex than WSW, the next column in (30). However, the data do appear to support the view that the most complex half-line is WS (the last column of (30)), which is generated by invoking the second alternative of both the abstract metrical pattern (29aiii) and the correspondence rule (29bi).

When we examine the statistics of occurrence of first half-lines, we find that these are somewhat less perspicuous. The numbers in the first column of (30) give the following order of initial half-lines: SS, S, SW, WS, SSW, WSS, SWS. The order of increasing complexity, however, is SS, S, SSW, WSS, SWS, SW, WS. Thus the order actually observed deviates from the expected order in that lines beginning with half-lines made up of three elements (SSW, WSS, SWS) are less frequent than lines beginning with half-lines made up of two elements (SW, WS). This deviation appears to us to be a "local phenomenon," the result of an idiosyncratic avoidance by the *Beowulf* poet of lines with long initial half-lines. If we are correct, this departure from the expected order will not be found in other examples of Old English alliterative verse. We are at present not in a position to perform counts like those in (30) on the entire Old English poetic corpus. Therefore, we cannot exclude the possibility that the deviation under discussion reflects a fundamental structural property of Old English alliterative verse that we have failed to take into account properly.

Regardless of how this issue is ultimately resolved, however, the data of (30) suggest rather strongly that claim (33) is correct, that is, that the complexity of a line type as defined here is intimately related to the frequency with which it occurs. This in turn provides additional support for the metrical theory (29) that has been advanced here. Of the 35 verse patterns allowed by (29), we were able to find only 29 in *Beowulf*. At first sight this might suggest that (29) needs to be further restricted to rule out the six unattested patterns. Note, however, that the unattested patterns are among the most complex generated by the theory (29). In view of the claim (33) that complexity is inversely related to frequency, it is to be expected that the line types under discussion will be extremely rare. In fact, it is not surprising that they are not at all attested in a relatively small corpus such as *Beowulf*; rather, their nonoccurrence is totally compatible with (29).

In sum, then, an examination of the line types in *Beowulf* suggests that there is a natural correlation between frequency of occurrence and line complexity as defined by (29), namely, that set forth in (33). However, in order to maintain this relationship, it is necessary to assume for *Beowulf* the principles of evaluation in (34):

(34) FOR THE *Beowulf* POET:
  (a) Later alternatives of the abstract metrical pattern rules increase complexity less than later alternatives of the correspondence rules
  (b) In the first half-line, three-entity sequences are always more complex than two-entity sequences.

It seems to us rather striking that it is possible to impose so coherent an order on the frequency of lines as that in (30), even given the need for the additional principles of (34). The question of whether these principles are too high a price to pay for the order of (30) must await further research.

We now turn to the condition (29ci), that is, the requirement that half-lines be at least two syllables long. This constraint rules out lines such as (35), which are nowhere attested:

(35) *hḗold héal*
he held the hall

According to Sievers' theory (1885), on the other hand, the half-line is normally at least four syllables long, but this forces Sievers either to declare as unmetrical or to emend half-lines such as those in (36):

(36) (a) *hrēas blāc*   (*B.2488*)
    he fell pale
  (b) *man geþēon*   (*B.25*)
    one (shall) prosper
  (c) *hāt in gān*   (*B.386*)
    bid them come in
  (d) *nēan bīdan*   (*B.528*)
    await at close quarters

The restriction (29ci) does not lead to these undesirable consequences and is therefore to be preferred.[8]

It was noted in Keyser (1969b) that another major inconvenience of Sievers' theory is that it forces us to emend lines which in the text are perfectly clear and make excellent sense semantically as well as syntactically. Among such lines are the five quoted in (37), which, as shown, are handled without difficulty by the theory proposed here:[9]

(37) (a) *líssa gelóng; ic lýt háfo*   *(B.2150)*
       S   S   S W
     favor at hand; I have little

    (b) *méaglum wórdum. Méoduscencum*   *(B.1980)*
       S   W   S
     earnestly in words. With the mead-cup

    (c) *sécg bétsta, mē for súnu wýlle*   *(B.947)*
       S   W   S   W
     best of men, I desire as a son

    (d) *Sórh is mē tō sécganne on séfan mínum*   *(B.473)*
       S   S   S W
     It is a sorrow to me to tell in my heart

    (e) *hréas blác; hónd gemúnde*   *(B.2488)*
       S   W   S   W
     he fell pale; his hand remembered

---

[8] In Keyser (1969a) a further observation was made which was incorporated there into a separate metrical constraint, namely, the last S in a verse always has a vowel of lesser stress somewhere to the right. This constraint prohibits a line from ending in a single alliterating monosyllable, thereby rendering unmetrical a line such as (35), though allowing a line such as *héal héoldon* (they held the hall). Within the present theory the need for this constraint
    S   S
is no longer clear.

[9] For a full discussion of these and similar lines with respect to Sievers' system, see Keyser (1969a).

In as yet unpublished work, Mrs. Reed (see note 7) has subjected to metrical analysis the poetic formulas in Old English poetry that have been collected in Watts (1969). Given the metrical theory of (29), the formulas could be classified as having the metrical patterns SS, SSW, WSW, SW, among others. Formulas having the metrical pattern SS or SSW were found only in the first half-line of poems; formulas with the pattern WSW were found only in the second half-line; formulas of the remaining types were found in either of the two half-lines, e.g., of the 322 formulas of the pattern SW, 175 are found in the second half-line, whereas 147 are found in the first half-line.

This result is readily understood in the light of (29) since the theory allows the patterns SS or SSW only in the first half-line and the pattern WSW only in the second half-line, while it allows SW in both half-lines. Given Sievers' theory, on the other hand, the restrictions just noted appear totally ad hoc since half-lines are classified in accordance with the distribution of stressed and unstressed syllables, specifically disregarding the presence or absence of alliterating staves in the half-lines.

We complete our discussion of *Beowulf* by listing in (38) examples of the attested line types predicted by (29).[10] (The order of lines in (38) follows the chart in (30), beginning with the first row and moving from left to right.)

(38) (a) SSSW

    mónegum mǽgþum méodosetla oftéah   *(B.5)*
    S   S   S   W

    wrested the mead-set from many tribes

   (b) SSS

    éaforum Écgwelan, Ǽr-Scyldingum   *(B.1710)*
    S   S   S

    the offspring of Ecgwela, the glorious Scyldings

   (c) SSSWW

    Béowulf wæs bréme—blǽd wíde spráng   *(B.18)*
    S   S   S   W   W

    Beowulf was renowned—his fame ranged afar—

   (d) SSWSW

    héah ofer héafod, léton hólm béran   *(B.48)*
    S   S   W   S   W

    high over his head, they let the sea carry

   (e) SSWS

    æþele ond éacen. Hét him ýðlidan   *(B.198)*
    S   S   W   S

    noble and great. He commanded a ship for him

   (f) SSW

    sē for ándrysnum éalle bewéotede   *(B.1796)*
       S   S   W

    who in courtesy watched over all

   (g) SS

    þone sélestan sǽcyninga   *(B.2382)*
       S   S

    the best of sea-kings

   (h) SSWW

    Gecýste þā cýning æþelum gód   *(B.1870)*
    S   S   W   W

    then the king kissed, noble in lineage

(Continued on p. 162)

---

[10] The system of prosody outlined here differs in one important respect from that described in Keyser (1969a). In the earlier work secondary stress was considered to be metrically significant. A consequence of this assumption was that certain morphemes such as finite verbs and the second element of compounds were treated as being sometimes metrically significant and sometimes not. Moreover, in lines which contained more than four major lexical items, it was necessary to resort to various types of stress subordination, either linguistic or metrical. Both of these consequences are avoided in the framework of (29).

38 (*Continued*)

(i) SWSW

Éormenrīces, gecéas écne rǽd   (*B.1201*)
  S   W   S   W

of Eormenric, he chose eternal gain

(j) SWS

ǽfenrǽste; wíste þǽm áhlǽcan   (*B.646*)
  S   W   S

to his evening rest; he knew by the evil spirit

(k) SWSW

Gréndles mágan gáng scéawigan   (*B.1391*)
    S   W   S   W

to examine the track of Grendel's kinsman

(l) SWS

þē hīe ǽr drúgon áldor[lē]ase   (*B.15*)
     S   W   S

which they endured before, without a lord

(m) SWSWW

þrýðum déalle. Þégn nýtte behéold   (*B.494*)
    S   W   S   W   W

proud in might. A servant did his duty

(n) SWWSW

fréan Scýldinga. Gewítaþ fórð béran   (*B.291*)
   S   W   W   S   W

lord of the Scyldings. Go forth bearing

(o) SWWS

mǽg Ǽlfheres; geséah his móndryhten   (*B.2604*)
   S   W   W   S

kinsmen of Ælfhere; he beheld his lord

(p) WSSW

"*Ne frín þū æfter sǽlum! Sórh is geníwod*   (*B.1322*)
   W   S   S   W

"Do not ask after happiness! Sorrow is renewed

(q) WSS

Cwóm þā tō flóde félamōdigra   (*B.1888*)
   W   S   S

then came to the flood a very brave

(r) WSSWW

Gewíton him þā féran,—flóta stílle bád   (*B.301*)
   W   S   S   W   W

Then they started out,—the ship remained still

(s) WSWSW

Ðā cóm ín gân éaldor ðégna   *(B.1644)*
 W   S W S   W

Then entered in the chief of the thanes

(t) WSWS

þénden hǽlo ābéad héorðgenēatum   *(B.2418)*
 W   S   W   S

then he saluted his retainers

(u) SSWSW

Fýrst fórð gewát; flóta wæs on ýðum   *(B.210)*
 S   S   W   S   W

Time passed on; the ship was on the waves

(v) SSWS

ǽscholt úfan grǽg; wæs se írenþrēat   *(B.330)*
 S   S   W   S

the ash spear gray above; the armored troop was

(w) SSWSWW

drǽfan déop wǽter, Déna lánd ofgéaf   *(B.1904)*
 S   S   W   S   W   W

to stir up the deep water, it left the Danish land

(x) SSWWSW

héard hǽr cúmen, sóhte hóldne wíne   *(B.376)*
 S   S   W   W   S   W

come boldly here, and visited a trusty friend

(y) SSWWS

bǽdde býre géonge; óft hīo béahwriðan   *(B.2018)*
 S   S   W   W   S

she urged the young men; often she a ring

(z) WSSSW

þæt hē hǽfde mód mícel, þéah þe hē his mágum nǽre   *(B.1167)*
  W   S   S   ·   S   W

that he had much courage, though he might not have been with his kinsmen

(a′) WSSS

hǽfde máre mágen. Þā hine on mórgentīd   *(B.518)*
 W   S   S   S

he had greater strength. Then him in the morning

(b′) WSSSWW

(unattested)

(Continued on p. 164)

38 (*Continued*)

(c′) WSSWSW

(unattested)

(d′) WSSWS

(unattested)

(e′) SWSSW

fíf níhta fýrst, oþ þæt unc flŏd tōdráf   (B.545)
 S W   S   S   W

a space of five nights, until the flood separated us

(f′) SWSS

dŏmes ǽr dĕaþe; þæt bið dríhtguman   (B.1388)
 S   W   S   S

glory before death; that shall be for the warrior

(g′) SWSSWW

(unattested)

(h′) SWSWSW

(unattested)

(i′) SWSWS

(unattested)

3. Iambic Pentameter

The meter we have just discussed is characterized by a set of correspondence rules which regulate the assignment of stressed syllables to abstract metrical entities while leaving the unstressed syllables in the line essentially free. We now turn to the meter in which correspondence rules assign all syllables in a line, stressed and unstressed, to abstract metrical entities. This meter, the iambic pentameter, has been the favorite of English poets since the time of Chaucer, and it is probably not a coincidence that its appearance coincides with the incorporation of the Romance Stress Rule into the English language. We may state the abstract metrical pattern underlying the iambic pentameter as in (39), where parenthesized entities are optional:

(39)   WSWSWSWSWS(W)(W)

This pattern is in turn related to concrete lines of verse by correspondence rules such as those illustrated in (40):[11]

---

[11] In (40) we follow the definition for syllable given in note 1 of this chapter.

By "stressed syllable" we mean any syllable (see note 1) which contains a fully stressed vowel (see note 3). As before, we shall be concerned only with full stress, lumping together all syllables with lesser stressed and unstressed vowels under the heading of "unstressed syllables."

(40) (a) Each abstract entity (W,S) corresponds to a single syllable
(b) Fully stressed syllables occur in S positions only and in all S positions

We scan particular lines by utilizing (40) to establish a correspondence between the syllables of the line and the abstract entities in the pattern (39). Lines are judged metrical if such a correspondence can be established exhaustively without violating the applicable correspondence rules, as is the case, for example, with the well-known line (41) from Gray's *Elegy Written in a Country Churchyard*:

(41) *The cúrfew tólls the knéll of párting dáy*
      W SW S   W   S W SW   S

The characterization of the iambic pentameter that has been given by means of the pattern (39) and the correspondence rules (40) is essentially a more formal statement of the description to be found in many of the standard treatises. Thus in Bridges' important *Milton's Prosody* (1921), we are told that the normal iambic line can be defined as in (42):

(42) A decasyllabic line on a disyllabic basis and in rising rhythm (i.e., with accents of stresses on the alternate even syllables); and the disyllabic units may be called *feet* (p. 1).

We discuss the question of "feet" directly. At this point we wish only to note that the normal iambic line as defined by (42) or, equivalently, by (39) and (40), does not characterize (1b) cited earlier, or any of a huge number of lines that appear commonly in iambic pentameter verses, such as those in (43)–(46):

(43) *Ăs óok, fírre, bĭrch, áspe, álder, hólm, pŏplér,*
      Wýlŭgh, élm, pláne, ássh, bóx, chásteўn, lýnde, laŭrér,
      Mápŭl, thórn, béch, hásĕl, éw, whíppĕltreé—

(CHAUCER, *A.Kn.2921–3*)

(44) *Báttĕr mў heárt, thrée-pérsŏn'd Gód, fŏr yŏu*
      Ăs yĕt bŭt knóck, bréathe, shíne, ănd seek tŏ ménd;
      Thăt Ĭ măy ríse, ănd stánd, o'erthrów mĕ, ănd bénd
      Yŏur fórce tŏ bréak, blów, búrn, ănd máke mĕ néw.

(DONNE, *Holy Sonnet 14*)

(45) *Ó wĭld Wést Wĭnd, thŏu bréath ŏf Aútŭmn's bĕing*
      Thŏu frŏm whŏse únseĕn présĕnce thĕ leáves deád
      Ăre drĭvĕn, lĭke ghósts frŏm ăn ĕnchántĕr fleéĭng,

(SHELLEY, *Ode to the West Wind*)

(46) *Spéech ăftĕr lóng silĕnce; ĭt ĭs ríght,*
  Ăll óthĕr lóvĕrs bĕíng ĕstrángĕd ŏr déad,

(YEATS, *After Long Silence*)

The existence of such lines, of course, did not escape the attention of Bridges or of any other serious student of prosody. In fact, immediately below the definition (42), Bridges notes that in Milton one may find three types of exceptions to the norm:

> I Exceptions to the number of syllables being ten,
> II Exceptions to the number of stresses being five,
> III Exceptions in the positions of the stresses.

In other words, each of the three properties of the line that are specifically regulated in the definition (42) is violated on some occasion in the iambic pentameter of Milton's *Paradise Lost*.

To account for these exceptions, Bridges and many other metrists supplement the definition of the norm with a list of allowable deviations which commonly includes the items in (47):

(47) (a) unstressed foot (pyrrhic)
  (b) heavy foot (spondee)
  (c) initial foot inverted (trochee)
  (d) verse-medial foot inverted (trochee)
  (e) extra slack syllable inserted verse-medially
  (f) dropping of verse-initial slack syllable (headless)

We shall refer to the account based on the norm (42) (or, equivalently, (39) and (40)) and the allowable deviations (47) as the standard theory of the iambic pentameter. In order to demonstrate the functioning of the standard theory, we now examine the lines in (43)–(46).

The lines from Chaucer (43) are metrical by a liberal invocation of the deviation (47b), for heavy feet abound in these lines. Moreover, there is an initial trochee (47c) in the last two lines, and an extra slack syllable (47e) in the second line.

The first line of Donne's sonnet (44) has an initial trochee (47c) as well as a verse-medial heavy foot (47b) in the phrase *three-person'd God* and a verse-final pyrrhic (47a). The second line also contains a spondee (47b), as does the fourth line; whereas the third line has an initial pyrrhic foot (47a) and an extra slack syllable (47e), *me and*.

The first line of Shelley's poem (45) exhibits two spondees (47b).

The second line contains an initial trochee (47c) and the pyrrhic foot (47a) *-ence the*, as well as a verse-final spondee (47b). The third line has an extra slack syllable (47e), *-en* in *driven*, and a pyrrhic (47a).

In the Yeats verses (46), the first line is headless (47f) and contains one verse-medial spondee (47b) and a pyrrhic (47a). The second line contains an extra slack syllable (47e), *being*.

Although the standard theory consisting of the abstract pattern (39), the correspondence rules (40), and the list of allowable deviations (47) correctly establishes the lines in (43)–(46) as metrical, it has a number of inadequacies that suggest rather fundamental revisions. Consider first the line (1a) which we referred to earlier as an example of an unmetrical line and which is repeated here for convenience as (48):

(48) *Óde to the Wést Wínd by Pércy Býsshe Shélley*

The line contains an inverted first foot (47c), a heavy foot (47b), and two verse-medial trochaic substitutions (47d). Since all these are admissible deviations, (48) must be judged metrical by the standard theory. But this surely is an unacceptable consequence.

The difficulty arises from the fact that the standard theory formulates allowable deviations in terms of feet. (In fact, it is mainly in this domain that the entity "foot" plays a significant role.) Implicit in this formulation is the view that deviations in one foot are independent of deviations in adjoining feet. This is not the case, however. Thus, although trochaic feet are admissible in iambic lines, they must not be consecutive, for consecutive trochaic feet render the line unmetrical, as in (48). It is, of course, possible to modify (47d) so as to exclude this possibility. But if adjoining feet are not independent, one must seriously question the postulation of feet as entities intermediate between the line and the weak and strong positions that constitute the foot. We shall propose here an account that does not make use of the concept "foot," and we shall attempt to show that such an account is superior to the standard theory even where the latter is patched up to handle cases like the one just discussed.

We have just noted that a shortcoming of the standard theory is that it deals with allowable deviations by means of a list, thus implying that there is nothing in common among the allowable deviations since there are no qualifications for membership in this list. Moreover, the list as given in (47) is incomplete, for it fails to explain certain facts about English verse which an adequate theory would be expected to take account of. It was observed many years ago by Jespersen (1933, p. 262) that whereas an iambic line could tolerate a trochee in the first two syllables, a trochaic line could not tolerate an analogous iambic substitution in the first two syllables.[12] He cites the lines in (49) from Longfellow's *A Psalm of Life* and observes that the second line may not be replaced by (50):

(49)   *Tell me not, in mournful numbers*
       Life is but an empty dream

(50)   *A life's but an empty dream*

There is no explanation offered for this phenomenon in the standard theory.

There is a further systematic correlation which is suggested by Jespersen's observation. If iambic verse permits the dropping of an initial slack syllable (see lines (66b) and (66c)), trochaic verse admits of an extra-metrical slack syllable at the beginning of a line. The trochaic couplet in (51) from Keats' *Fancy* is illustrative:

(51)   *All the buds and bells of May*
       From dewy sward or thorny spray

Indeed, if one did not know that *Fancy* was written in trochaic meter, this couplet would be metrically ambiguous since it can easily occur in an iambic tetrameter poem. This second correlation between iambic and trochaic verse also remains unexplained in the standard theory.

Thirdly, Jespersen (1933, p. 255) notes that major syntactic breaks—what he refers to as "pauses"—appear to play an important role in the metrical behavior of a line. Such breaks are commonly indicated ortho-graphically by a comma, semicolon, or period. It is noteworthy that two of the categories on the allowable deviation list are commonly associated with major syntactic breaks: internal trochaic substitution, which often occurs after a major syntactic break (see lines (66b) and (66c)), and the heavy foot, which is composed of two positions separated by a major syntactic break (see (43)). Once again a deeper generalization is hinted at here which the standard theory does not capture.

To meet the objections just sketched, we propose to replace the abstract metrical pattern (39) and the correspondence rules (40) by the account in (52):

---

[12] In addition, Wimsatt (in Sebeok (1960, p. 206)): ". . . it is not at all clear to me why the trochaic substitution in the first foot is so acceptable in the iambic line. I'm never able to make up my mind whether it is because it just happened, as Mr. Ransom, I think, suggests, sort of got established, or whether there is some peculiar reason."

(52) (a) ABSTRACT METRICAL PATTERN

(W)*S WS WS WS WS (X)(X)

where elements enclosed in parentheses may be omitted and where each X position may be occupied only by an unstressed syllable

(b) CORRESPONDENCE RULES

(i) A position (S, W, or X) corresponds to a single syllable

OR

to a sonorant sequence incorporating at most two vowels (immediately adjoining or separated by a sonorant consonant)

DEFINITION: When a fully stressed syllable occurs between two unstressed syllables in the same syntactic constituent within a line of verse, this syllable is called a "stress maximum"

(ii) Fully stressed syllables occur in S positions only and in all S positions

OR

Fully stressed syllables occur in S positions only but not in all S positions

OR

Stress maxima occur in S positions only but not in all S positions[13]

[13] In previous studies (e.g., Halle and Keyser (1966)) we proposed that a "stress maximum" is constituted by a stressed syllable located between two syllables with lesser stress. The definition given here limits more narrowly the syllables that can be stress maxima. Since in metrical lines stress maxima may *not* correspond to W positions, an immediate consequence of the more restrictive definition is to admit as metrical certain lines that previously had been judged as unmetrical. For example, from Chaucer:

With this quyksilver, *shortly for to sayn*	(*G.CY.1111*)
(cf. *For* quyksilver, *that we it hadde anon*)	(*G.CY.1103*)
He was short-sholdred, *brood, a thikke knarre*	(*A.Prol.549*)
There nas quyk-silver, *lytarge, ne* brymstoon	(*A.Prol.629*)

from Spenser:

Ne let house-fyres, *nor lightnings helplesse harmes*	(*Epithalamion, st.19,7*)

from John Donne:

Askt not of rootes, nor of cock-sparrows, *leave*	(*Progress of the Soule, 217*)
Th'hydroptique drunkard, and night-scouting *thiefe*	(*Holy Sonnet 3,9*)

Although lines of this kind are not too frequent, they do occur and thereby provide justification for "weakening" the theory in the manner outlined here. The need for a revision of the definition of stress maximum given in Halle and Keyser (1966) was noted independently by Meadors (1969).

We must now show how lines are scanned within the revised theory. The procedure is as follows. In each line we first establish position occupancy by numbering the different syllables in the line from left to right.[14] If the number is ten, a one-to-one occupancy of positions by syllables is assumed, in accordance with the first alternative of (52bi). If the number is one less than ten, a check is made to determine if a one-to-one syllable-to-position assignment can be made by assuming that the first W is missing (a headless line). If the number of syllables is more than ten, a check is made to determine whether the line contains any extra-metrical syllables or whether two adjacent syllables may be assigned to a single position in accordance with the second alternative of (52bi).

Having established the syllable-to-position assignments, we next locate stressed and unstressed syllables in the line. We then check to see if the location of stressed and unstressed syllables satisfies one of the three alternatives of (52bii). We begin by checking the first alternative and underlining all positions in which it is not satisfied, that is, we underline each position where an S is occupied by an unstressed syllable or a W by a stressed syllable. Next we examine the line in terms of the second alternative of (52bii) and underline all positions where this is violated, that is, a W occupied by a stressed syllable now receives a double underline. Finally, we check out the third alternative; if any position violates this—that is, if any W is occupied by a stress maximum —the line is judged unmetrical. In checking we count full and unstressed vowels only. We now illustrate the procedure just outlined.

) *The cúrfew tólls the knéll of párting dáy*
   W SW   S   W   SW   SW   S

Line (53) satisfies the first alternative of both (52bi) and (52bii).

) *And léaves the wórld to dárkness and to me*
  W   S   W S   W S W S̄   W S̄

In line (54) the fourth S and fifth S violate the first but not the second alternative of (52bii).

) *Bátter my héart, thrée-pérson'd Gód, for you*
  W̿S   W S   W̿ SW   S   W S

In (55) the first and last S violate the first alternative of (52bii) but not the second; and the first and third W violate the second alternative but are

[14] It is important to keep in mind that extra-metrical syllables, both in verse-initial and verse-final positions, are not included in the numbering. On the other hand, the missing first syllable in headless lines must be counted.

allowed by the third alternative: the word *three* does not constitute a stress maximum because it is not located between two unstressed syllables in the same syntactic constituent; it may therefore occupy a W position.

   An example where all three alternatives are violated is provided by the triply underlined and barred position in line (56). Such lines are unmetrical.

(56) *Óde to the Wést Wind by Pércy Býsshe Shélley*
       W   S W   S   W   S W S W   S X

   The revised theory (52) brings out the fact that the iambic pattern allows for a great deal of freedom while at the same time providing sufficient constraints to make the art form an interesting one for the poet to work in. It is for this reason that when one finds a poet moving outside of the restrictions of the meter, one is tempted to search for aesthetic motivation for his doing so. Consider, in this regard, the opening line from a sonnet by Keats given in (57):

(57) *Hów many bárds gíld the lápses of tíme*
       W   SW S   W   SW S W S

   Line (57) is unmetrical since it has a stress maximum in the fourth W position in violation of the last alternative of (52bii). However, it seems quite clear that the poet is purposely moving outside of the meter in order to caricature metrically the sense of the line. The line is literally what it speaks of figuratively, a "lapse of time." This metrical joke requires that the line be treated as unmetrical.

   Returning to metrical lines, we note Donne's line (58) as an instance where later alternatives of both (52bi) and (52bii) apply:

(58) *Yet déarly I lóve you and would be lóvĕd fáin*
       W S W S   W   S   W SW S

   The second and third W in (58) violate the first alternative of (52bi) but not the second, while the third S violates the first but not the second alternative of (52bii). Note that the assignment of two syllables to a single position has to take place in the manner shown in (58). If different syllables were to be assigned to a single position, the line would be unmetrical because the stress maxima would occupy W positions.

   The assignment of syllables to positions is, of course, strictly metrical. It does not imply that the syllables assigned to a single position should be slurred or elided when the verse is recited. The correspondence rules are not instructions for poetry recitations. They are, rather, abstract principles of verse construction whose effect on the sound of the recited verse is indirect.

It is obvious that the second alternative of (52bi) subsumes the first alternative as a special case. Poets appear to differ a great deal as to the precise extension of the second alternative. For example, Chaucer not only makes use of elision, that is, assigns to a single position two consecutive syllables when no true consonant intervenes, but he also allows for monosyllabic words to be assigned to a single position along with an adjacent syllable under certain conditions.[15] Other poets seem to modify elision as defined in (52bi) by allowing it to operate on two vowels separated by an optional fricative consonant (*s*, *f*, *v*, etc.) as well as across an optional sonorant.[16] Still other poets allow for an extra-metrical syllable internally before a major syntactic break, as in the examples in (59) (and in (63)):

(59)　(a)　*And as I past I worshipt: if those you seek*　　　(MILTON, *Comus,302*)

　　　(b)　*From mine own knowledge. As nearly as I may*　　　(SHAKESPEARE, *AC,II,2*)

Whatever the usages may be from one poet to another, they can readily be accounted for by suitable extensions of the correspondence rules. As they appear to have only limited general theoretical interest, we shall not attempt to deal further with these adjustments here.

We recall that in rejecting the standard theory we stressed the fact that the list of allowable deviations (47) was not otherwise restricted. Thus, there was no mechanism for excluding from the list such obviously absurd items as (60):

(60)　(a)　Insertion of a parenthetic phrase in a line

　　　(b)　Trochaic foot followed by a dactyl

　　　(c)　Elision of exactly three syllables verse-finally

We must now show that the allowed deviations (47) of the standard theory are in fact subsumed by the various alternatives of the revised theory advanced here and that the absurdities collected in (60) are excluded.

---

[15] For a detailed discussion of Chaucer's rule, see Halle and Keyser (1966), and for a criticism of the rule as given there see Hascall (1969). Hascall's modification is based upon the observation that in the overwhelming number of instances in which a monosyllabic word is assigned with another syllable to a single position, the monosyllabic word is not a member of a major lexical category (i.e., not an adjective, noun, adverb, verb). This seems to us a correct observation and requires a revision of the rule along the lines specified by Hascall.

[16] Extensions of the class of consonants which participate in elision are suggested in Hascall (1969) and in Freeman (1968). One of Bridges' (1921) contributions was to show that in Milton's metrical practice the content of this rule actually changes between *Paradise Lost* and *Samson Agonistes*.

It can be seen immediately that the revised theory presented in (52) excludes (60) since there is no natural way in which even the last (i.e., most general) alternatives of (52bi) and (52bii) can be stretched so as to include these items. It is equally evident that (47e), which allows an extra slack syllable in the line, and (47f), which admits headless lines, are included by the revised theory. The latter is specifically permitted by (52a), where the first W is parenthesized and therefore optional. It should be noted here that the omission of the line-initial W contributes to the complexity of the line, whereas the omission of the line-final extra-metrical syllable leaves the complexity of the line unaffected. Although we have reflected this difference between the two parenthesized subsequences by adding an asterisk to the first set of parentheses in (52a), we have at this point no explanation for the distinction. Examples of headless lines in iambic pentameter are given in (61):

(61) (a) —*Twénty bóokes clád in blák or réed*   (CHAUCER, *A.Prol.294*)
         (W)*S W S W   S W   S W S

     (b) —*Spéech after lóng sílence; it is ríght*   (YEATS, *After Long Silence*)
         (W)*S   W S W   SW   S W S

Extra slack syllables (47e) in the line are allowed by the later alternatives of (52bi), as we have already seen in our discussion of (58). The third line of (44), repeated here as (62), is an additional example:

(62) *That I may ríse, and stánd, o'erthrów me, and bénd*
      W S W S W   S   W   S   W   S

Turning now to the remaining allowable deviations, we recall that the unstressed foot, (47a), has already been illustrated in (54). Shelley's line (63) offers an additional example:

(63) *Are dríven, like ghósts from an enchánter fléeing*
      W   S   W   S   W S W S W SX

Here the third S contains an unstressed syllable, a realization allowed by the second alternative of (52bii). (For the assignment of *driven* to a single position, see the discussion preceding (59).)

The next allowable deviation, (47b), is the heavy foot (spondee). This requires the last alternative of (52bii), which we have already invoked in our discussion of (55). Notice, however, that this alternative must be utilized in each of the three lines from Chaucer quoted in (43), the second of which is repeated in (64) by way of illustration:

(64) *Wýlugh, élm, pláne, ássh, bóx, chásteyn, lýnde, laurér*
      W   S   W   S   W   S W   S   W S

In (64) the first W violates the first alternative of (52bi) and both the first and second alternatives of (52bii). The second and third W's violate the first two alternatives of (52bii) but are allowed by the last alternative.

A somewhat different type of spondee is exemplified in the lines in (65), from Chaucer, Shakespeare, and Tennyson:

(65) (a) *The Míllere was a stóut cárl for the nónes*   (*A.Prol.545*)
           W SW   S W S   W S   W S X

      (b) *The cóurse of trúe lóve never díd rún smóoth*   (*Mids.I.1.134*)
           W S   W   S   W   SW S W   S

      (c) *Dówn the lóng tówer stáirs hésitating*   (*Lancelot and Elaine*)
           W   S W   S W   S   WSWS

Two fully stressed syllables back to back as in *stóut cárl, trúe lóve, lóng tówer* may correspond to any verse-internal WS or SW sequence by virtue of the last alternative of (52bii). In the first two of these the first stressed syllable corresponds to an S position while the second corresponds to a W position. In the third the first stressed syllable corresponds to a W position while the second corresponds to an S position.

The final two allowable deviations of the standard theory concern inverted feet: by (47c) these are allowed verse-initially; by (47d) they are allowed verse-medially. We have already scanned examples of this type in (55) to show how they would be treated by the revised theory. Additional examples, one from Keats and two from Shakespeare, are given in (66):

(66) (a) *Sílent upon a péak in Dárien*   (*On First Looking into Chapman's Homer*)
           WS WS W S W   SWS

      (b) *Appéare in pérson hére in cóurt. Sílence.*   (*Wint.Tale,III.1.10*)
           W   S   W S W   S W S   WS

      (c) *Fríends, Rómans, cóuntrymen, lénd me your éars*   (*J.C.III.2.78*)
           W   S W   S   W S W   S W   S

It is an interesting fact that inverted feet appear only under the following conditions in an iambic pentameter line: verse-initially, after a fully stressed syllable (see (55)), and after a major syntactic boundary (see the discussion of Jespersen preceding (52)), across which the stress subordination

rules of English do not operate. In the standard theory this is just another
fact, to be noted down, of course, but not to be endowed with any special
significance. In the revised theory, on the other hand, the three environments
are those where a stressed syllable will not constitute a stress maximum and
hence where a stressed syllable may occupy a W position. Note, in particular,
that line (66c) would be unmetrical were there no syntactic boundary before
lend. Thus, in the light of the revised theory the restriction of inverted feet to
the three environments mentioned is anything but a curious coincidence;
rather, it reflects a significant property of the meter and is thus one of the
reasons for our assertion that the revised theory is to be preferred over the
standard theory.

Finally, the asymmetry between trochaic and iambic lines with regard
to the admissibility of inverted feet in verse-initial position (see the discussion
of (49) and (50)) finds a ready explanation in the light of the revised theory.
The abstract metrical pattern for a trochaic line must be of the form (67)
with the correspondence rules (52b):

(67) SWSWSWS

If one allows an inverted foot (i.e., an iamb) at the beginning of a
trochaic line, one places a stress maximum in a W position, thereby violating
the last alternative of (52bii). We illustrate this with the help of the line (68)
concocted by Jespersen on the model of Longfellow's *A Psalm of Life*:

(68) *A life's but an empty dream*
      S W   S W S W S

Here the second syllable violates all three of the alternatives of
(52bii) and hence renders the line unmetrical.[17] As we have already seen, the
same does not happen when a trochee is substituted for the first iamb in an
iambic line. Such lines (see (66)) are allowed by the third alternative of
(52bii) and are therefore perfectly metrical.

Notice also that the introduction of an initial extra-metrical syllable
will have no effect on a trochaic line, but its inclusion in an iambic line will
be largely limited to lines without inverted first feet since otherwise a stress
maximum could be realized in a W position in violation of the last alternative

---

[17] It must also be noted that Jespersen's example (68) contains a stressless vowel in the third
position. If this position were occupied by a fully stressed word, the line would have been
metrical, as is, for example, the following modification of (68):

Your life lacked an empty dream

of (52bii).[18] Once again the revised theory shows certain facts to be lawful consequences of certain other facts and thus provides a more adequate explanation for the phenomena than does the standard theory.

The final argument in favor of the theory proposed here is that, as already noted, it affords a relatively straightforward way to reconstruct the notion of metrical complexity or tension. In the standard theory it is possible to attribute increasing complexity to each succeeding item in the list of allowable deviations. This procedure, however, is quite ad hoc. There is no independent justification for ordering the allowable deviations as in (47); hence nothing can be deduced from that order. This does not hold for the order of the alternatives in the correspondence rules (52b). Here the alternatives are ordered in increasing generality, beginning with the least general and ending with the most general. As already remarked, the degree of difficulty that a reader will experience in discerning the abstract metrical pattern in a line can be plausibly assumed to be directly related to the richness and variety of the means that can be employed in actualizing the pattern. It should follow, therefore, that when a greater variety of correspondences is allowed, the pattern is more difficult to perceive. The number of underlines in the different lines scanned in accordance with our procedure can then be taken as a measure of the complexity of the line. As we have demonstrated, this measure works properly in extreme cases. Whether it works properly in all cases cannot yet be determined. Questions can naturally be raised about our decision to assign equal complexity to later alternatives regardless of source. It is perfectly conceivable that the increase in complexity due to the need to invoke the third rather than the second alternative of the correspondence rule (52bii) should be a fraction of that resulting from the invocation

---

[18] It would be possible to construct a metrical iambic line with an extra-metrical syllable preceding a verse whose initial foot is inverted provided that a major syntactic break separates the first position from the second position, thereby preventing the first position from becoming a stress maximum. Such a line would be extremely rare, however, in view of the marked tendency in iambic verse to avoid a major syntactic break after the first position.

The occurrence of an extra-metrical syllable in verse-initial position in a trochaic line will have the same effect as a verse-final extra-metrical syllable in an iambic line, namely, both may turn a main stress into a stress maximum. This suggests that stress maxima in these positions are not crucial to the meter, which would then be a purely internal matter. If this is so, the last position of an iambic line and the first position of a trochaic line would have to be given a rather different theoretical status. Bridges (1921, p. 39) was aware of this: "Tyrwhitt is quoted as saying that one of the indispensable conditions of English blank verse was that the last syllable should be strongly accented. The truth seems to be that its metrical position in a manner exonerates it from requiring any accent. —Whether the 'last foot' may be inverted is another question. —A weak syllable can very well hold its own in this tenth place, and the last essential accent of the verse may be that of the 'fourth foot'. The analogy with the dipody of the classical iambic, and with the four minim bar of the old alla breve time in music is evident."

of the second alternative. Such questions, however, can be answered only when a massive body of verse has been subjected to the type of analysis proposed. The best that can be done at this point is to list in order of increasing complexity a variety of lines, all of which have been analyzed here, so as to show that the judgments made by our scheme are not totally implausible.[19] We give such a list in (69):

(69)   COMPLEXITY

(53)	*The curfew tolls the knell of parting day*	0
(61)	*Twenty bookes clad in blak or reed*	1
(54)	*And leaves the world to darkness and to me*	2
(63)	*Are driven, like ghosts from an enchanter fleeing*	2
(58)	*Yet dearly I love you and would be loved fain*	3
(66)	*Appear in person here in court. Silence.*	3
(65)	*The Millere was a stout carl for the nones*	4

(Continued on p. 178)

---

[19] Recent studies (see Beaver (1968) and Freeman (1968)) have dealt with the question of metrical style in terms other than line complexity. They have taken into account such factors as the number and position of stress maxima and the number and position of unactualized S positions. For example, in a discussion of the following lines from Pope's *An Essay on Criticism*:

When Ájax stríves sóme róck's vást wéight to thrów
The líne tóo lábours, and the wórds móve slów.

Freeman notes that the heavy stresses back to back contribute to the overall impression of slowness: "Stress neutralization is at work even more clearly in another of Pope's deliberately and exaggeratedly 'slow' lines:

(1)
And ten low words oft creep in one dull line
W   S W   S   W   S W S   W S

The line is perfectly metrical, but the monosyllabic Adjective-Noun and Adverb-Verb combinations create so much stress neutralization that no stress maxima, or at most one, are actualized in the line" (p. 78).

It is perhaps worth noting that while the large number of heavy stresses back to back in this line is in part responsible for the impression of slowness, it is not in itself a sufficient condition. Thus, we can paraphrase this line by a simple permutation, and while the complexity level remains the same the line seems impressionistically quite different:

And ten low words in one dull line oft creep

Conversely, note that line (55) can be made to seem much slower by performing a similar inversion which leaves the complexity level unchanged:

Batter my heart for you, three-person'd God

The precise relationship to a theory of metrical style of such factors as line complexity and the arrangement of syntactic structures within the line remains to be explored. It is our hope, however, that the revised theory provides an adequate tool for such explorations.

69 (*Continued*)

(61)	*Speech after long silence; it is right*	5
(66)	*Silent upon a peak in Darien*	5
(55)	*Batter my heart, three-person'd God, for you*	6
(66)	*Friends, Romans, countrymen, lend me your ears*	6
(64)	*Wylugh, elm, plane, assh, box, chasteyn, lynde, laurer*	7
(65)	*Down the long tower stairs hesitating*	9

The lines in (69) vary in complexity from zero to nine. Lines with considerably greater complexity can readily be invented (see (70), with a complexity of 17), but such lines do not appear to be attested in the poets. The theory thus allows for a greater variety of line than anyone has ever found use for. When faced with such a fact, one may attribute it to inadequacies in the theory and attempt to revise the theoretical framework so as to restrict the number of unattested cases that are allowed. Alternatively, one may attempt to account for the unattested cases in some plausible fashion, leaving the theory intact. It seems to us that the absence of lines of greater complexity can be explained adequately within the theory. If it is granted that the complexity of a line is directly related to the difficulty that it poses for the reader, and if one further supposes that poets normally do not wish to turn their poems into difficult crossword puzzles, the artistry of which cannot be appreciated without laborious pencil and paper calculations, then it is not unreasonable to assume further that there is an upper bound on the complexity that a given poet would ever wish to impose on his lines. A supposition of this sort is perfectly natural in the case of syntax: while clearly there is no upper bound on the number of nouns that can be conjoined in a noun phrase, it would surprise no one to learn that a perusal of the collected works of all American novelists from Hawthorne to Henry James did not reveal a single conjoined noun phrase composed of more than 27 (or 69) nouns. The case of the iambic pentameter does not appear to us so dissimilar as to rule out an analogous explanation for the absence of lines such as (70):

(70) *Bíllows, bíllows, seréne mírror of the maríne bóroughs, remóte wíllows*

W S W S W S W S WS

To illustrate the metrical theory developed here,[20] we conclude with a

[20] At the time the present work went to press, two articles appeared, Wimsatt (1970) and Magnuson and Ryder (1970), which take issue with the theory of prosody set forth in Halle and Keyser (1966) and Keyser (1968). The theory presented in (52) here anticipates in certain instances the objections raised by Wimsatt and by Magnuson and Ryder. A more direct and detailed reaction to these critics, which also touches upon a number of points not treated here, appears in Halle and Keyser (forthcoming).

detailed scansion in (71) of a passage from the Prologue to the *Canterbury Tales.*

(71) *A Clérk ther was of Óxenfórd alsó,*
W S   W   S W S W S   W S
That unto lógyk hadde lónge ygó.
 W S W SW   S WS ⩔ S
As léene was his hórs as is a ráke,
W S W S   W S   W S W SX
And he nas nat ríght fát, I undertáke,
W   S W S W   S WS W S X
But lóoked hólwe, and therto sóbrely.
 W S W   S ⩔   S W S WS
Ful thrédbáre was his óvereste courtepý;
   W   S W   S W SW   S W S
For he hadde géten hym yet no benefíce,
 W S W   S W   S W S WSX
Ne was so wórldly for to have offíce.
  W S W S   W S   W S   W SX
For hym was lévere have at his béddes héed
 W   S   W S   W   S W S W S
—Twénty bóokes, clád in blák or réed,
W   S WS W   S W   S W S
Of Áristotle and his philosophíe,
W SWS ⩔   S WSW SX
Than róbes ríche, or fíthele, or gáy sautríe
  W S WS   W S   ⩔   S W SX
But al be that he was a philosóphre,
W S W S W SW   SWS   X
Yet hadde he but lítel góld in cófre;
 W S W S W SW S W S X
But al that he myghte of his fréendes hénte,
 W S W   S W   S W S W S X
On bóokes and on lérnynge he it spénte,
W S W S W S W   SW S X

(Continued on p. 180)

71 (*Continued*)

And bísily gan for the sóules préye
W SWS W S WSW S X

Of hem that yáf hym wherwith to scoléye.
W S W S W   S W S WS X

Of stúdie tóok he móost cúre and móost héede.
W SWS W S W S W   S X

—Noght ó wórd spák he more than was néede,
W S W S W S W   S W S X

And that was sáyd in fórme and reverénce,
W   S W S W S   W   SWS X

And shórt and qúyk and fúl of hý senténce;
W   S W S W SW SWS X

Sównynge in móral vértu was his spéche,
W S W SW SW S W S X

And gládly wolde he lérne and gládly téche.   (*A. Prol. 285-308*)
W   SWS WS W   SWS X

Bibliography

Bibliography

Anderson, S. (1969), *West Scandinavian Vowel Systems and the Ordering of Phonological Rules*, unpublished Doctoral dissertation, MIT.

Anonymous (1797), *A Vocabulary of Such Words in the English Language as are of Dubious or Unsettled Pronunciation*, reprinted 1967, Scolar Press Ltd., no. 46, Menston, England.

Babcock, C. (1914), "Study of the Metrical Use of Inflectional E in Middle English with Particular Reference to Chaucer and Lydgate," *PMLA*, *29*, 59–92.

Baehr, R. (1962), *Spanische Verslehre auf historischer Grundlage*, Tübingen.

Bartina, S., S. J. (1955), *Tratado de métrica castellana*, Barcelona.

Bartlett, J. (1937), *A New and Complete Concordance or Verbal Index to Words, Phrases, and Passages in the Dramatic Works of Shakespeare*, London.

Baum, P. F. (1961), *Chaucer's Verse*, Durham.

Beaver, J. C. (1968), "A Grammar of Prosody," *College English*, *29*, 310–321.

Bergsten, N. (1911), *Compound Suffixes in English*, Uppsala.

Bischoff, O. (1897), *Uber zweisilbige Senkung und epische Caesur bei Chaucer*, Darmstadt.

Bliss, A. J. (1958), *The Metre of Beowulf*, Oxford.

Bliss, A. J. (1962), *An Introduction to Old English Metre*, Oxford.

Bloomfield, L. (1933), *Language*, New York.

Borowski, B. (1921), *Zum Nebenakzent beim altenglischen Nominal-kompositum*, Halle.

Borroff, M. (1962), *Sir Gawain and the Green Knight*, New Haven.

Bradley, C. B. (1922), "The Accentuation of the *Research*-Group Words," *University of California Publications in Modern Philology*, vol. XI, pp. 3–23.

Brame, M. (1969), "On the Abstractness of Phonology," unpublished paper, MIT.

Bresnan, J. W. (1970), "On Sentence Stress and Syntactic Transformations," *Language*, *46*.

Bridges, R. (1921), *Milton's Prosody*, Oxford.

Bridges, R. (1966), "A Letter to a Musician on English Prosody," in Gross (1966), pp. 86–101.

Burling, R. (1966), "The Metrics of Children's Verse: A Cross Linguistic Study," *American Anthropologist*, *68*, 1418–1441.

Butler, C. (1634), see Eichler (1910).

Campbell, A. (1959), *Old English Grammar*, Oxford.

Chomsky, N. and M. Halle (1968), *The Sound Pattern of English*, New York.

Coles, E. (1647), *The Compleat English Schoolmaster*, reprinted 1967, Scolar Press Ltd., no. 26, Menston, England.

Cooper (1685), see Jones (1911).

Cooper (1687), see Sundby (1954).

Creed, R. P. (1966), "A New Approach to the Rhythm of Beowulf," *PMLA*, *81*, 23–33.

Danielsson, B. (1948), *Studies on the Accentuation of Polysyllabic Latin, Greek, and Romance Loan-Words in English*, Stockholm.

Dobson, E. J. (1968), *English Pronunciation 1500–1700*, 2nd ed., London.

Donaldson, E. T. (1948), "Chaucer's Final-E," *PMLA*, *63*, 1101–1125.

Eckhardt, E. (1942), "Der Übergang zur germanischen Betonung bei den Wörtern französischer Herkunft im Mittelenglischen," *Englischen Studien*, *75*, nos. 1, 3.

Eichler, A. (1910), *Charles Butler's English Grammar* (1634), Halle.

Ekwall, E. (1907), *Dr. John Jones's Practical Phonography* (1701), Halle.

Ellis, A. J. (1869–1889), *On Early English Pronunciation*, (vols. 1–5), London.

Fidelholtz, J. (1967), "English Vowel Reduction," unpublished paper, MIT.

Flint, see Kökeritz (1944).

Freeman, D. C. (1968), "On the Primes of Metrical Style," *Language and Style, 1*, 63–101.

Freudenberger, M. (1889), *Das Fehlen des Auftakts in Chaucers heroischem Verse*, Leipzig.

Gross, H. (1966), *The Structure of Verse*, Greenwich, Conn.

Halle, M. (1962), "Phonology in a Generative Grammar," *Word, 18*, 54–72; reprinted in *The Structure of Language: Readings in the Philosophy of Language*, J. A. Fodor and J. J. Katz, eds., 1964, Englewood Cliffs, N. J.

Halle, M. (1966), "On the Metrics of Pre-Islamic Arabic Poetry," *Quarterly Progress Report of the Research Laboratory of Electronics*, MIT, no. 83, 113–116.

Halle, M. (1968), "Žirmunskij's Theory of Verse: A Review Article," *The Slavic and East European Review, 12*, 213–218

Halle, M. (in press), "On Meter and Prosody," *Recent Developments in Linguistics*, The Hague.

Halle, M. and S. J. Keyser (1966), "Chaucer and the Study of Prosody," *College English, 28*, 187–219.

Halle, M. and S. J. Keyser (forthcoming), "Further Explorations Toward a Theory of Iambic Pentameter," *College English*.

Hammond, E. P. (1908), *Chaucer: A Bibliographical Manual*, New York.

Harrison, T. P. (1892), *The Separable Prefixes in Anglo-Saxon*, Baltimore.

Hascall, D. (1969), "Some Contributions to the Halle-Keyser Theory of Prosody," *College English, 30*, 357–365.

Hodges, R. (1644), *The English Primrose*, reprinted 1930, H. Kauter, ed., Heidelberg.

Huguenin, J. (1901), *Secondary Stress in Anglo-Saxon* (*Determined by Metrical Criteria*), Baltimore.

Jakobson, R. (1932), "Über den Versbau der serbokroatischen Volksepen," *Selected Writings IV*, The Hague, pp. 51–60.

Jakobson, R. (1952), "Slavic Epic Verse: Studies in Comparative Metrics," *Selected Writings IV*, The Hague, pp. 414–465.

Jespersen, O. (1909), *A Modern English Grammar on Historical Principles, Part 1: Sounds and Spellings*, Heidelberg.

Jespersen, O. (1928), *Monosyllabism in English*, Biennial Lecture on English Philology, British Academy, London.

Jespersen, O. (1933), "Notes on Meter," *Linguistica*, Copenhagen.

Joerden, O. (1915), "Das Verhältnis von Wort-, Satz-, und Versakzent in Chaucer's Canterbury Tales," *Studien zur englischen Philologie*, Heft LV, Halle.

Johnston, W. (1764), *A Pronouncing and Spelling Dictionary*, reprinted 1968, Scolar Press Ltd., no. 95, Menston, England.

Jones, D. (1956a), *Outline of English Phonetics*, New York.

Jones, D. (1956b), *The Pronunciation of English*, Cambridge, England.

Jones, Dr. J. (1701), see Ekwall (1907).

Jones, J. D. (1911), *Cooper's Grammatica linguae Anglicanae* (1685), Halle.

Kenyon, J. S. and T. A. Knott (1944), *A Pronouncing Dictionary of American English*, Springfield, Mass.

Keyser, S. J. (1968), "The Linguistic Basis of English Prosody," *Modern Studies in English*, S. Schane and D. Reibel, eds., Englewood Cliffs, N. J.

Keyser, S. J. (1969a), "Old English Prosody," *College English, 30*, 331–356.

Keyser, S. J. (1969b), "Old English Prosody: A Reply," *College English, 31*, 74–80.

Kingdon, R. (1958), *The Groundwork of English Stress*, London.

Kisseberth, C. (1970), "On the Functional Unity of Phonological Rules," *Linguistic Inquiry, 1*, 291–306.

Kittredge, G. L. (1891), *Observations on the Language of Chaucer's Troilus*, London.

Klaeber, F. (1922), *Beowulf and the Fight at Finnsburg*, New York.

Kökeritz, H. (1944), *Mather Flint on Eighteenth Century English Pronunciation*, Uppsala.

Kökeritz, H. (1953), *Shakespeare's Pronunciation*, New Haven.

Lachmann, K. (1876), *Kleinere Schriften zur deutschen Philologie*, Berlin.

Langenhove, G. C. van (1925), *On the Origin of the Gerund in English*, Paris.

Learned, H. D. (1922), "The Accentuation of Old French Loanwords in English," *PMLA, 37*, 707–721.

Lehmann, W. P. (1956), *The Development of Germanic Verse Form*, Austin.

Levins, P. (1570), *Manipulus vocabulorum: A Rhyming Dictionary of the English Language*, reprinted 1867, H. B. Wheatley, ed., London.

Lieberman, P. (1967), *Intonation, Perception, and Language*, Cambridge, Mass.

Lowe, S. (1755), *The Critical Spelling Book*, reprinted 1967, Scolar Press Ltd., no. 7, Leeds, England.

Luick, K. (1896), *Untersuchungen zur englischen Lautgeschichte*, Strassburg.

Luick, K. (1914), "Zur mittelenglischen Verslehre," *Anglia, 38*, 269–348.

Luick, K. (1921), *Historische Grammatik der englischen Sprache*, Halle.

McJimsey, R. (1942), *Chaucer's Irregular -E, A Demonstration among Monosyllabic Nouns of the Exceptions to Grammatical and Metrical Harmony*, New York.

Magnuson, K. and F. G. Ryder (1970), "The Study of English Prosody: An Alternative Proposal," *College English, 31*, 789–820.

Manly, J. M. (1893), "Observations on the Language of Chaucer's *Legend of Good Women*," *Studies and Notes in Philology and Literature*, vol. II, Boston.

Meadors, J. (1969), "On Defining the Stress Maximum," unpublished paper, MIT.

Meillet, A. (1923), *Les Origines Indo-Européennes des Mètres Grecs*, Paris.

Meyer-Lübke, W. (1890), *Romanische Lautlehre*, Leipzig.

Meyer-Lübke, W. (1920), *Einführung in das Studium der romanische Sprachwissenschaft*, Heidelberg.

Nares, R. (1784), *The Elements of Orthoepy*, London.

Paul, H. (1879), "Zur Geschichte des germanischen Vocalismus," *Beiträge zur Geschichte der deutschen Sprache und Literatur, VI*, Halle.

Pope, J. C. (1942), *The Rhythm of Beowulf*, New Haven.

Pope, M. K. (1934), *From Latin to Modern French*, Manchester.

Prince, F. T. (1954), *The Italian Element in Milton's Verse*, Oxford.

Riquer, M. de (1950), *Resumen de versificación española*, Barcelona.

Robinson, F. N. (1933), *The Poetical Works of Geoffrey Chaucer*, Boston.

Sebeok, T. A., ed. (1960), *Style in Language*, Cambridge, Mass.

Sievers, E. (1879), "Zur Accent- und Lautlehre der germanischen Sprachen," *Beiträge zur Geschichte der deutschen Sprache und Literatur, IV*, Halle.

Sievers, E. (1885), "Zur Rhythmik des germanischen Alliterationsverses," *Beiträge zur Geschichte der deutschen Sprache und Literatur, X*, Halle.

Sievers, E. (1905), "Altgermanische Metrik," *Grundriss der germanischen Philologie*, Hermann Paul, ed., vol. 2, no. 2, pp. 1–38, Strassburg.

Sievers, E. and K. Brunner (1951), *Altenglische Grammatik*, Halle.

Skeat, W. W. (1891), *Rime-Index to Chaucer's Troilus and Criseyde*, London.

Skeat, W. W. (1894), *Chaucer's Works*, Oxford.

Sledd, J. (1969), "Old English Prosody: A Demurrer," *College English, 31*, 71–74.

Smith, J. (1674), *Grammatica Quadrilinguis*, London.

Sundby, B. (1954), *Christopher Cooper's English Teacher* (1687), Copenhagen.

Sweet, H. (1891), *A History of English Sounds*, Oxford.

Tamson, G. (1898), "Word-Stress in English: A Short Treatise on the Accentuation of Words in Middle-English as Compared with the Stress in Old and Modern English," *Studien zur englischen Philologie*, Heft III, Halle.

Tatlock, J. S. P. and A. G. Kennedy (1927), *A Concordance to the Complete Works of Geoffrey Chaucer and to the Romaunt of the Rose*, reprinted 1963, Gloucester, Mass.

Ten Brink, B. (1901), *The Language and Meter of Chaucer*, 2nd. ed., F. Kluge, trans., London.

Tolkien, J. R. R. and E. V. Gordon (1925), *Sir Gawain and the Green Knight*, Oxford.

Tyrwhitt, T. (1798), *Canterbury Tales of Chaucer*, vol. I, 2nd ed., Oxford.

Waldo, G. S. (1968), *Stress the Right Syllable: The Accentuation of English Words with Special Reference to their Structure (Morphology)*, monograph, University of Alberta.

Walker, J. (1791), *A Critical Pronouncing Dictionary, and Expositor of the English Language*, London.

Watts, A. C. (1969), *The Lyre and the Harp*, New Haven.

Weil, G. (1960), "Arūd," *Encyclopedia of Islam*, vol. I, Leiden, pp. 667–677.

Weyhe, H. (1904), *Kleine Beiträge zur westgermanischen Grammatik*, Halle.

Wimsatt, W. K., ed. (in press), *Metrical Studies*, New York.

Wright, J. (1925), *Old English Grammar*, Oxford.

Zeps, V. J. (1963), "The Meter of the So-called Trochaic Latvian Folksongs," *Journal of Slavic Linguistics and Poetics, 7*, 123–128.

Indexes

Word Index

LATE MIDDLE ENGLISH

MODERN ENGLISH

Affix Index

Subject Index

Abstract metrical patterns, *see* Metrical patterns (abstract)

Adjectives
  modern English 76–77
  Old English, 92, 93, 95–96

Adverbs
  Old English, 92, 96

Alliterative
  defined, 147, 154
  Germanic poetry, in Middle English, 107
  poetry, 86, 147, 153–154
  syllables, 88, 147

Alternating Stress Rule, 27–28, 31, 32, 34, 38, 39, 68n, 70
  cyclical application of, 39
  differences between Main Stress Rule and, 34n, 42, 54n, 62–63, 66, 67–70, 75n
  evolution of, 135

Arrow notation, 5, 11

Auxiliary Reduction Rules
  compared with *Sound Pattern of English* treatment, 59
  order of, 54–55
  I, 35, 48, 49
  II, 44, 45, 49
  III, 33, 50, 74n

Bartholomae's Law, 73n

Bisyllabic words, 10, 38, 39, 61–65, 66, 67, 69, 70, 71, 72, 80, 81
  with final stress in Chaucer, 101
  with lax final vowel, 82, 110, 121
  in Levine, 116, 118
  retraction of stress in, 61–65, 70, 73
  in Shakespeare, 120
  with tense final vowel, 70

Boundaries, 5, 12, 106, 123n
  in complex words (=), 5, 37–40, 55n, 59, 68n, 69, 118
  internal (#), 90n, 110, 112, 118, 120
  morpheme (+), 5, 37n
  and rule application, 5
  word (##), 5, 12, 19–20, 27, 38, 43, 90n

Brace notation, 19, 33

Brackets, 17
  labeled, 17n

C (symbol), 5

Capital letter notation, 5, 19, 20

Cæsura, 153, 155, 156

Cluster deaspiration, 73n

Complaint of Venus, 105

Complex words, 37–40, 74, 75n, 79
  evolution of stress pattern in, 112n, 118, 119–120, 122–123, 134n
  in Old English, 88–89, 90–91
  See also Boundaries

Complexity, *see* Conciseness; Correspondence rules; Metrical complexity

Compound and Nuclear Stress Rules, 24–26, 28, 43
  Compound Rule, modern English, 15–16, 19, 21, 22, 23, 26n, 31
  Compound Rule, Old English, 95, 97, 108, 109
  Nuclear Stress Rule, 23–24, 26
  See also Stress Adjustment Rule

Compound words
  in Chaucer, 108–109
  in Old English, 88, 93n, 95, 96, 148
  See also Compound and Nuclear Stress Rules

Conciseness, 7, 8, 9, 22

Conjugational endings, 91, 92, 112

Conjunctive ordering, 33

Constituent structure, 17, 20, 39, 55, 56, 63, 75, 90, 91, 92, 108

Correspondence rules, 140–144, 146, 147, 149, 157, 164, 175
  for iambic pentameter, 164, 165, 167, 168–169, 172, 175, 176
  metrical complexity and, 142, 157, 159, 176–177
  for Old English verse, 147, 153–154, 157, 158

Cycle, principle of, 16–17, 25, 51–53, 56, 83, 90

Dactyl, 172

Decasyllabic line, 165

Declensional endings, 91, 92, 112

Dental consonants, 72n, 82

Diacritic features, 36, 41, 42, 64, 67, 68, 75n

Diphthongization, after palatal consonants, 89, 93

71 72 73 74   7 6 5 4 3 2 1